TOBIAS SMOLLETT

Tobias Smollett

Essays of Two Decades

by

G. S. Rousseau

Professor of Eighteenth-Century Studies
in the University of California,
at Los Angeles

T. & T. CLARK
36 GEORGE STREET, EDINBURGH

Printed in England by
Billing and Sons Limited
Guildford, London and Worcester
for
T. & T. Clark Ltd., Edinburgh

ISBN 0 567 09330 1

First printed 1982

Contents

Also by G. S. Rousseau

Acknowledgements

Chapter

I. Towards Maturity and Mental Collapse
originally appeared as: "Tobias Smollett: Doctor by Design, Writer by Choice," *Journal of the American Medical Association*, CCXVI (1971), pp. 85–89

II. Tobias Smollett and Laurence Sterne: A Revaluation
originally appeared as: "Smollett and Sterne: A Revaluation," *Archiv*, CCVIII (April, 1972), pp. 286–297

III. Smollett's London
originally appeared as a discussion of: André Parreaux, *Smollett's London*, Paris, A. G. Nizet, 1965, *Philological Quarterly*, XLV (1966)

IV. Smollett and the Society of Arts of London
originally appeared as: " 'No Boasted Academy of Christendom': Smollett and the Society of Arts," *Journal of the Royal Society of Arts*, vol. ccxii (June, July, August 1973), pp. 468–475; 532–535; 623–628

V. Smollett as a Letter Writer
originally appeared as: "Shades of Obscurity: Tobias Smollett Correspondence," *Studies in Burke and His Time*, XII (1970), pp. 1714–1720.

VI. Smollett and the Form of Picaresque Literature
originally appeared as: "Smollett and the Picaresque: Some Questions About a Label," *Studies in Burke and His Time*, XII (Spring, 1971), pp. 1886–1904

VII. Beef and Bouillon: Smollett's Achievement as a Thinker
originally appeared as "Beef and Bouillon: A Voice for Tobias Smollett, With Comments on his Life, Works and Modern Critics," *The British Studies Monitor*, VII (Winter, 1977), pp. 4–56

VIII. Original chapter

IX. Smollett and Politics (I)
originally appeared as: (With Roger Hambridge) "Smollett and Politics: Originals for the Election Scenes in *Sir Launcelot Greaves*," *English Language Notes*, XIV, pp. 32–37

X. Smollett and the Eighteenth-Century Sulphur Controversy
originally appeared as: "Matt Bramble and the Sulphur Controversy in the Eighteenth Century: Some Medical Background of Humphry Clinker," *Journal of the History of Ideas*, XXVII (1967), pp. 577–589

XI. Smollett and Paracelsian Medicine
originally appeared as: "Smollett's *acidum vagum*," *Isis*, LVIII (1967), pp. 244–245

XII. Smollett's Wit and the Traditions of Learning in Medicine
originally appeared as: "Pineapples, Pregnancy, Pica, and *Peregrine Pickle*," in *Tobias Smollett: Bicentennial Essays Presented to Lewis M. Knapp*, ed. by G. S. Rousseau with P. G. Boucé (New York: Oxford University Press, 1971), pp. 79–109

XIII. Smollett and Roger Dibon
originally appeared as: "Tobias Smollett and Roger Dibon: The Case of the Elusive Translation," *Notes ond Queries*, N.S., XVIII (February, 1971)

XIV. Smollett and a Victorian Editor
originally appeared as: (With Roger Hambridge) "David Herbert: Victorian Editor of Smollett," *Library Review*, XXV (Spring, 1975), pp. 17–20

XV. Smollett and the Scholars
originally appeared as a discussion: "Smollettiana," in *Eighteenth-Century Studies*, IV (1971), pp. 336–342

Preface

These essays composed over a span of two decades have been gathered under one cover in order that students might read them in a convenient and inexpensive form. I offer no argument for their collective coherence, nor may they possess any; and although I have grouped them according to my sense of the reader's needs—Smollett's life, works, problems related to the interpretation of his remarkable fictions, specialized areas for further criticism and scholarship—I would certainly not maintain that they naturally flow into one another, or that when combined they constitute a unified book. A collection of essays written over a long period of time need not have the kind of large coherence a single long essay, say of three or four hundred pages, ought to possess. Such a long and coherent essay about Smollett remains to be written, as I dared to suggest some years ago. *Essays of Two Decades* is not that book, although some day in the future I hope to write a long essay about Smollett.

My editorial procedure has been to print the essays as they originally appeared except for alterations in some of the titles, and not to worry about the repetitions and overlappings. The reader of one essay may not be the reader of another, and I have not attempted to predict who would read a particular chapter. Moreover, even the reader who pursues a majority of these essays, or all of them, will not read them at one sitting; and he may consequently appreciate the casual reminder that Smollett travelled, for example, to France in the spring of 1749 or revised *Peregrine Pickle* during 1757, without feeling imposed upon because he has been offered this bit of information a hundred pages earlier.

My scheme for presentation of the essays is not chronological: I have thought it more advisable to guide the reader by beginning with the most general and biographical piece, "Towards Maturity and Mental Collapse," and thereby to educate him and equip him to approach the more difficult essays, such as "Beef and Bouillon: Smollett's Achievement as a Thinker." But I am not apologetic for the variety of audiences addressed: the essays were originally written with different audiences in mind, and I see no reason to diminish the reader's intelligence by presuming he is not wise enough to decide which essay is or is not for him. A collection of essays spanning two decades need not be addressed to a single audience. I do not think, therefore, that a general reader interested in Smollett's works will object to the chatty allusiveness of "Smollett and Sterne: A Revaluation," or that teachers of literature and their students will turn away from the detailed pieces on pineapples and pregnancy, sulphur, politicians, charlatans, ghost translators, French collaborators, Victorian editors and the like, merely because these essays are not concerned primarily with the forms of literary expression.

Finally, the chronology printed at the beginning of the volume contains no new information: it merely hopes to serve as a brief but useful reference guide for non-specialists and to refresh the memory of Smollettians who already know the details of Smollett's life.

My indebtedness to P. G. Boucé, O. M. Brack, Robert Adams Day, Roger Hambridge, M. E. Novak and R. D. Spector, with all of whom I have been privileged to discuss Smollett for over a decade, is everywhere evident.

UCLA   G. S. ROUSSEAU

August 1979

A Chronology of Tobias George Smollett

1721 (19 March)	Baptized in the parish church of Cardross, Dumbartonshire, Scotland
Dates uncertain	Attended Dumbarton grammar school, and later Glasgow University
1735 (November)	Working in a dispensatory in Glasgow
1736 (30 May)	Apprenticed to William Stirling and John Gordon, surgeons of Glasgow
1739 (some time after June)	Travelled to London
1740 (10 March)	Received warrant as surgeon's second mate in the Navy—first served on the Chichester in the Carthagena expedition
1741 (September)	Returned to England
1741–4	Movements uncertain. May have returned to West Indies. Married Anne Lassells, daughter of a Jamaica planter
1744 (May)	Set up as a surgeon in London
1746	Published a short poem, 'The Tears of Scotland'
1746 (September)	*Advice*, a Juvenalian verse satire
1747 (January)	*Reproof*, another verse satire
1747–8	Translating Le Sage's *Gil Blas* (in the press, Nov. 1748)
1748 (January)	*The Adventures of Roderick Random*
1749 (June)	Published *The Regicide* after fruitless struggles to get it produced
1750 (Summer)	Visited Paris and the Low Countries
1751 (25 February)	*The Adventures of Peregrine Pickle*
1752 (January)	*Habbakkuk Hilding*, perhaps by Smollett
1752 (March)	*An Essay on the External Use of Water*
1753 (February)	*The Adventures of Ferdinand Count Fathom*
1755 (February)	Translation of *Don Quixote* (begun at least by 1748)

1755–7	Working on *A Complete History of England*
1756 (March)	Involved in launching the *Critical Review.* An active editor until 1763
1756 (April)	Edited *A Compendium of Authentic and Entertaining Voyages* (7 vols.)
1757 (January)	*The Reprisal*, a farce, presented at Drury Lane
1760 (January)	Began *British Magazine.* In it, from January 1760 to December 1761, appeared *The Adventures of Sir Launcelot Greaves*
1760 (November to late February 1761)	In the King's Bench Prison for libel of Admiral Knowles
1760–5	Working on *Continuation of the Complete History of England* (5 vols.)
1761–5	Joint Editor of The Works of Voltaire
1762 (29 May to 12 February, 1763)	Editing *The Briton* in support of Lord Bute—health deteriorating
1763 (3 April)	Only child, Elizabeth, dies, aged 15
1763 (June)	Travelled to France with wife and friends, then to Italy
1765 (July)	Returned to England
1766 (May)	*Travels through France and Italy*
1766 (May–August)	Travelled to Scotland and then back to Bath and London
1768	Completing *The Present State of All Nations* (8 vols.), on which he had been working since 1760
1768 (Autumn)	Left England for Italy, finally settling near Leghorn
1769 (April)	*The History and Adventures of an Atom*, a violent political satire
1771 (June)	*The Expedition of Humphry Clinker*
1771 (17 September)	Died near Leghorn. Buried in English cemetery there
1773	*Ode to Independence*, published posthumously
1776	Translation of Fenelon's *Adventures of Telemachus*, published posthumously

I
Towards Maturity and Mental Collapse

Physicians, in addition to their medical skill, often possess talents in music and literature. Few doctors do not either play musical instruments competently or at least enjoy classical music; and the last three centuries attest to the extraordinary literary gifts of men of medicine: Boyle, Smollett, Goldsmith, Keats, our own William Carlos Williams, to mention a few. As early as the 17th century, Bartholinus compiled a list of medieval and Renaissance physicians who had been poets, and Pierre Bayle was so deeply impressed with his findings that he reprinted the list in his *Dictionary*. The reasons for these particular leanings, rather than, say, painting, sculpture, or the dance, are not perfectly clear, but a number of theories exists, ranging from broad social factors to individual psychological ones. And yet the matter remains something of a mystery.

Tobias Smollett (1721–1771), a contemporary of Fielding, Richardson, Sterne, Goldsmith, and Dr. Johnson, is a case in point.[1] He did not spring from a literary family (his grandfather was a military man who rarely opened a book of poetry, and his father, a business man, was impressed by the talk of merchants more often than of artists); nor did Tobias display literary talent at an early age. Born and raised in Dumbartonshire, Scotland, he was educated in the local grammar school, and at the age of 15 entered Glasgow University. Here, apparently acting on his own, he chose the study of medicine, although possibly his family influenced him in this matter. Whatever the case—and no certainty exists—he is next found apprenticed to two prominent Glasgow surgeons, Drs. John Gordon and William Stirling, both connected with the university's newly formed Department of Anatomy. He continued as an apprentice for four years (1736–1739) but left Glasgow in 1739 without a degree, for reasons that remain murky. Perhaps he, like other young Scots of the time, ran out of money; but the magnetic lure of London may also have loomed large in his decision. Wanderlust may have been an impelling factor.

Journeying by land and with only a little money, he arrived in London in 1739 and almost immediately attached himself to dis-

tinguished Scottish medical men—William and John Hunter, James
and John Douglas, William Smellie. Exposure to these doctors must
have introduced him to some of the most advanced medical theories
of the day. With this advantage Smollett could be expected to distinguish himself in medicine. Marriage to Anne Lassells, a Creole
heiress, also proved an advantage. But naval service in the Caribbean,
while it offered the young surgeon experience, interrupted his professional advancement by removing him from London and his medical
sponsors. How otherwise can his total lack of medical achievement
be explained, especially since he was neither shy nor recalcitrant
towards his associates: he knew that they appreciated the ordeals of
a Scotsman in cosmopolitan though hostile London, and prominent
men like the Hunters and Douglases made every effort to encourage
the young Scot to carry on. Books, money, letters of introduction, a
proper image of the dignity of the Hippocratic profession—all were
at his disposal. Indeed there were few men in the 18th century who
could rival Tobias Smollett's fortune in coming under the aegis of
such patrons.

Smollett's medical career in the 1740s cannot be described as
distinguished. Yet during these years (1740–1750) he attended some
anatomical lectures delivered in Covent Garden by the Hunter
brothers; he displayed a modicum of concern for obstetrics, his
favourite branch of medicine; and he began to edit the collected
writings of Dr. William Smellie, in whose library he spent time. As
he prepared Smellie's works for the publishers, he read, perhaps
extensively, in obstetrics, not so much out of scientific curiosity as
from profound responsibility toward the man who had been so
benevolent to him. During these years he also practiced medicine
and, as was customary for surgeons, consulted with apothecaries.
He attracted an undue amount of attention through envy of rival
doctors, mostly Englishmen, who were denied easy access to the
"greats" (the Hunters, Douglases, Smellie) in whose company he
was often seen, as further evidenced by the portrait painted by an
unknown hand. By the mid 1740s the young Smollett was in a position
to reap every advantage that propinquity to the great and encouragement by the mighty could yield. Through his Scottish circle he had
met the celebrated James Thomson, poet of the *Seasons*, and had
fraternized with many lights, especially female lights of London's
theatrical world. In the London medical world, Smollett was virtually
unique in having easy access to those who could facilitate his career.

But at that moment he veered from medicine and chose another
walk of life; he turned away from a professional life that offered
status and relative financial security, and embraced a literary career
with a precarious future.

Precisely when Smollett was smitten with the desire to write is unknown but it must have been around 1739, when he was in his late teens. By 1746 the itch to write extended to the composition of poetic satires in partial imitation of Dryden and Pope; shortly afterwards he tried his hand at plays; and in 1747 he finished a full-length novel called *The Adventures of Roderick Random*, the experiences at sea of a ship surgeon. This novel, magnificently written, was an instantaneous best-seller and prompted critics to proclaim the advent of a Leviathan on the literary horizon. Almost overnight, Smollett was being compared to Fielding, who had just published *Tom Jones*, and was urged by his friends to write another in the same vein.

During the next five years, 1748–1752, Smollett continued to lead a double life, practicing medicine and writing novels. But there could be no doubt about his real passion: he could be enticed by medicine but he would not yield to it; his practice dwindled, and there were periods when he did not practice very much at all— preferring impoverishment to the risk of dulling his literary acumen. Writing for him was not sublimation; it was his way of making order out of a confusing world that soon threatened, as Pope had noted in *The Dunciad* (1743), "Universal Darkness." His determination to find time for both callings, when he performed both, is enviable though not surprising; he was energetic, as his pathologically ebullient prose style indicates, industrious, and, most noteworthy, intensely ambitious. And yet in the period during which he interchangeably donned two hats, his literary achievement proved remarkable: he translated *Gil Blas* into English, reviewed books for leading magazines, and published a second and third novel, *Peregrine Pickle* and *Ferdinand Count Fathom*, totalling more than half a million words in the space of three or four years. He befriended musicians and opera stars, and even found time to compose lyrics for their music. He left humble lodgings in the Strand, and moved into a splendid though somewhat small house in Chelsea with a court overlooking the Thames Embankment. Here the Smolletts entertained moderately among a selected few, some of them parishioners, others Scottish exiles living in London.

Smollett's medical achievement during these years is far less impressive. He saw the Hunters and Douglases less and less, and by 1750 probably ceased to attend their medical gatherings. He did, however, publish an original medical work, *An Essay on the External Use of Water* (1752), which argues for the valuable effects of pure water bathing, but the purport of this work is less scientific than its title implies: a close study shows its purpose to be the vindication of certain physicians at Bath and the indictment of others, and it is not in any case a purely scientific piece of writing. He immersed himself in obstetrical and gynecological literature in preparation for the editing of Dr. Smellie's works, but no original thought of his own issued, certainly not among his published works.

The passage of time has made it increasingly difficult to learn precisely what role Smollett played in editing Smellie's *Collection of Cases and Observations in Midwifery*; yet in view of Smollett's limited knowledge of the history of medicine and of experimental research, it is unlikely to have been more than an editorial function. His own stance was neutral: he did not disagree with Smellie, nor did he take the initiative to conduct research in obstetrics. At one point early in the 1750s, shortly after receiving his M.D. degree, it seemed that he was virtually on the verge of making a small discovery about the separation of the pubic joint in pregnancy, but this proved abortive since his theory was not really new at all. Although he may have attended many patients, several of whom were an overflow from Dr. Smellie's practice, Tobias Smollett can and must be classified as an average doctor, very far from a Mead, Sloane, or Radcliffe, or the Hunters, Douglases, or Smellie. He would not submit to the demands of total dedication to the medical profession.

From this point forward the enigma of Smollett begins; by contrast the events surrounding his life up to about 1750 are relatively clear, even if partially clouded for lack of evidence. Sometime after the early 1750s, Smollett, now about 30 years of age, began to experience what we can reasonably interpret as an "identity crisis." If this critical moment had appeared ten years earlier when he, then in his early twenties, was both medical practitioner and writer, his biographers could write more plausibly about their subject's dilemma in choosing between medicine and literature. But by 1750–1752 Smollett was an established author, his two novels already facts of literary history, and such a niche, now securely carved, could not escape his notice, modest though he was. He had already published two important novels, poems, a play, periodical literature, reviews, commentary, and in his mind's eye he pictured himself within reach of Parnassus. What other novelist in the early 1750s had so radiant a future? Richardson and Fielding had already written their masterpieces; Swift was dead and Jane Austen not yet born; only Sterne (older than Smollett but still an unknown country parson), who would publish *Tristram Shandy* in the next decade, can be described as having his whole future before him. Yet Smollett, at this critical moment of his career, must have envisaged his own apocalypse. He knew that medicine was a refuge. Though having no profound medical interests, he nonetheless had trained in the field and could resort to it when necessity beckoned. Literature, in contrast, was his favourite by choice; by his own volition he had turned away from medicine toward this new passion; he had taken his chances and conquered. In his own mind then, he had steered out of a sheltered cove—medicine—into an open sea—literature—which, it seems, gave greater challenge to his own energies—a challenge that would ultimately bring rewards.

Depression over transient concerns, whether financial, literary, or familial cannot rationally explain this crisis which mirrored his entire past and even seemed to foretell quite distant events of his future. Naturally, his biographers display caution in answering this difficult question. The paucity of extant documents leaves modern students in darkness, with few clues. Only a handful of contemporary accounts about Smollett during these years survives, and these are not particularly enlightening. His wife Anne wrote few letters that tell anything about her husband, and Smollett's own correspondence does not reveal much more. Unlike some of his contemporaries—Horace Walpole, Alexander Pope, Thomas Gray, Lady Mary Wortley Montagu—he was temperamentally not the type of letter writer who dissected himself in letters. And only a few disclosures of a genuinely autobiographical nature are found in his novels, *Roderick Random* notwithstanding. It is almost as if he wished himself unknown to posterity.

The day-by-day facts of his life after 1752 are plain enough, but they do not shape into a pattern that might help us understand the crisis and subsequent depression. After 1752, he seems to have stopped practicing medicine, and devoted himself exclusively to writing, despite the certainty that an already tottering financial condition would leave him impecunious. Few Grub Street hacks of the mid-18th century—not even the great Samuel Johnson—were financially solvent; and most, like the "Doctor," whom Smollett called "the great Cham of literature," passed their lives in wretched circumstances in dirty garrets. Could Smollett of Monmouth House, Chelsea, continue to live in high style among his neighbours, associating with aristocratic circles that spent their afternoons in Vauxhall and Ranelagh and their evenings in some of the most exclusive drawing rooms in town, if he were to devote all his time to writing? He could if subsequent novels were to sell as well as *Roderick Random*. But this was the unknown factor.

Peregrine Pickle, published early in 1751, was the precursor of a literary decline which was in part Smollett's trouble. "Sir" John Hill, a fellow hack who was as priggish as Smollett was modest, had learned through his own publishers that Smollett's forthcoming novel would contain "The Memoirs of Lady Vane," a lengthy account of a "woman of quality". In record time Hill shrewdly composed another set of intimate memoirs—of a pseudonymous "Lady Frail"—and thereby beat Smollett to publication. Hill announced that his memoirs were authentic and Smollett's spurious. Lady Frail's memoirs, by virtue of their greater sensual appeal, attained wide popularity, and cut the sales of Smollett's book considerably. The imitation proved financially more successful than the original. Smollett made little money through royalties and desperately hoped his next novel would turn the tide of his fortune. But this too was fruitless, for his third novel, *Ferdinand Count Fathom*, was a dismal failure: few readers are known to have enjoyed it and it was unnoticed by the critics.

An environment of financial worry and constant pressure, in conjunction with a steadily declining literary eminence, took its toll physically and mentally. Illness hounded him: he grew thin, wan, and (to use his own word) ulcerated. He was attacked by "sickness"—just which sicknesses are unclear, but from his self-diagnosis they included gout and consumption. Possibly his wife implored him not to abandon medicine forever until his literary eminence, and consequently his financial standing, were more firmly established. But that too, like so much of his life, is shrouded in conjecture. He would not yield the conviction that he possessed the qualities and abilities of a great novelist; and as long as he was convinced that he could achieve fame as a novelist, and join the ranks of Richardson and Fielding, then anyone's objections would fall on deaf ears. Despite adversity and sickness he would not relinquish the belief that his next novel would be as well received as *Roderick Random* had been. This expectation, coupled to a new sense of the presence of evil in human nature, accounts for his massive experimentalism and for his altered style in *Count Fathom*.

Yet depression lingered and introspective brooding occupied much of his time. For a period of several months he grew irritable, nasty, vindictive, almost to the point of a full-blown "identity crisis." I use this term in quotation marks because evidence does not exist to identify it as a proper identity crisis in the modern psychiatric sense. During this brief period (the end of 1752) he fed the myth that he was intrinsically unapproachable and that none who crossed his path would come away unscathed. He wrote quickly but not always well; certainly not so well as in the late 1740s when a depressive mood might have been understandable. At 27 *Roderick Random* had taken London by storm and nothing he did ever again would match that sense of thrill and glitter. At best the future would be a repetition of the past.

But derogation was not confined to himself; he seemed to despise others as well. Ebullient since childhood, he grew increasingly so, and the emotional crisis at hand further stimulated his energy, rendering him uncontrollable at times. He lashed out at others, especially religious fanatics and enthusiasts, seemingly persuaded that he alone recognized the supreme value of rational control over emotion and passion. And yet his most human qualities were the very ones he professed to loathe: pride, energy, tenacity, jealousy, irascibility. By the middle of 1752 he was so very much enmeshed within himself, so severely depressed, that he committed an unconventional and unexpected act in the preface to *Count Fathom*—he dedicated the novel to himself! In no previous novel had the dedication ever contained such venom together with savage self-indictment: the narrator in a characteristic mood of bitterness blended with romanticism engages in a dialogue with himself, his *ego* lashing out at his *alter ego*:

> Know, then, I can despise your pride while I honour your integrity; and applaud your taste, while I am shocked at your ostentation. I have known you trifling, superficial and obstinate in dispute; meanly jealous, and awkwardly reserved; rash and haughty in your resentments; and coarse and lowly in your connections. I have blushed at the weakness of your conversation, at the errors of your conduct. Yet as I own you possess certain good qualities, which overbalance these defects, and distinguish you on this occasion as a person for whom I have the most perfect attachment and esteem, you have no cause to complain of the indelicacy with which your faults are reprehended; and as they are chiefly the excesses of a sanguine disposition and looseness of thought, impatient of caution or control, you may, thus stimulated, watch over your own intemperance.

In this passage there is something truly epic and tragic. It is Smollett's most revealing autobiographical statement, far more confessional than anything in his correspondence; and despite its fictional context its contents are too significant to be overlooked. The "I" and the "you" only seem to converge, only seem to ambulate in "perfect attachment"; in actuality each goes its separate way, the *ego* charging the *alter ego* with fraudulent sovereignty. Such bifurcation of personality reveals forces within Smollett that had not come to the surface before. He was torn by forces over which the *ego* and *alter ego* each claimed dominion, and yet the precise nature of these forces is now lost.

His "indelicacy" of tone is but the emblem of his own true life style and temperament. He was harsh with others but harshest with himself, often addressing his inner self with unabashed tactlessness. If a "sanguine disposition" and "looseness of thought" were inextricably his chief flaws, they were relatively recent weaknesses, unknown to the Smollett of the forties. And while a pallid but lingering sullenness characterizes him well enough (in sharp contrast, for example, to the flamboyant Sterne of *Tristram Shandy* fame), "looseness of thought" is not a quality his contemporaries would have used to describe Tobias Smollett—certainly not those physicians who just ten years before had opened doors for him and lost no opportunity to aid his medical career. The narrator's command that the *alter ego* take charge of itself points to Smollett's most serious indictment of himself: an inability to feel whole and to love himself— to treat himself with anything but "indelicacy."

Time was not much kinder to him; nor were most of his biographers: *Count Fathom*, with its grotesque vision of evil and all reality, was an unequivocal failure, or so the critics agreed, and its reception hurled him deeper into despair. He did not compose another novel for eight years. And when *Sir Launcelot Greaves* appeared, it made no more than a slight impression on the London literary world, a world then much too preoccupied with the salty prurience of *Tristram Shandy* to take notice of still another quixotic romance. "It is not worthy of the author of *Roderick Random*" one critic exclaimed and Smollett, now consumptive, gouty, and broken in spirit, abandoned novel writing altogether and escaped forever to the sunny Mediterranean in search of health. His personality had suffered some trauma, and he hoped that time and sun should heal the wound, would at least remove the mephitic elements preying upon him. In Italy there was hope for a new life, but to many he remained, as to Sterne, merely the irritable "Smelfungus Smollett."

There is another turn of the screw, one that lends poetic justice to the tale but does not explain away the enigma. In his very last years while living abroad and now almost 50, Smollett decided to make a comeback. His decision to write a final great novel was influenced by the knowledge that he was seriously consumptive and had little time to live. Perhaps he was also prompted by the fact that he had written at least one great novel, *Roderick Random*, and if he had achieved eminence once he could scale the heights again. Therefore in 1766, or thereabout, he began writing an epistolary novel about an itinerant family, the *Brambles* headed by Matthew, a splenetic, gouty old man with a tough exterior and a heart of gold. *Humphry Clinker* was published only two or three months before his death and although it is not likely that Smollett still in Italy, saw many reviews of his novel or heard from many of his friends about it, critics in England and Scotland were acclaiming his eminence as they had not before. *Humphry Clinker* was immediately deemed, like *Roderick Random*, to be a masterpiece, the best production of its author. Smollett did not survive to enjoy its financial success or literary acclaim. Had he lived, there is every reason to believe that the nagging depression of his middle period would have been at least alleviated. Instead, he died without the knowledge of a renewed public approval; yet he might have had the consolation that time would tell the truth—as it has—that he himself best knew the literary worth of his novels.

NOTE

1. The year 1971 marks the bicentenary of Smollett's death. In commemoration a definitive Bicentennial Edition of his works is in preparation, under the editorship of O. M. Brack and others.

My materials in this essay derive from a longer essay and make use of the authoritative biography of Smollett by Lewis M. Knapp, Smollett's most learned student of this century. *Tobias Smollett* (Princeton, 1949). Additional information relating to his life is found in these works chronologically listed: George Kahrl: *Tobias Smollett, Traveler-Novelist* (Chicago, 1945); G. S. Rousseau: *Doctors and Medicine in the Novels of Tobias Smollett* (Princeton, 1966); *The Letters of Tobias Smollett*, edited by L. M. Knapp (Oxford 1970); *Tobias Smollett: Essays on the Man and His Works*, edited by G. S. Rousseau with P. G. Boucé (Oxford, 1971). I am indebted to Professor Knapp for making his Smollett library available to me, to Miss Jessie Dobson of the Hunterian Museum for sending me information about Smollett and the Hunter brothers, to Eric Gaskell of the Wellcome Institute of the History of Medicine, London, and to more than a half-dozen psychiatrists, here and abroad, with whom I have discussed Smollett's psychological case history.

II

Tobias Smollett and Laurence Sterne: A Revaluation*

We have all come to praise Caesar and yet we know that a centenary can be a fete worse than death. At best it provides a good occasion to settle accounts, not just with the celebrity but with his critics and interpreters. This is all the truer in our case because we have only recently recovered from the splendours of the Sterne bicentenary (1968) held in York, and such propinquity of a Smollett and Sterne jubilee permits taking stock of all ourselves.

If we look around us, we can see, palpably and tangibly, that we are busy. We are engaged in compiling large editions—scholarly editions that will lend both authors a credibility unknown before and grant them an abiding permanence; we have been writing books (twelve on Sterne in the last decade, seven on Smollett); we are at work on historical and literary studies, critical checklists, and descriptive bibliographies. Yorick-the-flamboyant would have been exhilarated at all this fuss made over him; the more modest and less colourful "Smelfungus Smollett"—as Sterne called him—would have been embarrassed at this activity.

And yet this occasion also provides an opportunity for the sane to take negative stock. We have perhaps answered to our satisfaction Thackeray's charge of Laurence's prurience, but not his lesser known branding of Tobias as simple-minded. We have quoted again and again that Virginia Woolf, Elizabeth Bowen, Thomas Wolfe, and Katherine Anne Porter—as well as a host of others—have taken delight in the way Sterne's prose "leads us to the very brink of the precipice",[1] but muted the fact that these writers have not uttered so much as a single word of praise for Smollett and for an embarrassing—embarrassing, that is, to themselves as well as to our celebrity—variety of reasons ranging from their not having read him to their belief that he simply was not important enough to be *read*. Sterne, on the other hand, has been in the public domain since his death and

* Delivered on December 29, 1970 in New York City at the annual meetings of the MLA.

to an extent never enjoyed by Smollett, with the possible exception of the first two decades of the nineteenth century. Among ingenues what passes as paradigmatic for Sterne's fictive world is tacitly assumed also to be true of Smollett's because they were contemporaries, born almost nine years apart. But whereas Sterne is an "original", Smollett is a mere "influence". Pick up any single volume of criticism of the novel, and references, however brief, will be found to the heteroclite parson and his bizarre masterpiece. Smelfungus Smollett is rarely discovered in indexes, and still more rarely as the subject of sentences solely about him or his novels. If one scrutinizes the works of David Cecil, Ian Watt, Wayne Booth, J. M. S. Tompkins, Arnold Kettle, V. S. Prichett, Frank Kermode, and dozens of other influential critics, it is soon evident that Smollett's name is used to buttress vapid generalities about eighteenth-century novels generalities usually of the rhetorical cast: "this technique may be seen at work in the fiction of Fielding, Richardson, and Smollett".[2]

Henry James is known to have thought highly of George Eliot's fiction; would he have wasted his time with Tobias Smollett? Would he have read him through and taken the time to write an entire essay about him? Three decades ago Dr. Leavis relegated Dickens to a footnote in *The Great Tradition* (1948) of English novelists, but one searches in vain for any mention of a Tobias Smollett. The express train from Sterne to Joyce is heavily travelled these days; which novelists of consequence (excepting Dickens) has Smelfungus influenced? Somewhere I have seen a three line note about Smollett and Shaw, and more recently a tiny note suggesting a possible echo of Smollett in Melville, but scholars agree that both parallels are tenuous—at best it can be said that Shaw had read *Peregrine Pickle*. But that is "Hyperion to a Satyr"! After 1760, there were literally dozens of imitations of *Tristram Shandy*; *Humphry Clinker* has claimed only a handful, and this fact of literary history must be viewed in the bleak light that it is much easier to imitate the latter. Sterne has often been called a latter-day Swift as is made apparent by the number of studies embracing both men; Smollett, on the other hand, has no such eminent prototype and for want of one is said to be a second-rate Fielding. His detractors note that if one wishes Fieldingesque experience, why not read the better of the two writers? Yorick is the founder of a whole movement in the novel— some critics of sentimentalism incorrectly assert—and whether or not they are historically correct he is at least thought to have started *something*. No such accolade embraces Tobias, too long a forgotten and misunderstood novelist, even to the experts. A mere editor? A hack? An amateur? . . .

Sterne was well read, especially in philosophy, and knew of and used for purposes of learned wit the writings of Locke and the Associationists. His characters, unlike Smollett's, are amazingly attuned to the New Psychology of the day, as Swift's had been, (there is that old comparison cropping out again!), and reflect contemporary uneasiness about new and somewhat frightening realms of mind expansion. Sterne wrote immensely enjoyable letters in whose maze the reader can lose himself for days; Smollett's correspondence, by comparison, is read in a few hours and very little of it is worth recommending, is anything but topical irrelevance to the larger concerns of life.[3] To move from letters to the content of his fiction: scholars today cannot even show that Smollett read about or knew the works of his own native Scottish Common Sense School;[4] that he knew how to use rhetoric effectively, or yoke (in the best sense of that term) form to content. A well-known English critic, speaking of English novelists and their letters in a BBC afternoon lecture this last autumn, called Smollett one of the worst letter writers in three hundred years, and if one has no axe to grind it must be admitted that there is some meat in the assertion.

I remember an elderly lady professor in the North Library of the British Museum—whose name you would all know*—who confessed to me that she read Sterne annually because Yorick's combination of prurience and nonsense amused her; but she would not dream of rereading the few works by Smollett she had read at the university as a girl because, even then, in the peak of adolescence, he "bored the tears off her". I also remember a distinguished Johnson scholar in Johnson's house in Gough Square, who at a dinner of the Johnson Club, confessed he knew little about that writer who called his hero the "Great Cham of Literature", and, to add insult to injury, that no Johnsonian needed to!

If we ourselves could become parsonical for a moment, we might consider: who in these troubled times reads *Launcelot Greaves*, *Count Fathom*, or the *History of England*? How many critics of the English novel sincerely enjoy *Peregrine Pickle* as they relish the fictive worlds of Conrad or D. H. Lawrence? My father, no scholar, roars reading *Tristram*; he pours over *Random* in silence. It is not enough to flatter ourselves as period specialists within the profession of English letters that we have read this novelist. If Smollett is to gain footing as important in the heritage of English literature, it must be unequivocally demonstrated that his appeal is not merely to a small and remotely élite group of readers unrepresentative of wide taste and value, but that he succeeds, as every great novelist must succeed, by appealing to universal concerns throughout many ages and to wide varieties of readers.

---

* The late Frances Yates.

Some of Sterne's popularity and Smollett's unpopularity can be demonstrated to be historically a matter of aggregative biography, myths, and anecdotes. Smelfungus, unfortunately the author of only one hundred extant letters, has none of the charm of the heteroclite parson: none of his delectable vagaries, wheedling, flamboyance, colour, turpitude, unflagging conquests, penchant for the lewd in sex, *rondeur* about the joys of promiscuity. Sterne may or may not be a *poseur*, but what a time he has trying to persuade us! Witness his drawing room in Toulouse, for example, or compare both men at Montpellier. "I have been for eight weeks smitten," he wrote to Eliza in May 1764, "with the tenderest passion that ever tender wight underwent." On another occasion when suffering from an unnameable disease, he apparently ran into Anne Stuart, Lady Warkworth, in Hyde Park, whom he designated as Sheba:

"Come, come to me soon my Eliza and save me" [he said to her]...
"I fear your wife is dead," quoth Sheba
"No, you don't fear it, Sheba," said I
"Upon my word, Solomon! I would quarrel with you, was you not so ill."—
"If you knew the cause of my illness, Sheba," replied I, "you would quarrel but the more with me."—
"You lie, Solomon," answered Sheba, "for I know the cause already—and am so little out of charity with you upon it—that I give you leave to come and drink tea with me before you leave town."
"You're a good honest creature, Sheba!"
"No, you rascal, I am Not—But I'm in love, as much as you can be for your life."
"I'm glad of it, Sheba," said I.
"You lie," said Sheba, and so cantered away.[5]

Just how much of Sterne's life story is a pack of lies we may never know, but so long as Lothario-Yorick continues to make an impression on generations of men by his deepest self-revelations as acts of play and oblique stance, he will command the area. Smelfungus, on the other hand, is direct, harsh, introverted, and not infrequently a brooder. Witness by contrast this sanguinary self-portrait, Smollett's analysis of himself:

Know then, I can despise your pride, while I honour your integrity; and applaud your taste, while I am shocked at your ostentation. I have known you trifling, superficial and obstinate in dispute; meanly jealous, and awkwardly reserved; rash and haughty in your resentments; and coarse and lowly in your connections. I have blushed at the weakness of your conversation, and trembled at the errors of your conduct. Yet as I own you possess certain good qualities, which overbalance these defects, and, distinguish you on this occasion as a person for whom I have the most perfect attachment and esteem, you have no cause to complain of the indelicacy with which your faults are reprehended; and as they are chiefly the excesses of a sanguine disposition and looseness of thought, impatient of caution or control, you may, thus stimulated, watch over your own intemperance and infirmity with redoubled vigilance and consideration, and for the future profit by the severity of my reproof.[6]

Smollett's temperamental weaknesses are minor in comparison with his deficiences of personality, especially a lack of charisma; while Yorick, his apparent antithesis, the ultimate *poseur*, appeals to citizens of the whole world, not merely to a select few. A terrible moral self-consciousness ruled Smollett's life; Sterne's was self-assured, even smug, hardly "moral". In Smollett's life there had been *no* Belle Indian, *no* mad Queen of Bohemia, *no* Shandy Hall, *no* playing of the devil at Bath, *no* narcissistic delight in his own sensibility, *no* Kitty, *no* Eliza, *no* hordes of acolytes, *no* inveterate optimism, *no* ostentatious boasting. While Sterne grew more, Smollett grew less prurient. Yorick—and by now it is clear that I am using his name synonymously with Sterne's intentionally to defy the heresy of confusing author and narrator—could plagiarize even from himself; at best, Smollett could compose introspective self-dedications. Matt Bramble, tender-hearted though he is, has no delectable wound in the groin. Yorick's combination of sick black humour, exuding penis symbols, and a positively incomparable and inimitable speaking style the rhetoric of which has still not been perfectly deciphered, render him, as Virginia Woolf has said, "a dragonfly with method in his flight". But she is also known to have commented to Sir Herbert Read about the flatness of Smollett's letters (in contrast to Sterne's), and on Smelfungus' lack of self-revelation.

But one hundred or so letters are all we have of Tobias', and there is no likelihood we will discover a Malahide Castle. We have a biography of Tobias[7] that is remarkable for vacuum-cleaner thoroughness, but for all the sympathy—or understanding—it shows a man of flesh and blood, and for its portrait of a human being, it might as well never have been written. And yet, the culprit is not so much Smollett's present biographers or biographers of the future —but the man himself. His personality lacked colour and we might as well forget about its perennial interest. If he lacked technique in the novel, he also lacked life-style, charisma, charm, poise—briefly all those qualities one dotes on in the case of Sterne.

Far more vulnerable and fallible than the biographers have been his critics: especially Victorians who made no sense whatever of his works, but also twentieth-century critics who have egregiously become bogged down in matters that are needless challenges to the sanest readers because, in addition to boredom, they ask questions that lead nowhere.

What is it? asked Alice in Wonderland: is it a tree, a house, a cheshire cat? No! The petulantly inquisitive Alice was wrong: it is a *picaresque*! Is *all* of it picaresque, *some* of it, *one* of it, *part* of it, or what? Is it picaresque or quixotic or roguish, or more roguish and less picaresque?

These and other similar concocted questions are being asked about Smollett's fiction and others less barbaric and solemn (like which parts of his novels are read with pleasure?), left by the wayside to rot. Profound questions pertaining to his sense of plot, to what I have called elsewhere his pathologically energetic words, and to the unusual way his narratives strike the imagination of readers; all have been sadly ignored, but particularly the last has gone begging while theoretical critic after critic, wading in the unsifted muck of concretes and universals, tinkers superficially in a paragraph here or there with picaresques and discriminations of picaresques and further discriminations of picaresques.

If Smollett is a truly great novelist, and I am not certain he is, then one cannot dismiss the often asked and somewhat embarrassing question about his amateurish sense of form and shape. Only those who fabricate out of every Defoe a Shakespeare, out of every Rochester a Keats, will elevate Smelfungus to Yorick, Smollett to Sterne; but those who are wiser and sounder and few know that Smollett is far from a Dickens: has not the richness of content, the intellectual and symbolic substratum of textual fabric, nor so perfect a sense of form. One thinks of the preposterous and gimmicky ending tagged on to *Roderick Random* in the pious name of "Providence" and wonders what would accrue if Professor Frank Kermode's test of an artist's worth judged by his sense of an ending[8] were here applied. Surely no writer whose vision of reality is so bizarre and marvellous (in the eighteenth-century sense), nor who scotch tapes (not to say imposes) endings like that, however comic his mode, ought to have a thing called a bicentenary:

> . . . yes when I put the rose in my hair like the Andalusian girls used or shall I wear a red yes and how he kissed me under the Moorish wall and I thought well as well him as another and then I asked him with my eyes to ask again yes and then he asked me would I yes to say yes my mountain flower and first I put my arms around him yes and drew him down to me so he could feel my breasts all perfume yes and his heart was going like mad and yes I said yes I will Yes[9]

If Molly and Leopold appear endless in their levels of awareness, Smollett's admittedly ribald figures (heroes and heroines introduce a nonexistent element into his fiction) display none of the subterranean currents of Sterne's: the key to any depth Smollett's figures possess is measured by their ingenious ability to conjure playful and grotesque stratagems and to repeat these in all possible combinations and permutations. Until recently this view of man has not been popular, and, to add to an already immodest indictment, there is little evidence in Smollett's fictions that he was aware in the slightest degree of executing anything more than the telling of stories.

Until we discover how Smollett's grotesques impinge upon the reading imagination, we cannot know—and this is just the point— what he did achieve artistically and if he is anything more than a stylist—anything of the magnitude of a Joyce or Dickens or even Defoe in *Moll Flanders*. After all, his cities have none of the vast symbolic density of Dickens' London, or, to turn inwards, the mind's holographic landscape in Sterne's Toby, Wadman, or Tristram. If formalist critics astutely remark that Tobias' fiction is thoroughly anomalous when compared to the dominant—dominant in that between them they shared fiction's planet—Richardsonian–Fieldingesque form of plot, realism, and judgment, a classification sufficiently describing the novels of both writers, what then is a proper formalistic description of Smollett's novels, different though they are from each other? We have laboured almost too far to the nitty gritty facts of Smollett's pale existence and not bothered to look at the shape of his fictions and their precise impact on our imagination.

Sterne's art, in contrast, is more perfect by virtue of a more enticing (and eccentrically intrusive) narrator and because of character distortions that are surely more original, less grotesque, and—most important—less repetitive than Smollett's. "Writing", says Sterne in *Tristram Shandy*, "when properly managed (as you may be sure I think mine is) is but a different name for *conversation*: and no one, who knows what he is about in good company, would venture to talk all;—so, no author, who understands the just boundaries of decorum and good breeding, would presume to think all." Yorick-Sterne *can* think almost all, or so he convinces us, and "properly" records the most intimate conversations and intimations; whereas Tobias, whose grotesque caricatures blend after a while into one another like the white fences in a Vermont landscape, is limited— and even when his writing is "properly managed", properly adjusted to the level of inflation or deflation he desires, he himself is too harsh, too caustic, too pungent, too brutal a narrator for the ordinary reader and, besides, recedes too far into a distant background to appear as a felt presence. So much so, that only those critics willing to commit the exegetical heresy of inverted autobiography, that is in discovering in every Random or Pickle a Tobias, etch out a comprehensive Smollett whose narrative and historical identities merge into one blurry nucleus. That cannot pass as modern-day criticism. Nor does it help us to assess Smollett's literary achievement.

More often than not, his writing is not "properly managed" unless writing is defined in the most reductionistic and simple-minded terms as mere rhetoric. Stiff doctrines—especially that good old cause Providence—are made to account for vast turns of plot and action, and this charge has nothing to do with imposing post-Jamesian criteria, as one insensitive critic has noted, on pre-Jamesian fiction. Smollett learned much from Fielding about low-life characters, especially as they interact within family structures, and about the thematic organization of a novel; but in total achievement he could not rival Fielding because his vision of reality was too oblique and because personal virulence caused him to view the world as a bizarre accumulation of insane caricatures. His fiction deflects reality too much because he ultimately believed the whole world was insane. His great flaw, therefore, lay in the superimposition of a *deus ex machina* who constantly (and bafflingly) bails the world out of its age-old misery, which Smollett believed so sad as to be grossly comic. A man who does this we cannot love. Nor will his style console us.

Moreover, if we take away his first and last novel, the rest is subject to confounded nadirs. *Peregrine Pickle*, by far the best of the middle three, has its great comic moments and memorable caricatures (fancy tacking up the street en route to one's wedding!), but as all its readers know it rambles in prodigious disorganization and cannot control an already loose form. As for Smollett's other two middle novels: *Ferdinand Count Fathom*, a dismally massive experiment in the hybridization of low-life realism and gothic melodrama, is as unpopular and neglected now as it was in 1753, and *Sir Launcelot Greaves*, perhaps the least distinguished novel ever conceived by a reputedly major author, knows not its own significance or ends and greatly suffers from an immense miscalculation, namely that novel readers accustomed to at least two decades of realism (i.e., probable plots) would willingly withdraw from the concerns of real life into its preposterous terrain and ossific quixotic orb.[10]

But Sterne could not write poorly, never misjudged so fantastically as Smollett in *Count Fathom* or *Launcelot Greaves*. His was a great life ensconced in great art giving maximum pleasure to the common reader. Tobias-the-irascible, the brutal cynic whose pungent personality forever remained a mystery to the man himself, had at best an unornamented life and only occasionally wrote well: this estimate is accurate whether he is judged solely on technical grounds (e.g., plot, character, realism, endings, diction, prose rhythm, intrinsic inventiveness, etc.), and not as Sir Walter Scott so often judged him[11]—on extrinsic bases of every variety ranging from nationality and regionality to certain types of topicality (e.g. the prevailing fashion of the mid-eighteenth century to read novels for comic amusement) which Scott erroneously thought would sustain perennial interest. The Victorians and Edwardians were to crush that expectation. If Sterne's private god, unlike Smollett's, was the hole in the wall behind the barn (as Thackeray intimated) and all the delicious joys thereunto, his public god—that deity within him that he sensed would long outlive himself—was doubtlessly the perfection of the art of the novel: the marriage of stories, people, and language into a seemingly perfect harmony; perfect for its own purposes and for posterity's, and moreover one that persuades us of more substance than mirth and grotesquerie. No one can call Sterne, or for that matter Fielding, an amateur, and those readers like Mr. Leavis, for whom novel reading commences with Jane Austen, can only plead, however imperceptibly, that their imaginations and moral senses are are not sufficiently stirred by the stories of a Fielding or Sterne. But Tobias is another matter. He *was* an amateur more often than not, and when he wrote well, as in *Humphry Clinker*, it has never been made clear precisely what his crowning achievement was. The point to be gathered, then, is first that Smollettian uniqueness, artistry, and profundity (if there is profundity) have not as yet been established, and second, that although all of us in this room have a vague intui- tion (although we may not be able to verbalize it clinically and analytically) of the nature and scope of this uniqueness, artistry, and profundity, it is not perfectly clear just if and why these are worth passing on from generation to generation.

What remains but to acknowledge excellence and merit where they appear? We must admit, even vaunt the fact, as has often been done, that Smollett was first and foremost a stylist. Where in his novels are there objectionable sentences, unfit logomachies, inappropriate diction, obscure syntax, unsuitable metaphors, inept images? But style alone, however broadly conceived,[12] does not guarantee eminence or immortality to a novelist. Novelists, like poets, after all, must be read equally for their omissions as for their inclusions. And a balanced estimate of his works shows that Smollett's range, like Prévost's or Trollope's, is limited; even more limited is his *métier*: a gallery of grotesque rogues; unlike Herman Melville, rarely is his theme mighty. Comic grotesques like Mrs. Grizzle or Mrs. Tabitha Bramble, ribald and mirthful though they are, cannot constitute the entire fabric of character of a distinguished oeuvre, however "relevant" they appear today to a world obsessed by figures like Gogo, Didi, and Marat Sade. We as critics have perhaps erred by concentrating too much on Smollett's caricatures and grotesques—but what else is there if these are subtracted?—when his greater achievement within the history of English fiction, or so it seems to me, is stylistic. Like the Trollope of *Barchester Towers*, he is a considerable stylist and ought to be enjoyed, page by page, for a variegated style that commands a broad spectrum of image, metaphor, and rhythm. But as I have already stated too many times, style in and of itself does not sustain novelists whose appeal, if they are to endure, must transcend topical relevance and daily fashion; does not insure the greatness of a Dickens—great for many reasons in addition to style—let alone the metaphysical greatness of a Lawrence, Proust, or Tolstoy.

I have intentionally played the devil and focused on Smollett's weakest sides to paint a dim picture and disburden my audience of the inebriation of a centenary; but also because no critic or scholar of integrity can face such a solemn occasion without anticipating objections raised by his soberest listeners. But I have not painted the bleakest picture. To do that would entail, for example, playing the tapes of sessions with several large American paperback companies in which the hard economic facts of paperback sales of Smollett's fiction are recorded; or revealing what the jet-set thinks of this writer (i.e., those members of the jet-set who have stooped to read him). Not wishing to shock my many friends present, I shall keep this arcane material in abeyance for another day.

This is where we stand on the advent of 1971. In conclusion, I must sincerely profess that my comparisons of Sterne and Smollett are tentative, pending the necessary critical toil in the vineyards that will accurately pinpoint Smollett's contribution to English fiction and establish once and forever his niche. It is naturally my great hope that when this labour has been accomplished we can reconvene and place garlands around Caesar's tomb.

NOTES

1. Virginia Woolf, introduction to *The World's Classics* edition of *A Sentimental Journey* (London, 1928), p. xii.
2. E.g., Sir Herbert Read, *English Prose Style* (London, 1952), pp. 78–79: "Fielding, Smollett, Richardson, Thackeray, Trollope, George Eliot, Dickens, Meredith, Hardy, —there is a vivid immediacy in the work of all these authors. There is a quickness of observation, a fund of comedy or humour, an invention of character or plot, and—in different degrees—a philosophy of life." Another example is Giorgio Melchiori, *The Tightrope Walkers* (London, 1956), p. 49: "Swift, Fielding, Sterne and Smollett set out deliberately as humorous writers, since the novel was taken to be mainly a vehicle for light entertainment." Northrop Frye comments only once on Smollett in the *Anatomy*

of Criticism (Princeton, 1957), p. 159 and notes his simple-mindedness: "In Smollett's *Humphry Clinker* (I select this because no one will suspect Smollett of deliberate mythopoeia but only of following convention, at least as far as his plot is concerned), the main characters are nearly drowned in an accident with an upset carriage; they are then taken to a nearby house to dry off, and a *cognito* takes place, in the course of which their family relationships are regrouped, secrets of birth brought to light, and names changed. Similar points of ritual death may be marked in almost any story that imprisons the hero." George Steiner, another influential critic, also comments on Smollett only once in his printed works and demonstrates unequivocally that he cannot have grasped anything of Smollett's art; *The Death of Tragedy* (New York, 1961), p. 264: "The novels of Smollett show money being made and lost in rational and technical ways."

3. See G. S. Rousseau, "Smollettiana", *Eighteenth Century Studies*, 4 (1971), pp. 336–342.

4. Reviews, especially the one by David Daiches, of Milton A. Goldberg's book *Smollett and the Scottish School* (Albuquerque, 1959) have made this point abundantly clear.

5. "The Journal to Eliza", May 1, 1767, quoted in *Letters of Laurence Sterne*, ed. Lewis Perry Curtis (Oxford: Clarendon Press, 1967, rev. ed.), p. 335. Sterne's personality might best be described as follows: mercurial, amorous, somewhat unreliable, confident, amoral, gregarious, immodest, egotistical, humorous, impulsive, erratically generous, flamboyant, self-derisive. Unlike Smollett, he found his negative qualities amusing. However wrongheaded Albert Pollard's Victorian notions of the eighteenth century were, he is surely right to note in his *DNB* Life of Sterne that "Morality, which ordinarily checks the free play of feeling and passion by the exercise of virtuous reason, lay, he admitted, outside his sphere".

6. Preface to *Count Fathom* (London, 1753), dedicated "To Dr. S . . ." For a recent psychoanalytical case history of Smollett's life, see G. S. Rousseau, *Journal of the American Medical Association* (April 1971), 85–89.

7. Lewis M. Knapp, *Tobias Smollett: Doctor of Men and Manners* (Princeton, 1949).

8. Frank Kermode, *The Sense of an Ending: Studies in the Theory of Fiction* (Oxford, 1967). Kermode never refers to Smollett in this book or elsewhere, and the fault is partly Smollett's. His novels, like Haydn's comic opera *The Apothecary* but unlike Mozart's comic opera *Don Giovanni*, compel analytical readers ultimately to abandon their twentieth-century perspective and adopt historical categories (e.g., Hogarth's comic painting, caricature drawing, grotesque depiction) now antiquated because of monumental changes in the progress of realism. If one performs an experiment in the form of testing Smollett's novels by criteria of modern realism (e.g., George J. Becker, *Documents of Modern Literary Realism* [Princeton, 1963]) all one can say after close scrutiny is that Smollett's fiction, like some recent novels and films, depicts ugliness. Smollett therefore suffers when one grasps the age-old paradigm that artistic works demanding analysis in the context of the time of their composition are simply not as universal as their opposites. Witness, for example, the plays of Shakespeare.

9. James Joyce, *Ulysses* (New York: Modern Library Edition, 1934), p. 768.

10. They withdrew into *Rasselas*, two years earlier, for other reasons, especially because the imagination did not perceive it as a novel. Furthermore, allegories and oriental tales were then more highly esteemed than low-life quixotic romances.

11. "Tobias Smollett" in *Lives of the Novelists: Prefaces to Ballantyne's Novelists' Library* (1821–4).

12. E.g., Walter Pater's *Essay on Style* (London, 1889).

III
Smollett's London*

As the titlepage indicates, *Smollett's London* was a course of lectures delivered at the University of Paris during 1963–64. The author, the professor of English there, has selected Smollett's time rather than some other period of the eighteenth century because "the fifty years when Smollett lived, from 1721 to 1771, may be regarded as the turning point of the age: Smollett's time was a time of change." Having stated his belief, Parreaux proceeds to discuss the growth of London, especially bridge and edifice building, street life, the mob, the underworld, the criminal world, the "tricks of the town," scandal and vice, and London's amusements. It may be that most historians will not agree with Professor Parreaux's basic assumption about the transitional nature of Smollett's time. One wonders, after all, if the period from 1721 to 1771 was any more transitional than that of 1688–1744, the years coinciding with Pope's lifetime, or of 1709–1784, those of Johnson's. Thus one searches still for a book on Pope's London and Johnson's London. Despite the weakness of this starting point—weak from an historiographical vantage—Parreaux's book is informative for many details that the student of eighteenth-century literature finds difficult to locate elsewhere. This is all the more emphatic as students continue to be intrigued by tensions between town and country in that century, and by the symbolic associations of evil and moral chaos with city life.

Given that the city is an extremely important zone in the mental landscape of the major English writers of the eighteenth century, it is useful to learn that "globular lamps for street-lighting were introduced as early as 1709. And about 1740 there were 4200 lamps, apart from those wanted for public buildings. They were fixed at twenty-five yards distance on each side of the way in the high streets, and at thirty-five in lesser streets and lanes." Elsewhere one discovers that "after the shock of an earthquake in 1750, which was felt in London, a fanatic prophesied that the next shock would occur on the same day of April the 8th and totally destroy the cities

* This piece originally appeared as a review of André Parreaux's *Smollett's London* (Paris: Nizet, 1965).

of London and Westminster." The implications of these occurrences to the imagination of writers is not followed through—one wonders how *apocalypsis imminentis* struck the rascalish and irritable Smollett; but everywhere suggestions in the form of facts abound that must give rise to better thinking about the remarkable fictions of the as yet barely understood Smollett. There is no question that the city —London beyond Glasgow or Edinburgh—is a symbol of evil for Smollett, and that in his early works, especially his two poetic satires, the city promotes vice of the worst sorts. What is curious and what contributes to the importance of this little book is Smollett's socio-logical imagination: from the start of his literary career, Smollett seems to have sensed that evil centres on groups of persons, not on individuals. Smollett has no sophisticated hypothesis about the reasons for this belief until his mature fictions in the 1750s. Neverthe-less, it is useful now to have a book that documents the facts of the symbol, as it were.

IV
Smollett and the Society of Arts of London

Tobias Smollett, author of *Roderick Random*, *Peregrine Pickle*, and *Humphry Clinker*, never became a member of this Society, but he commented on its virtues and defects—the former more so than the latter—four times in his published works. It is not extraordinary for Dr. Smollett, a physician by training but a writer by profession, to have praised this group: in an epoch devoted to the encouragement of arts, manufactures and commerce this was typical. But for Smollett, unlike Johnson, Boswell, Burke, Sterne, Richardson, Goldsmith, Horace Walpole, and dozens of other literary men of his generation, to elect never to affiliate himself must give us pause. At the least, we want to know his reasons.

Before answering this question, however, we must delve into Smollett's estimate of the Society, this "elegant, useful, and noble society", as Boswell called it.[1] Nor is it fanciful to link the two men's opinions at the outset, for Smollett was equally enthusiastic but not in regard to all societies. A non "clubable" man, Smollett usually speaks about other societies baldly and flaccidly. His usual nervous tone denoting approbation is lacking. But when referring to the Society of Arts, he regains energy and adopts his not uncommon optimistic voice employed when commenting on the possibility of progress: man can have a future and happy destiny. Is this stance not curious for a man who maintained grave doubts about the human condition? whose sense of man was largely determined by the harsh reality of economic competition that often reduced heaps of mankind to poverty, rags, and death?—a game of warfare Smollett once dubbed men preying on other men like animals.[2]

I

Smollett's first and lengthiest discussion of the Society of Arts appears in his *History of England, From the Revolution in 1688 to the Death of George II*, published in 1758 as a continuation of Hume's *History*. This fact is significant considering that only two societies are mentioned in all five volumes covering over seventy years (1688–

1760) and totalling over a million words. The other is the Society for the Reformation of Manners (1698), briefly discussed in connection with "a contagious and infectious immorality sweeping over England",[3] especially London. But it is a brief mention containing little of the substance found in the passage on the Society of Arts. In the former, Smollett meditates on civilization under the long reign of George II:

"Nor was encouragement refused to those who distinguished themselves by extraordinary talents in any branch of the liberal and useful arts and sciences, though no Maecenas appeared among the ministers, and not the least ray of patronage glimmered from the throne. The protection, countenance, and gratification secured in other countries by the institution of academies, and the liberalities of princes, the ingenious in England derived from the generosity of a public, endued [sic] with taste and sensibility, eager for improvement, and proud of patronizing extraordinary merit. Several years had already elapsed since a society of private persons was instituted at London, for the encouragement of arts, manufactures, and commerce. It consisted of a president, vice-president, secretary, register, collector, and other officers, elected from a very considerable number of members, who pay a certain yearly contribution for the purposes of the institution"[4]

Then follows a detailed description of the administration and activities of the Society, a subject Smollett must have thought warranted extensive treatment within the overall architecture of his *History*.[5] The passage is so carefully wrought that it is worth quoting *in toto*:

"In the course of every year they held eight general meetings in a large assembly-room, built and furnished at the common expence; besides the ordinary meetings of the society, held every week, from the second Wednesday in November to the last Wednesday in May; and in the intermediate time, on the first and third Wednesday of every month. At these ordinary meetings, provided the number then present exceeded ten, the members had a right to proceed on business, and power to appoint such committees as they should think necessary. The money contributed by this association, after the necessary expence of the society had been deducted, was expended in premiums for planting and husbandry; for discoveries and improvements in chemistry, dyeing and mineralogy; for promoting the ingenious arts of drawing, engraving, casting, painting, statuary, and sculpture; for the improvement of manufactures, and machines in the various articles of hats, crapes, druggets, mills, marbled-paper, ship-blocks, spinning-wheels, toys, yarn, knitting, and weaving. They likewise allotted sums for the advantage of the British colonies in America, and bestowed premiums on those settlers who should excel in curing

cochineal, planting logwood-trees, cultivating olive-trees, producing myrtle-wax, making potash, preserving raisins, curing
safflour, making silk and wines, importing sturgeon, preparing
isinglass, planting hemp and cinnamon, extracting opium and
the gum of the persimon-tree, collecting stones of the mango,
which should be found to vegetate in the West Indies; raising
silk-grass, and laying out provincial gardens. They moreover,
allowed a gold medal, in honour of him who should compose the
best treatise on the arts of peace, containing an historical account
of the progressive improvements of agriculture, manufactures,
and commerce in the kingdom of England, with the effects of
those improvements on the *morals* and *manners* of the people,
and pointing out the most proper means for their future advancement. In a word, the society is so numerous, the contributions so
considerable, the plan so judiciously laid, and executed with such
discretion and spirit, as to promise much more effectual and
extensive advantage to the public than ever accrued from all the
boasted academies of Christendom."[6]

After this passage (typical of Smollett's best prose as, for example,
in the number of its pleonasms) follows another, almost as long, on
the group of artists within the Society who were trying to organize
themselves into an Academy of Artists. Smollett's interest in their
formation reflects his concern with the social history of taste but,
even there, he emphasizes that they were an offshoot of the main
Society. His logic in building up both passages is sensible: proceeding
from the general to the minute, he surveys the aspirations and attainments of an epoch. Nor does he omit to embellish his prose with
fine images. We can readily comprehend the effect of his light and
dark imagery, for example, in describing patronage under George
II: "no Maecenas appeared among the ministers, and not the least
ray of patronage *glimmered* from the throne".

   Dark clouds make an impression over the landscape of Georgian
history; one indeed combs in vain through the printed annals of that
age for instances of royal or aristocratic support of the *practical* arts,
commerce, manufacture and trade.[3] The ministries of Walpole,
Pelham, and Pitt, of Lords Chesterfield and Hardwicke, and of the
Duke of Newcastle, boasted victory over France and unprecedented
gain in the treasury, but not one spoke about his own or his countrymen's collective achievement so far as the *applied* arts were concerned
How could they? Not one was a Maecenas. Burlingtons and Bathursts
and their ilk, patrons of the fine arts, had left an indelible mark on
the visual landscape of the British Isles.[7] Their support was given
to poets like Pope, painters like Guelfi, and composers like Handel—
but never, so far as can be discovered, to encouraging the applied
arts.

Understandably then, Smollett uses Maecenas' name: allusively, ironically, ambitiously. He doesn't suggest that some new Maecenas appearing on the horizon as a patron of the *practical* or *fine* arts, or for that matter *practical* sciences or *theoretical* sciences, can magically solve England's most pressing problems and ensure her continued greatness; that will require, as he implies elsewhere in the *History*, much more concerted effort and foresight. But he is troubled by the direction of patronage, especially the encouragement of certain activities and the neglect of others.[8] To express his unease, he draws an analogy between the fine and applied arts linked together in the 1750s, he believes, by the image of a modern Maecenas, plodding ahead without wisdom or foresight, decisive but imprudent and neglecting the crying needs of the common man.

Richard Rolt, author of the first English *Dictionary of Trade and Commerce* (1756), used a similar analogy in the opening sentence of his introduction, which was written by Johnson, but his Maecenas is fiercely decisive, nationalistic and—of course—French: "Trade and Commerce always fly for protection to the Great and God. And Colbert, by giving them encouragement in France, obtained as much permanent honour and glory, as MAECENAS by his patronizing the Muses in Rome . . .". The same could not have been said of England in 1755; Colbert had no equivalent, nor did one appear in sight. In December 1755, the month in which Johnson composed this preface, the Society of Arts had just been born and its future was uncertain. No such adamant mind as Colbert's could shape its career, and whatever early success it had was owing to laymen like Shipley, not great men like Colbert.

Smollett's image viewed against this background becomes sharp and clearly formed. Not only does he contrast the fine and applied arts but he implies that national contrasts (England and France, England and Holland, and so forth) are best viewed within this context. And it is perhaps for this reason—his belief about the importance of national societies—that Smollett is so highly selective in his *History of England*. At the time he wrote his *History* the Royal Society, founded and endowed with a charter by Charles II in 1660, was almost a hundred years old.[9] Dedicated to the advancement of pure, not applied, science, its spokesmen in the century from 1662 to 1762 grew increasingly sceptical of the Society's original aims. But scepticism produced nothing more than propaganda; there was no programme to branch out, no financial encouragement to theoretical scientists to apply their learning for gain. In other countries, Smollett observes, "the liberality of princes" actually patronizes and financially supports the *applied* arts, while in England advancement is owing to "the generosity of a public endued with taste and sensibility, eager for improvement, and proud of patronizing extraordinary merit".[10] In this alert public of the 1750s Smollett discovered the source of national prosperity and hope for the future. He could not agree with Pope that the last word of praise should go to Burlington, Bathurst and Boyle: those men had somehow forgotten the common man who looks to the future, not to the past. This alert public in fact had an enormous influence, as historians of science are beginning to show, on the technological progress of the late eighteenth and nineteenth centuries, and Smollett is therefore on sound historical ground to extol it in contrasting England with the other nations of Europe.

The French Academy, founded by Louis XIII in 1635, promoted nothing less than the glory of France. Ostensibly it was also dedicated to language and literature and sometimes encouraged the natural sciences, but the government alone (as Rolt expressed it in comparing Colbert to Maecenas) endorsed trade and commerce.[11] After a few decades it became evident that *belles lettres* was its only genuine activity and that science, in any shape or form, played no significant role. Men outside Paris called it "*l'Académie des beaux esprits*" or "*l'Académie de l'Eloquence*," more accurately describing its daily programme than the original name did: but it was not in the French national temper in 1640 to promote natural science on a big scale, not even if it could be purely *French* science. The Academy's charge was to preserve the French language, eject foreignisms, abjure Anglicisms, compile dictionaries and textbooks; in brief to dedicate itself to the opposite ends set down in the motto of the Royal Society, *nullius in verba*. The Germans likewise had no official academy corresponding to the French or English, but their "princes", as Smollett notes, were usually beneficent patrons, especially to naturalists.[12] In the Low Countries and Spain the situation was somewhat similar to that in Germany: neither royal nor private societies abetted the fine or applied arts; this was peacefully left to the regent and his noblemen, who enacted the role of Maecenas by encouraging a Boerhaave or supporting a Goya.

Only in England was the situation different. Monarch, noblemen and private patrons had encouraged the natural sciences, had formed a Royal Society for their propagation, but could not know that social conditions as well as opposition from various segments of the public, not merely the Church, would unite to debunk its foolish practitioners. When it became evident by the first quarter of the eighteenth century that certain promises of science—not solutions to concrete problems but a change in the total quality of life itself—would not be fulfilled, envy and malice set in. Swift and Pope, members of an intellectual élite profoundly interested in progress achieved through scientific advancement, now gloomily speculated about the researches of Newton's colleagues.[13] It is against this background that Smollett locates the Society of Arts and summarizes its attainment—against a distinct pattern of promise and disappointment, enthusiasm and revolt. By the time reaction set in Smollett was a young man, and he knew that petition of the old would solve nothing. The possible resuscitation of the Royal Society in the 1740s and 1750s might enhance learning and kindle certain kinds of hopes again, but it would not in itself lead to continued English glory. In this regard Smollett is much more prophetic of the nineteenth century than he has been given credit for. And when he pondered the question of distinguished English societies while writing his *History*, he could see only two, and the first of these, the Royal Society, had fallen on hard times; had been transformed into a kind of obsolescent anti-quarian establishment, performing research, to be sure, but of a specious nature and without any clear value to the common man.

The historian surveying this epoch cannot omit some word, however brief, about the Society of Antiquaries. This is all the more pertinent in Smollett's case because he knew so many of its members and some of their activities must have been known to him. Even if he is silent about this body in his *History*, the organization merits consideration as part of the panorama.[14] Smollett would have been the first to acknowledge that the Antiquaries were beginning to flourish under the leadership of William Stukeley and Martin Folkes, but he could not have tolerated their fierce eclecticism based on birth and education, nor their subject of study. An ardent democrat living in a country with a long democratic tradition, Smollett would have criticized their basic intentions: a select body of men committed to segregating its ranks from the vulgar crowd, to limiting membership to one hundred and to deriving pleasure from a lost, if not largely mythical, world. Not prepared to castigate the Antiquaries publicly, he kept silent.

In contrast, the Society of Arts suffered from none of these defects. Smollett could see that it was egalitarian, realistic, urban-minded, and concerned with the present; but, most salient, it captured modern man's imagination, especially in regard to his daily, personal comfort. Malachy Postlethwayt, Archdeacon of Norwich and author of a *Universal Dictionary of Trade and Commerce* (1751–5), a compendium expressing the spirit of his age more precisely than Johnson's lexicographical work, wrote in his preface that "Labour and arts are a great means to purchase to us [i.e. Englishmen] one of the greatest blessings upon earth, health and the length of days; for it both prolongs life, and prevents untimely death".[15] Rolt, author of the *Dictionary* mentioned earlier, commented in a similar vein that "the predictions of an author are very far from infallibility; but in some degree of confidence it may be properly observed, that there was never from the earliest ages a time in which *trade* so much engaged the attention of mankind, or commercial gain was sought with such general emulation".[16]

Such sweeping generalizations epitomized beliefs prevalent for several decades and in some form or fashion could not have escaped the ears of Smollett, growing up in the 1730s in Scotland and observing the London scene in the 1740s. Smollett also heard a good deal of talk about theoretical versus applied science in the Scottish medical circle he frequented. During his most formative years he listened to the talk of the famous Hunters, Douglases, Smellie, to Akenside and Thomson the poets, to writers, actors, men in the street—all interested in the new attitude of mind to the advantages of a more comfortable life; he listened to talk about the "spirit of the age" (to borrow from Hazlitt), as evidenced in trade and commerce, to talk about the decline of "natural philosophy", scientific theory and first-rate minds, and of course to talk about the forlorn condition of the Royal Society, a perpetual topic of conversation among medical men. Smollett, a friend of several Fellows, especially Henry Baker, knew about dissatisfaction inside and outside the Royal Society; indeed, he could not help hearing about this.

But where did it lead him? After all, he also knew that the Royal Society had never been pledged to indulge popular sentiment regardless of its validity. After Newton's death in 1727 scientific activity was gradually transformed within its ranks and by the 1750s there was little evidence of a still healthy collection of great minds. Several modern historians have commented,[17] most intuitively, that during this inert period its *Philosophical Transactions* read like schoolboy chronicles concerned with petty feuds and personal advancement much more than with breaking the knowledge barrier and improving the lot of man. For reasons already given, the Society of Antiquaries could not even be compared with the Royal Society. As Smollett surveyed the scene in connection with his various historical works he naturally examined other learned, especially literary, societies like the Gentlemen's Society at Spalding, a type of provincial antiquarian group which tried hard but produced nothing which seems concrete and impressive to the onlooker. The Spalding Society was weighted down with administrative difficulties stemming from constitutional weaknesses; its members, usually drawn from local Peterborough schools and the surrounding clergymen, talked profusely but educed no convincing programme; and while it was incontestably more egalitarian than the London Antiquaries, its members shared similar interests. In short, it was the type of society,

Smollett reasoned, which would always interest historians like himself and other historians (John Nichols, author of *Literary Anecdotes of the Eighteenth Century*) for the ideals it embraced, but not for any solid or utilitarian achievement.

The Society of Arts, on the other hand, seemed to Smollett altogether different from these; in purpose, potential, and organization it was radical, as the *History* reveals. It was grounded in the "generosity of the [English] public",[18] a statement one could not even make about the Royal Society, for all its Baconian idealism and utterances about the advancement of knowledge.[19] Democratic from the start, the Society of Arts suffered from an opposite danger in its potential of being too much subjected to the mob. Here we must recall that the Society of Arts did not acquire Royal patronage until the nineteenth century and that it remained throughout Smollett's lifetime precisely "a society of *private* persons". True, this rank and file included a plethora of noblemen and clergymen, as evidenced even in its first meeting at Rawthmell's Coffee House, Henrietta Street, on 22nd March 1754: the eleven men present were distinct in their rank and attainment: Viscount Folkestone, Lord Romney, Dr. Stephen Hales, Henry Baker, Gustavus Brander, James Short, John Goodchild, Nicholas Crisp, Charles Lawrence, Husband Messiter, and William Shipley, who became the group's secretary.[20] Four (statistically over a third of the total) were Fellows of the Royal Society, and this fact ought to reveal something in itself about the loss of faith in that institution in 1754. No sensible historian, certainly not Smollett, would argue that these men came together *because* (i.e. cause and effect) they were discontented with the ancient and established society to which they already belonged, but clearly they cannot have been thoroughly convinced of its programme if they were so enthusiastic to start a new society, not even if all four were receptive to any suggestion that crossed their desks. The literature of the epoch reveals that something else was needed. And close biographical scrutiny of these four men discloses pertinent factors: Hales was an eminent physiologist and inventor; Baker's microscope and his own microscopic research were important for the advancement of the common man; Brander, a director of the Bank of England, had adamantly refused to donate personal wealth to the Royal Society but grew enraptured at the idea of this new group; James Short the astronomer was distinguished in optics.

Smollett, briefed by Henry Baker and others, knew about these original meetings, had taken care to learn everything he could about the newly formed group. And it was a conscious act of will when he decided to omit from his *History* all mention of the Royal Society. He knew that eyebrows would be raised, if not upon publication then later. One might compare the omission to a chronicle of the progress of learning in England 1660–1760 which made no mention of Oxford or Cambridge. Even if one took these institutions for granted, some word, however brief, would be expected. But not so Smollett: persuaded that omissions and inclusions are significant aspects of historical writing—as Donald Greene has recently shown[21]—he wilfully omitted the mother institution and documented the child. Over the course of time, the prudence of this decision would become evident; viewed even in the strictly historical aspect, however, Smollett was equally prudent. As one recent historian has put it, "the English populace of mid-century, especially outside London, was awakening to a new sense of the possibilities of progress through trade, manufacture, and commerce, and to this bulging new class science counted for little unless its practical aspects could clearly be viewed".[22]

Before leaving Smollett's first commentary, there remains the question of the accuracy of his details. In general, he has taken meticulous care. Viscount Folkestone was the first President of the Society, Lord Romney, Charles Whitworth, James Theobald and Stephen Hales were Vice-Presidents, William Shipley was the Secretary, John Goodchild the Treasurer, and after the initial year 1754–5 these officers were democratically selected from large numbers. Women were not excluded, though few in fact joined. In the space of five years (1754–8) membership swelled from 17 to 110 to 708. By the time Smollett composed this section of his *History* dealing with the year 1758, he could therefore state authoritatively that these officers "were elected from a very considerable number of members".[23]

Other facts are also accurate, and only a few need be mentioned here. Members paid no less than two guineas per annum and dues-payers were entitled to attend both "general" and "ordinary" meetings held on certain Wednesdays of each month, as Smollett states. If Smollett had been able to allot more space to the Society, perhaps he would have commented, as Trueman Wood does, on the important point that

> "The ordinary meetings were not competent to alter the 'rules and orders'. This could only be done at 'general meetings', the number of which seems to have varied from time to time. At the ordinary meetings all the regular business of the Society was transacted, members were proposed, balloted for, and elected, bills were ordered for payment, and expenditure was discussed."[24]

Smollett's description of premiums, an enticement of monetary rewards given to discoverers and inventors, is also meticulously accurate, as is his catalogue of projects ranging from mechanical improvements in agriculture to "a treatise on the arts of peace".[25] But his concluding statement about the "effects of [all] these improvements on the *morals* and *manners* of the people" genuinely captures his profoundest reasons for approbation and consequently deserves attention. Elsewhere in the *History*, especially while discussing the reigns of William and Anne, Smollett argues that higher economic standards pave the road to more scrupulous morals and manners. Although he was not the deepest philosopher of history the period produced, he nevertheless observed a pattern progressing in time and correlating the two; if the lot of the beggar and charwoman could be improved, and if the populace at large could earn and enjoy some continuous sense of economic well-being, other matters would gradually take care of themselves. Philosophers ranging from Locke and Mandeville to Adam Smith and the physiocrats had introduced specific programmes, most of which appeared fanciful to Smollett.[26] The real issue, he reasoned, was economic, simply monetary, and this basic belief figures prominently in all five of his novels as a result. Part of his conviction about this precept manifests itself in his tone: not one note of scepticism creeps into his final judgement. Nor is there anything conservative, reactionary, or nostalgic about this stance; at no time is the Society of Arts viewed within a context that wistfully glances back at a pastoral England unmarred by manufactories; nothing in Smollett's estimate betrays awareness of a previous golden-age grotesquely transformed into a landscape of "deserted villages", as Goldsmith piously grieved about the mythical Auburn. Nor would Smollett have understood the vociferous opponents of Adam Smith clamouring in the 1760s about the deleterious effects of luxury: if the long-range effect of the Society of Arts were to produce a nation of rich men profligate in their waste, this would be a condition preferable to the poverty he saw all around in every quarter of London.[27] True, Smollett was later to change his mind about some of these matters. In 1758, however, the Society of Arts was golden and everything it promised, even implicitly, seemed equally untarnished.

"In a word, the society is so numerous, the contributions so considerable, the plan so judiciously laid, and executed with such discretion and spirit, as to promise much more effectual and extensive advantage to the public than ever accrued from all the boasted academies of Christendom."[28] Nothing succeeds like promises, especially in a remote future, and Smollett's concluding phrase, "boasted academies of Christendom", captures his sense of space as well as time. Distant societies like the Imperial Academy of Sciences in St. Petersburg (1724),[29] the Dutch Mattschappij der Wetenschappen (1752), the Royal Danish Academy of Sciences and Letters (1742), the Royal Swedish Academy of Sciences (1739), and the Italian Academia delle Scienze (1757) had benefited mankind, but to Smollett they existed in another sphere. Perhaps they had helped the whole of mankind, but their palpability was minimal, their words more glittering than their deeds, and in certain cases their intentions demonstrably suspect. An ironist at heart, as readers of his novels know, Smollett could not forgo an opportunity to lash these "boasted academies of Christendom", even if gently.

NOTES TO PART I

1. James Boswell, *A London Journal* (Oxford, 1950), p. 60, entry for 1st Dec. 1762. Unless otherwise indicated, all places of publication are London.
2. *The Adventures of Ferdinand Count Fathom* (1753), I, 58.
3. *History of England* (1758–65; 1805, 6 vols.), I, p. 474.
4. Ibid., V, p. 447.
5. For some discussion of the making of his *History*, see Arnold Whitridge, *Tobias Smollett: A Study of his Miscellaneous Works* (n.p., 1925) and Lewis M. Knapp, *Tobias Smollett: Doctor of Men and Manners* (Princeton, 1949), pp. 186–193.
6. *History of England* (1805), V, pp. 448–9.
7. See Pope's *Moral Essays* (1730–35) and James Lees-Milne, *Earls of Creation: Five Great Patrons of Eighteenth-Century Art* (1962).
8. I.e., aristocratic support in the fields of painting, architecture, and landscape gardening but no encouragement of commerce and trade. The question of patronage in general in eighteenth-century England has never been adequately studied, certainly not the monetary allocations actually appropriated. For an interesting prolegomenon to the subject involving some debate over the meaning of the terms patron and patronage during Smollett's time, see a series of articles by Jacob Leed and P. J. Korshin in *Studies in Burke and his Time:* XII, pp. 1677–90, 1804–11, 1862–85; XIII, pp. 2011–15; XIV, pp. 5–22.
9. See the standard histories of the Royal Society by Thomas Sprat (1667), Thomas Birch (1756–7), C. R. Weld (1848), H. B. Wheatley (1905), and Sir Henry Lyons (1944). Recent historians (e.g., Marjorie Purver, *The Royal Society: Concept and Creation*, 1967) have aptly criticized these early histories for omitting any discussion of the social and cultural aspects of the Royal Society; that is, all these histories merely survey the Society's activities diachronically and by examining its own internal structure as recorded in its own transactions. The same is true of histories of the Society of Arts, as evidenced in the works by H. Trueman Wood (1913) and Derek Hudson and K. W. Luckhurst (1954).
10. *History of England* (1805), V, p. 447.
11. See the article entitled "Académie de Politique" in the *Dictionnaire Universel des Sciences Morale, Economique, Politique et Diplomatique* (1777), pp. 175–84 explaining French attitudes at this time. The standard histories of the French Academy should also be consulted for its activities during the period 1660–1760. Hume's brief estimate of the French Academy is insipid but still worth citing for purposes of contrast with the English Royal Society: "Though the French academy of sciences was directed, encouraged, and supported by the sovereign, there arose in England some men of superior genius, who were more than sufficient to cast the balance, and who drew on themselves and on their native country the regard and attention of Europe . . ." (*History of England*, 1763; 1830, VI, p. 340).
12. The Deutsche Akademie der Wissenschaften, founded in 1700 and elevated to the rank of a royal academy by Frederick the Great in 1743, did sponsor scientific activities, but on such a small scale in comparison to its English and French equivalents that it cannot be discussed with them; see Adolf Harnack, *Geschichte der königlich Preussischen Akademie der Wissenschaften* (Berlin, 1901), intro. and chapters i–iii for its origins and activities.

13. Especially in *Gulliver's Travels* (1726) and *An Essay on Man* (1733); see Marjorie Hope Nicolson and G. S. Rousseau, *This Long Disease, My Life: Alexander Pope and the Sciences* (Princeton, 1968).

14. The best account of its activities is Joan Evans' *A History of the Society of Antiquaries* (Oxford, 1956), but also see the extensive eighteenth-century account by John Nichols, *Literary Anecdotes of the Eighteenth Century* (1812), VI, pp. 140–62, and H. R. Steeves, *Learned Societies and English Literary Scholarship* (New York, 1913), pp. 60–98.

15. P. x.

16. P. ii. These words are, of course, Johnson's.

17. See Dorothy Stimson, *Scientists and Amateurs: A History of the Royal Society* (New York, 1949), pp. 133–45, but the best commentator on the subject was a mid eighteenth-century man, Dr. John Hill (1707–75), sometimes called "The Inspector" after a daily column he wrote by that name. In two satirical prose works, *A Dissertation on Royal Societies* (1750) and *A Review of the Works of the Royal Society* (1751), Hill severely criticized the Society's decline after Newton's death.

18. *History of England* (1805), V, p. 447.

19. An important question about the public's knowledge of the Royal Society's activities 1727–70 remains unanswered; mostly uneducated in scientific matters, the English public could not challenge any aspect of the Society's administration or activities.

20. See the excellent biography of Shipley by D. G. C. Allan (1968), which provides much important background material to the 1750s.

21. "Smollett the Historian: A Reappraisal", in *Tobias Smollett: Bicentennial Essays Presented to Lewis M. Knapp* (Oxford Univ. Press, 1971), pp. 25–56.

22. G. S. Rousseau, "Science and Science Books in Eighteenth-Century England", forthcoming. This idea is stated in a different form by H. Heaton, "Industry and Trade", in *Johnson's England*, ed. A. S. Turberville (Oxford, 1933), I, p. 247: "If one dare speak about the 'spirit of the age', that spirit of the mid eighteenth-century was one of the insatiable curiosity; and it hovered over the head-quarters of the Society, when it was not in the patent office."

23. *History of England* (1805), V, p. 447.

24. H. Trueman Wood, *A History of the Royal Society of Arts* (1913), pp. 18–19.

25. Entries for this prize were to be submitted on or before the second Wednesday in 1761.

26. As may be evidenced from his brief comments on these schemes in the *History of England* and *Present State of All Nations* (1768); but the real proof of Smollett's renouncement manifests itself in his early novels, especially in *Roderick Random* and *Ferdinand Count Fathom*. Here one views fictive figures in all stages of economic deprivation and luxuriousness, and one sees that the poor become more civil and humane only when they grow less poor.

27. See Dorothy Marshall, *The English Poor in the Eighteenth Century* (1926).

28. *History of England* (1805), V, p. 449.

29. Dates of establishment.

II

Smollett's second, third and fourth comments about the Society of Arts are more puzzling than his first. The second and third appear respectively in *The Present State of All Nations*,[1] a socio-cultural survey of the nations of Europe, and in the last volume of a *Continuation of the Complete History of England*.[2] In *The Present State* Smollett reiterates the portrait painted in his *History of England*. "It must be owned", he charges the Royal Society, "that of late years persons of very little merit or erudition have insinuated themselves",[3] and then proceeds to defend his accusation through personal knowledge: "The members seem to have degenerated in their studies; and some of the modern transactions [*Philosophical Transactions of the Royal Society*] have intailed ridicule and contempt upon the whole body".[4] This forlorn corporation is contrasted with the Society of Arts, its only hope for rescue in imitation: "The design of the institution would certainly be prosecuted with better success, were they endowed with a fund to bestow premiums on those who should distinguish themselves in the different branches of philosophy and mechanics."[5]

Smollett, so often poor in his life, could not imagine a better temptation than money. Nor was there anything ignoble or base about payment for intellectual discovery—at least Smollett saw none:

> "This defect in the Royal Society is, in some measure, compensated by a private society of persons established by public spirited persons of all ranks, for the encouragement of arts, manufactures, and commerce, in bestowing rewards, from time to time, on those who shall produce inventions and improvements that may tend to the increase of trade, the employment of the poor, and the propagation of industry, in this kingdom. Several improvements in arts and mechanics have already been offered to this Society; and the authors of them enjoyed the reward of their ingenuity, either in premiums of money, or honorary medals."[6]

Medals were fine but money was better, and it was the Society's landing upon this scheme of rewards that enabled Smollett to forecast a successful future. "As the society seems to be conducted with spirit and discretion, it will prosper in all probability, and by the accession of new funds, be enabled to extend its plan, and multiply its bounties."[7] Next time Smollett wrote about the Society, he persisted in this rosy view. In his *Continuation of the History* he considered England's industrial progress and the Society of Arts as inextricably intertwined. One reflected the other in the sense of spirit and matter being two states of the same potential form: "A spirit of industry, at this time [mid-Georgian England], seems to have succeeded that of war all over Europe. The society of noblemen and gentlemen for promoting arts, manufactures and commerce, though destitute of all public support, consisted of above two thousand five hundred members; by which they raised an annual fund, sufficient to encourage the highest enterprises and improvements for the good of the nation."[8] No question existed in Smollett's mind about the Society's genuine contribution to English progress: "The progress they made in the ends of their institution was such as must do honour, to their memory through all succeeding ages, as their institution is, perhaps, the most public-spirited that ever was formed." The absolute finality of Smollett's language reveals his degree of assurance about the Society's niche; and his phrase "the most public-spirited that ever was formed" further reflects his own concerns for Englishmen at large. Emblazed by England's ingenuity, other countries, jealous and wishing to advance themselves, imitated her Society, especially her system of rewards (premiums) for mechanical inventions and technical discoveries. "This ardour for useful improvements soon spread itself to Edinburgh and Dublin, where societies were planned on the like noble principles with that of London; and the French, the Danes, the Dutch, the Swedes, some of the states of Italy, Swisserland [sic] particularly, followed the same example."[9] Smollett, knowledgeable of French social and economic life (having travelled many times through France and observed her peculiar customs), naturally comments on France first: "The French king opened a free trade for gain through all his dominions, great encouragement was given to tillage and agriculture all over the kingdom, where the former laws, oppressive to trade,[10] were abrogated. A new taxation took place, by which imports were laid on more equally . . ." Having praised the Society, Smollett returns to the subject of commerce and industry; he could not imagine the development of one without the other, nor of either without the Society.

Smollett's fourth and final commentary appears in *The Expedition of Humphry Clinker*, published in June 1771 just three months before his death. "We are become members of the Society for the Encouragement of the Arts",[11] Jery Melford writes. By "we" he presumably means the whole Bramble family (Squire Bramble, Lydia, Tabitha and Jery) and he continues to comment that we "have assisted at some of their deliberations, which were conducted with equal spirit and sagacity—My uncle is extremely fond of the institution, which will certainly be productive of great advantages to the public, if, from its democratical form, it does not degenerate into cabal and corruption."

Before launching into a discussion of the obvious change in head and heart revealed here, it is necessary to consider the facts of composition of *Humphry Clinker*. Smollett probably began to write the book in 1765 or 1766, five or six years before actual publication; good reason exists to believe that the first two volumes containing the remarks about the Society of Arts were completed by 1768.[12] This is later than the date of composition and publication of his two other works, *The Present State of All Nations*, composed in the early 1760s but not published until June 1768,[13] and the fifth volume of the *Continuation*, written in the summer of 1765 and published in October.[14] In other words, it is possible that during the three years 1765–8 Smollett qualified his estimate with the serious charges quoted above. During these three years he spent much time in London and Bath and could have seen the "cabal and corruption" he describes. But it is also possible that although he held this idea all along, he withheld its insertion in the previous accounts for any number of reasons.[15]

Some facts about the Society also require brief comment before deciding about Smollett's final estimate. In 1758 the Society had 708 members, but by 1765 the membership soared. During this eight-year period, first under the secretaryship of Shipley and, after 1760, of Templeman, the Society conducted the totality of its business on a democratic basis, as Trueman Wood notes: "It [the Society] had no governing body. There were certain standing committees and others appointed from time to time for special purposes, but their duty was merely to prepare the work for the general body of members, by whom all the business was transacted."[16]

Wood also notes that "as will be seen later on, Smollett's fears were not without justification." The unending debate and equivocation referred to here unquestionably hurt the Society during the next three or four decades, causing it to degenerate further into disorder. Its meetings by 1780 were not unlike those in the House of Commons today in which the value of uncontrolled argumentation, colloquy, and even of obloquy and logomachy, is often questionable. Trueman Wood, the Society's most learned historian, notes how the organization subsequently diminished in numbers and needed a new constitution that would curb undisciplined talk: "It is certain that the main factor was the obsolete character alike of the Society's objects and of the manner in which they were carried into effect. Its constitution badly needed reform and until that reform was effected, as it was a few years later, the Society remained incapable of useful work, and was consequently not likely to receive public support."[17]

Chronology of Smollett's movements during 1760–70 and the above facts relating to the Society suggest that Smollett *did* change his mind. If the information published in his *History of England*[18] was supplied by friends who were members, his commentary in *Humphry Clinker* was most likely the result of direct observation of a Wednesday meeting around 1765, possibly a little later.[19] By that time the ranks had swelled enough to give any visitor pause; and Smollett himself had grown sufficiently irritable, partly because of physical illness, to be stricken by the mob. Thus, when Jery Melford, Bramble's nephew, appraises his uncle's view of the Society of Arts he notes to his correspondent:

"You are already acquainted with his aversion to the influence of the multitude, which, he [Bramble] affirms is incompatible with excellence, and subversive of order—Indeed his detestation of the mob has been heightened by fear, ever since he fainted in the room at Bath; and this apprehension has prevented him from going to the Little Theatre in the Hay-market, and other places of entertainment . . ."[20]

It may not seem so to us today, but to Squire Bramble the meeting rooms of the Society of Arts in Beaufort Buildings in the Strand seemed another rowdy "place of entertainment", no different from the noisy and smoky theatres in the Hay Market or Covent Garden.

NOTES TO PART II

1. Published in 1768, II, p. 232. The composition and publication of this work present problems that have been explored by Louis M. Martz in *The Later Career of Tobias Smollett* (New Haven, 1942), pp. 104–23. Smollett's chapter on "Commerce" in *The Present State*, pp. 233–50 is rich in historical materials and deserves more attention than it has received, especially from economic historians.

2. 1765, V, pp. 291–2. For complicated reasons partly owing to Smollett's treatment in this volume of George III's madness, volume V was suppressed shortly after publication. But the book is not so scarce as Lewis Knapp affirms; see *Tobias Smollett* (Princeton, 1949), p. 260 and "The Publication of Smollett's *Complete History* . . . and *Continuation*", *Transactions of the Bibliographical Society*, *The Library* (Dec.1935), pp. 306–15.

3. II, p. 232.

4. II, p. 232. The reference is to Sir John Hill's satires, *A Dissertation on Royal Societies* (1750) and *A Review of the Works of the Royal Society* (1751).

5. *Present State of All Nations*, II p. 232.

6. Ibid., II, p. 232.

7. Ibid., II, p. 232.

8. *Continuation of the History*, V, p. 291. The following quotations in this paragraph appear on pp. 291–2 of the *Continuation*.

9. Smollett had surveyed the history of trade and commerce of several of these countries in *The Present State of All Nations*.

10. Smollett's estimate here is not entirely borne out by the facts, and his view may be prejudiced by his universal dislike of France and French institutions; as his *Travels through France and Italy* (1766) make plain, Smollett was deeply curious about France but he lost few opportunities to savage her people and customs. For a more accurate contemporary estimate than Smollett's see M. P., *Relation contenant l'histoire de l'Académie Françoise* (Paris, 1671), the writings of the French physiocrats and the essays on commerce in the *Histoire de l'Académie Royale des Sciences* (Paris, 1702–––). Also, see Joseph Schumpeter, *A History of Economic Analysis* (1954), pp. 167–80 for a description of France's attitude to trade in comparison to England.

11. J. Melford to Sir Watkin Phillips, 5th June.

12. See Lewis Knapp, *Tobias Smollett* (Princeton, 1949), p. 289.

13. Both Martz and Knapp speculate about the date of composition, but it is not possible to be certain; internal evidence, however, makes it clear that some portions were written early in the 1760s.

14. See Knapp, *Tobias Smollett*, p. 260.

15. A further consideration is that the "ordinary" Wednesday meetings were not as boisterous in the early 1760s as they were later on when their size greatly increased. Does this mean that Smollett's account in *Humphry Clinker* is inaccurate if he visited the Society in 1761, for example, and describes it as it was then? There is no way of telling, since he was a visitor and no record of his attendance would have been kept. Besides, he may have visited the Society many times over a large span of years. Smollett's biographer, L. M. Knapp, knows nothing about Smollett's visit or visits.

16. *History of the Royal Society of Arts* (1913), p. 350. On p. 345 Wood comments: "The whole business of the Society was carried on in open meetings, which all members had a right to attend, and at which consequently the attendance was always varying. The natural result was that the less work there was to do, the greater was the expenditure of time and talk." It is not necessary to recount here the story of Lord Brougham's (Henry Peter Brougham, 1778–1868, Lord Chancellor) reaction to a Wednesday meeting; suffice it to say that his response was almost identical to Squire Bramble's and that he left declaring what he hoped to be his final doom if ever again he wasted time with a Society that spent all its time discussing "rules and orders".

17. Ibid., p. 345. By 1842 Smollett's prediction came true and the Society was on the verge of total dissolution. Until it had a governing body and a new mechanism for dispensing premiums, it could not hope to survive. Its Wednesday meetings, as Smollett anticipated, were now bogged down in endless debates about particular inventions and about problems of procedure, i.e., the Society's rules and orders.

18. Smollett's description is so accurate here that he must have been fed a great deal of information from members. The anonymous tract *A Concise Account of the Rise, Progress, and Present State of the Society for the Encouragement of Arts, Manufactures, and Commerce* appeared in 1763, too late for Smollett's use in the *History*. It is the first published account of the early years of the Society's history.

19. Unfortunately no portraits or other illustrations of Wednesday meetings are extant for the period discussed here *ca.* 1765.

20. J. Melford to Sir Watkin Phillips, 5th June.

III

No attempt has been made thus far to assess Smollett's comments about this Society. They have merely been set forth, briefly explained, and given something of a superficial historical context. But in no sense have they been evaluated or studied within a wider scope than mid eighteenth-century England or a broader perspective than Smollett's own vantage.[1] It remains to do this, especially by consulting the attitudes of Smollett's contemporaries and of modern historians since the eighteenth century.

The major literary figures of Georgian England are usually thought to include Johnson, Boswell, Goldsmith, Gray, Smollett, Sterne, Horace Walpole, Chesterfield, Joshua Reynolds, Burke, Garrick and Colman. All except Smollett were members and paid the minimum dues of £2 per annum. Goldsmith almost became Secretary, and even Sterne, who lived in Yorkshire (except for brief visits to the South and to London), was proposed and elected, and paid his dues. Unique among this group stands Smollett, who for reasons perhaps now lost to history, never joined. How can this be explained and, more importantly, can it be explained in the light of his four comments already discussed?

Smollett was by 1760—certainly by 1765—a gravely sick man suffering from a constellation of illnesses including consumption and cardiac arrest.[2] After the death of his daughter Elizabeth in 1763, he lost interest in many activities. There is no use in sentimentalizing his condition or exaggerating it; but it is equally foolish and biographically false to diminish it or pretend it did not exist. Except for brief periods in which he travelled about the country to various spas in search of health, Smollett lived in Chelsea, and his failure to join the Society may be answered by as simple a phenomenon as his dislike of travelling into town.[3] What explanation could be more straightforward? Straightforward and logical it may be, but it is no more than conjecture. During the 1760s Smollett was well enough (or sick enough, depending on how one views it) to ride into the city when business demanded it, and if he considered membership in the Society important one can reason equally cogently that he would have joined.

What about the possibility of Smollett's disliking organizations of any sort? I have already commented on his "non-club-ability," to coin a somewhat grotesque neologism, and as Smollett aged he grew increasingly similar to his semi-autobiographical fictional figure Squire Bramble, who, as we have already seen, disliked mob scenes of any sort, regardless of the worthiness of the mob's intention.[4] Smollett's reason for not joining may therefore have nothing to do with travelling into town. But here, again, conjecture has intruded, and to put this theory forward as historical probability rather than as one man's suggestion violates every attempt at finding out the truth.

No other biographical likelihoods suggest themselves, and if they do they are not persuasive. One can argue, for example, that Smollett was not friendly with too many of the Society's members or that he could not care less what other literary figures (Johnson, Boswell, Goldsmith) were doing or how they spent their time. But once again, these suggestions are not persuasive.[5] Nor is the one alleging that the shift in attitude reflected in the *History of England* and in *Humphry Clinker* parallels a personal change of heart; that he would have joined in the late 1750s but not after about 1765 when the Society's membership sky-rocketed. Why then did he not? Why did he wait? The answers cannot be supplied with any degree of confidence. One must resign himself to a position of doubt in this matter: unless further information comes to light we may never know.

But we can briefly explore the attitudes of some of Smollett's contemporaries. Although these men, some already mentioned, mostly joined the Society they frequently held opinions suggesting less than approbation and often embodying outright derogation:[6] men sometimes join organizations whose basic *raison d'être* they loathe, for reasons of prestige and personal advancement. An example is Horace Walpole, mentioned in our list of Georgian literary luminaries. This aristocratic antiquarian and brilliant memoirist had nothing whatsoever in common with the ideals of the Society; in fact, he was opposed to its most basic and cherished hope that England could be made a more comfortable country for the common man; and yet, despite his view of progress, he joined.[7] In February 1758, the same year Smollett wrote about the Society in his *History of England*, Walpole wrote to his perpetual confidant Horace Mann: "There is now established a Society for the Encouragement of Arts, Science, and Commerce, that are [sic] likely to be very serviceable."[8] Before rushing to conclusions, we must comment that Walpole is referring to the *artistic* branch of the Society, not to the Society at large. Twenty years later, in 1777, Walpole admitted to Mann what had been his true feelings from the start, and the disclosure supports a more general theory about the reasons illustrious men join organizations. "I never had patience for such solemn assemblies and have neglected that of the Arts and Sciences."[9] Solemn it was not, at least not according to Squire Bramble and Jery Melford, but the comment illustrates an attitude held among some of Smollett's luminous contemporaries. If we had merely noticed that these lights were members, we may have been led to generalize falsely. True, everyone except Smollett seems to have joined the Society; untrue, that they joined because they esteemed it or that Smollett failed to join because he dispraised it in *Humphry Clinker*.[10]

To turn elsewhere, Johnson's activities in the Society are known too well to be retold; so too are Boswell's.[11] Both men, unlike Horace Walpole, were genuinely interested in the Society's work, especially during the 1760s, and contributed some time and effort to its advancement. Burke and the brilliant third Duke of Richmond (Charles Lennox, 1735–1806) also believed in the Society's usefulness and attended meetings; their close proximity in the famous Barry painting of the Society still on the wall of the "Great Room" testifies to this.[12] Regarding Goldsmith, one is less certain: his financial condition was so perennially unstable that any attempt to assess his motives for wanting to become Secretary must be viewed askance; and he was so vain and proud that one cannot even accurately predict what he would have thought about the Society's ideals.[13] If he could speak at the Wednesday meetings and be called a "great wit", he would have adored the Society and all its members.

Even the eccentric and colourful Sir John Hill, variously dubbed by friends and enemies alike as the "Inspector" and the "Doctor", desired to join. But here was one luminary (so he appeared to some of his contemporaries) who found himself *hors de combat* after the attempt. This officious and impudent rascal, this self-advertising "paffer and puffer" as Christopher Smart the poet libelled him,[14] practically bribed the Earl of Northumberland to put his name forward.[15] He did and Hill failed to win enough votes. This astonishing fact, astonishing in that Hill was perhaps the only famous man in the age of George II to be turned down, grows less astonishing when we recollect that by 1755 Hill's name was already discredited. Dozens of writers had exposed his outrageous behaviour, including Smollett, who satirized him at length in the "College of Authors" in *Peregrine Pickle*.[16]

So far as I know, nothing unusual is recorded about the visits of Smollett's other literary contemporaries mentioned above, nor do the journals and diaries of foreigners abroad in London yield reports as one might expect.[17] Some, like Sterne and Garrick, attended a few meetings, as the manuscript archives in the Society show, but they are not known to have written about their experience, not even in letters or journals. Smollett, somewhat ironically, the only important literary man who did not belong, has left posterity with the most extensive accounts for the 1750s and 1760s: in his popular *History*, in the *Present State*, and in his final masterpiece *Humphry Clinker*. Dozens of semi-literary figures like William Windham (1750–1810), Pitt's Secretary for War in the mid 1790s, made visits with their families and recorded brief descriptions in their memoirs, but nothing more than a few words factually reporting the date of their expedition and sometimes the extent of the crowd.[18] Illustrious physicians such as William Hunter, sometimes called the most important surgeon of the eighteenth century, Peter Shaw, the fashionable London doctor and Physician-in-Ordinary to both George II and III, and Joshua ("Spot") Ward, whose statue, carved over many years by Agostino Carlini, still stands in the entrance hall of the Society, were members and presumably attended at least one meeting for curiosity's sake, but not one of these doctors nor of many other physicians who were also members has left even an unpublished fragment describing the occasion. Future historians of the Society will search in vain for authors like Smollett who have left behind them enough commentary to form at least a partial sketch of the first decade 1755–65.

This brings us to the last point, the Society and its historians then and now, as well as historians generally. The Royal Society of Arts has naturally had its own competent historians ranging from the anonymous author mentioned above[19] who brought out in 1763 a tract surveying the first decade, and Robert Dossie, whose *Memoirs of Agriculture and Other Oeconomical Arts* (1768–82) amount to an early history of the Society,[20] to twentieth-century historians such as Trueman Wood, Derek Hudson, Kenneth Luckhurst and D. G. C. Allan. These scholars have performed a useful service in bringing together disparate materials spanning several centuries;

yet, in fairness, it must be noted that their approach has been diachronic rather than synchronic and that they have only recently attempted to study the Society's origins from sociological, psychological and psycho-historical perspectives. Nor have other types of historians (economic, scientific, technological) considered including the Society as part of their grist; historians of medicine, for example, rarely, if ever, discuss the effects of progress in trade, commerce and manufacture on the social history of medicine in Georgian England. Traditional historians of medicine will include discussion, for example, of an obscure treatise like John Bellers' "An Essay Toward the Improvement of Physick" in *Proposals for Employing the Poor in a College of Industry* (1714) because it purportedly treats of medicine, but they normally do not entertain the possibility that the Society's usefulness radically altered the social dimensions of medicine, especially the manufacture of pharmaceuticals; and thus they consider it parergal to their own work.[21]

Nor have economic historians, among whom Smollett must be counted as one for the plethora of economic history in his six-volume *History of England*, fared better. Such standard reference works as Ephraim Lipson's *Economic History of England* (1915), Karl Polanyi's *Origins of Our Time: The Great Transformation* (1945), Milton Briggs's *Economic History of England* (1949, 5th ed.), and Joseph Schumpeter's *A History of Economic Analysis* (1954) are silent on this Society.[22] Even students of the history of luxury say nothing, and which official (not to say royal) organization of the last three centuries can hope to have done more to enhance English opulence than the Society of Arts?

Wars, conquest and imperialism have played their important roles in the accumulation of vast personal and national fortunes in this kingdom, but without the scientific and technological ability to harness natural and artificial resources, England could not have become the world power she until very recently was. In this area also, Smollett has left his imprint: large segments of *Humphry Clinker* deal topically with the dangerous effects of luxury, and close scrutiny of this book's structure reveals that the author's ideas on the subject have radically changed from those he held in the 1740s and 1750s, even at the time he was composing the early volumes of his *History*.[23] Smollett, by the very end of his life 1770–71, would have thoroughly agreed with, and put forward even more violently, the anti-luxury arguments of Horace Walpole:

"As I believe our virtues are extremely like those of our predecessors the Romans, so I am sure our luxury and extravagance are too. What do you think of a winter Ranelagh erecting in Oxford Road at the expense of sixty thousand pounds? The new bank, including the value of the ground and of the houses demolished to make room for it, will cost three hundred thousand; and erected, as my Lady Townley says, *by sober citizens too*! I have touched before to you on the incredible profusion of our young men of fashion. I know a younger brother who literally gives a flower woman half a guinea every morning for a bunch of roses for the nosegay in his buttonhole. There has lately been an auction of stuffed birds, and as natural history is in fashion, there are physicians and others who paid 40 and 50 guineas for a single Chinese pheasant . . . In short, we are at the height of extravagance and improvements, for we do improve rapidly in taste as well as in the former."[24] "

Willy-nilly the Society of Arts contributed its share to this state of affairs, although such diverse anatomists of luxury as Adam Smith the economist, Dr. John Brown the author of *An Estimate of the Manners and Principles of the Times* (1757–8), and sermonists of different persuasions like John Wesley, George Whitefield and Laurence Sterne were still too close in time to the new phenomenon of unprecedented luxury for the common man not to be blinded Nor could it be otherwise. The discovery of a plan of premiums, as Smollett intimated, was nothing short of genius and was bound to give incentive to the best schemes and inevitably to accelerate the rate of social change. Peter Laslett, the Cambridge University social scientist, has written admirably on "The world we have lost" in his anatomy of social change at the end of the seventeenth century.[25] But much remains to be researched and studied for the next century, especially outside London—trade, commerce, and manufacture as promoted by the Society lie close to the heart of the central agent generating this rapid change. Even Georgian patricians and opulent literary gentlemen removed from the cares of this world knew this as they meditated about the greatest issues of their day while on their country estates and in pastoral retreats.[26] But less wealthy men like Johnson and Boswell, Smollett and Goldsmith, also knew it. H. B. Wheatley has caught the essential appeal of the Society when he contrasts its lure with the appeals of a previous era:

"As the condition of England in the middle of the seventeenth century brought about the foundation of the Royal Society and the popular and widely-spread interest in the investigation of science, so the condition of the country in the middle of the eighteenth century brought about the formation of the Society of Arts for the encouragement of the applications of science for the general good. As Dryden, Waller, Evelyn, and the literary coterie of the Restoration period largely supported the Royal Society, so the circle that surrounded Dr. Johnson took a lively interest in the success of the Society of Arts."[27]

But if we are to do justice to Smollett's "boasted academy of Christendom" let us also not forget that democratic government and a democratic set of rules and regulations constituted the Society's daily regimen, and that this version of democracy had stirred deep questions in Smollett's mind. He had written, to be sure, at great length in his *History of England* about the effects of democracy on a monarchy like England, and we have every reason to believe that he deeply valued the institution. But here he was suspended, as it were, in a kind of ignorance about the Society's future—he was not sure it would or even could survive. Democracies, as Locke wrote two generations before Smollett's, existed in degrees of perfection and ranged from nations to small gatherings of men and families. Smollett, cantankerous but still percipient, gruff but intellectually flexible, wondered as his life drew to a close if any organization as poorly administered as this one could survive, no matter how noble its intentions.[28] At times its members seemed to Smollett to babble no more coherently than the lunatics at Bedlam. Accordingly and in the most rational fashion, he extracted the core of his objection; and no less seriously or intentionally than he had extracted so many other salient features of Georgian culture and then compressed them into an unusual literary form in *Humphry Clinker*.

He approved, of course, of the Society. But he was also sceptical, and time has proved him right. And yet, was his refusal to join based upon this profound scepticism? We shall probably never know.

NOTES TO PART III

1. I.e., the inverse of the so-called "Whig Interpretation of History" from the book by that title by Sir Herbert Butterfield. The advantages of permitting Smollett and his contemporaries to speak for themselves are obvious, but eventually one must step aside and survey the scene from other perspectives.

2. See L. Knapp, *Tobias Smollett: Doctor of Men and Manners* (Princeton, 1949), pp. 253–6, 266, 270–71, and a somewhat psychoanalytic case history of Smollett's life in *Journal of the American Medical Association* (April 1971), pp. 85–9. Smollett's extant correspondence for these years ought to persuade any sceptic; see *The Letters of Tobias Smollett*, ed. L. Knapp (Oxford, 1970), pp. 108–25.

3. Here one thinks of Pope, Smollett's near contemporary, who professed to be almost "jolted to death" every time he rode into town in a carriage.

4. See *Humphry Clinker*, J. Melford to Sir Watkin Phillips, 5th June.

5. Recently L. Knapp has gathered evidence to show that Smollett and Johnson were better friends and more interested in each other's activities than has previously been thought; see L. Knapp, "Smollett and Johnson, Never Cater-Cousins?", *Modern Philology*, LXVI (1968), pp. 152–4.

6. The best survey of their attitudes, although brief, is found in H. Trueman Wood's *A History of the Royal Society of Arts* (1913), Chapter II, pp. 26–52.

7. W. S. Lewis, Walpole's most learned student ever, says nothing about his membership or attitude to the Society; see his *Horace Walpole: The Mellon Lectures 1960* (New York: Bollingen Series XXXV, 1960).

8. *Horace Walpole's Correspondence*, ed. W. S. Lewis *et al.* (New Haven: Yale University Press, 1937–), V, p. 173, 9th Feb. 1758.

9. Ibid., XXIV, p. 284, 5th March 1777. Walpole's only attraction to the Society lay in Charles Lennox's (the 3rd Duke of Richmond) fine collection of antique statues and busts housed at Goodwood, Sussex. On 6th May 1770 Walpole commented to Mann that three artistic exhibitions were being held simultaneously in London, but he says nothing about the encouragement of trade and commerce. In the same letter cited here and dated 5th March 1777, Walpole dismisses the Society of Arts along with two other "societies" in his view equally ignominious: "I shut myself entirely out of the Antiquarian Society and Parliament, the archiepiscopal seats of folly and knavery." Walpole's "non-club-ability" is a chapter in itself, especially his malicious and bizarre quarrel with the Antiquaries.

10. As I attempted to demonstrate in Part II, Smollett at no time in his life dispraised the Society; he was merely anxious by the mid-1760s about its faulty rules and regulations.

11. For Johnson, see John L. Abbott, *Journal of the Royal Society of Arts*, 1967, CXV, pp. 395–400, 486–91; 645–9 and James L. Clifford, "Johnson and the Society of Artists", *The Augustan Milieu*, ed. H. K. Miller *et al.* (Oxford, 1970), pp. 333–48; the latter does not of course deal exclusively with the Society of Arts but Clifford, in documenting Johnson's support of the petitions of artists for exhibition space, says much about this Society in passing. For Boswell, see the scholarly editions of his *London Journal;* curiously, Boswell's most recent biographer, F. A. Pottle, is silent on his membership in *James Boswell: The Earlier Years 1740–1769* (New York, 1966).

12. Smollett does not appear anywhere in this panoramic view and it is difficult to know why not: by 1777–84, when Barry was singlehandedly painting this and his five other canvases, Smollett's reputation was at its zenith, his works were being translated into many languages and he was considered one of the greatest writers of Georgian England; on the other hand he was not a member of the Society, and this may have influenced Barry. So very little is known about Barry's mind and art, especially during these early years of his career, that the student must advance any theory about these great canvases—especially the fifth—sceptically. All six need to be studied in detail for their techniques as well as for the inclusion and exclusion of certain personages in the fifth. See Hudson and Luckhurst, *The Royal Society of Arts* (1954), pp. 22–3; D. G. C. Allan, "James Barry's Fifth Picture, some problems of identification", *Jnl. R.S.A.*, Vol. CXX (1972), p. 540.

13. No letters of any significance survive, and thus there is no possibility of firsthand commentary; all Goldsmith's biographers have speculated about his reasons.

14. In *The Hilliad; an Epic Poem* (1753) with "Notes Variorum" by Arthur Murphy, dramatist.

15. The story of his rejection has come down through the ages, although no record with which I am familiar recounts it, certainly not the extant manuscripts of Hugh Percy, the Earl of Northumberland. Trueman Wood, *A History of the Royal Society of Arts* (1913), pp. 45–6, comments: "He [Hill] does not appear to have been much affected by his rejection by the Society of Arts, though he wrote what was for him a temperate letter of protest." Where could Wood have seen this letter? It now seems to have disappeared, and I have not seen it referred to elsewhere.

16. 1751, Chapters CI–CII. For Smollett's relations to Hill, see "Controversy or Collusion? The 'Lady Vane' Tracts", *Notes and Queries*, XIX (Oct. 1972), pp. 375–8.

17. I have recently combed through a large part of these journals, especially works such as Samuel Sorbière's *Relation d'un voyage en Angleterre* (1667; 1709 trans. Eng.), and have been surprised to discover no comments worthy of quotation. Nor is there, surprisingly, a single reference to the Society in *Three Tours Through London in the Years 1748, 1776, 1797*, ed. W. S. Lewis (New Haven, 1941).

18. See R. W. Ketton-Cremer, *The Early Life and Diaries of William Windham* (1930), p. 47.

19. See Part II of the present study, n. 18.

20. Surely the most authoritative early history of the Society and on several counts the equivalent of Bishop Thomas Sprat's *History of the Royal Society* (1668). Probably William Bailey's *Descriptions of the Useful Machines and Models Contained in the Repository of the Society for the encouragement of Arts* (1776–9) should also be mentioned in this catalogue, although Bailey's historical abilities cannot vie with Dossie's.

21. An example is Sir George Clark, *A History of the Royal College of Physicians* (1964–6), II, p. 542.

22. I have searched for comments in histories of all varieties but have found very little. Witt Bowden's volume *Industrial Society in England Towards the End of the Eighteenth Century* (New York, 1925) is still the most extensive, especially his first chapter ("The Age of Invention") which devotes 30 pages to the Society, but it is in other aspects out of date. John Harris's recent inaugural lecture at the University of Birmingham, *Industry and Technology in the Eighteenth Century* (Birmingham Inaugural Lecture, 1972), says nothing.

23. I am grateful to Miss Deborah Smith, a graduate student at the University of California, whose unpublished study "Smollett's Attitudes to Luxury: 1747–71" persuaded me of the validity of this point.

24. *Horace Walpole's Correspondence*, ed. W. S. Lewis *et al.* (New Haven: Yale University Press, 1937–   ), XXIII, pp. 210–12, Walpole to Horace Mann, 6th May 1770; notice here that the year is significant.

25. *The World We Have Lost* (1965).

26. Had Alexander Pope survived another decade, i.e., 1744–54, he surely would have praised the Society and joined it (if he could have endured the ride from Twickenham!); an optimist at heart, Pope, like Smollett, would have seen the Society's value.

27. *Engineering*, LII (1891), p. 83.

28. While preparing this essay I had occasion to consult the constitutions of many similar societies around the world, and was struck by the cowardliness of most historians when commenting on this aspect. It seems that institutional historians grow sentimental about their pet institution and fail to note its genuine weaknesses. D. W. R. Bahlman, tracing the history of the Society for the Reformation of Manners in *The Moral Revolution of 1688* (New Haven, 1957), says nothing about its rules in the first two decades 1690 ff. A unique exception is J. M. Brewer, not an historian but a polemicist, who has written a witty volume called *Wellsprings of Democracy: Guidance for Local Societies* (Philadelphia, 1952). In his chapter "Making Business Meetings Democratic", he writes (p. 81): "In the USSR men are forced to attend evening meetings twice a week, for indoctrination in the glories of communism (really red fascism) and the failures of western democracy. Can you not, therefore, give up eight or ten evenings a year to the mass meetings of your democratic organization?"

V

Smollett as a Letter Writer

Letters do not always reveal the man. In theory they should, but actuality dictates otherwise. Even in the eighteenth century—the epistolary century par excellence—there are notable examples, Defoe, Gay, Richardson, Fielding, Goldsmith, Sterne, Priestley, to mention only a few of the eminent literary lights. Then, too, not every set of "letters should be published as curiosities," as Boswell once intimated to Johnson, nor does every correspondence read like the gossipy tidbits larded with female glitter of Elizabeth Carter and Catherine Talbot. For every Horace Walpole, or for that matter Voltaire (who documented everything in his life from specks on his china to his latest metaphysical precept), five correspondences (at least) of important figures exist that give modern students pause about their (the letters') right to be titled "a correspondence." Tobias Smollett's are a case in point.

His letters are as scarce as hen's teeth, in this aspect almost without rival (except for Fielding and Goldsmith). Lewis Knapp, whose name in this century has become almost synonymous with Smollett's, here prints 107 extant letters spanning from 1737 to 1771. While it is true that this represents a considerable addition to the 75 printed in 1926 by Edward S. Noyes, *Letters of Tobias Smollett* (1926), nevertheless it is a meagre show (to say the least) for a man of Tobias Smollett's stature.[1] Unless he was allergic to the epistolary form (could that be possible in eighteenth-century England among the *literati?*) or sparing of words (*Peregrine Pickle* gives the lie to that possibility), the paucity of his extant correspondence remains an enigma of the first order. And the enigma is not limited to a riddle concerning lost letters or unknown documents that one day may come to light.

The question of disappearance is (of course) fascinating. The facts are that during 1750–70 Smollett was considered among the ten best novelists then writing. *Roderick Random* (1748) was an all-time best seller and admitted him to the fame machine: Fielding and Richardson. After 1750 everything he wrote was read, closely scrutinized by the critics, and reread on grounds that he had carved for himself a permanent niche in the history of the English novel. But he was also "Grub-Street." Beginning in 1756, he edited the *Critical Review*, perhaps the single most powerful and influential literary machine of the age of Johnson, and wrote for most other periodicals; he was a member of the in-group among novelists, actors, and scholars, travelling smoothly and comfortably in all these circles, and was deemed the only man in Britain capable of continuing in 1757–58 Hume's *History of England*. He knew everyone of importance, and every English writer, significant and insignificant, in London and elsewhere, knew of him.

How then is it possible that only 107 letters survive? Granted, many must have disappeared, as happens with all writers, and granted his wife, Ann Lassells, was not extremely intelligent and made no known effort to preserve (or collect) the literary remains of her husband. Nonetheless, one would expect Smollett's correspondents to have kept his letters, if for no other reason than as souvenirs of a famous and great novelist; and after 1748, when he was twenty-seven, it was perfectly clear he was that. Other alternatives are equally puzzling: namely, that for reasons remaining unclear Smollett wrote unusually few letters; or that the particular persons with whom he corresponded (in order of numbers: 16 to Dr. John Moore, 16 to William Huggins, 9 to Dr. George Macaulay, 9 to Dr. William Hunter, 7 to John Wilkes, 6 to Samuel Richardson) were unaware of his claims on posterity; or even, and this alternative is more likely, that the papers of his correspondents were not kept intact after their death. If the letters of Swift and Pope survive in greater numbers, it is at least possible that this is occasioned by their constant correspondence with royalty and the aristocracy, with earls and dukes whose librarians knew better the needs of future students than did Mrs. Smollett or—to cite another example of a fellow novelist whose letters survive in even scantier numbers—Mrs. Fielding.

And yet, the possiblility that Smollett actually wrote few letters must not be discarded so quickly. Much of his writing labour was devoted to novels (he wrote quickly but was an incorrigible reviser), reviews, and, whenever he was in financial straits to ghosting and, as he himself admitted, this left no energy for familiar letters. The idea that some aspects of his temperament prevented him from writing letters is practically absurd; at any rate, it is impossible to prove. No, it is more likely that Smollett lived "through" his novels and for a brief period (1755–60) "through" the writing of history. At least the extant letters indicate that. He was not particularly egocentric and and believed that his own life would hold little interest for posterity. And he was right. Smollett-the-novelist is much more interesting than

Smollett-the-man. The case might be otherwise if more documents survived, but despite Knapp's sunny optimism ("It is the hope of all students of Smollett that eventually more of his correspondence will be found"—Preface) such abundant discovery is not likely to occur.

Smollett's correspondence as it stands today is impersonal and without many "leaks." It avoids the confessional mode that stamps the letters of Alexander Pope or John Keats; it refrains from the anecdotal idiom of Johnson and Boswell, and lacks the historical aspirations of Horace Walpole or (on a less grand scale) Lady Mary Wortley Montagu. It can be read in a single sitting of no more than a few hours, during which one often views Smollett complaining about his debt, health, or nostalgia for Scotland. The often discussed irascibility of the gentleman is indubitably present, but is not nearly so vitriolic as some critics have stated it. Irascibility is balanced here by a genuine, almost winning, shyness which the man possessed in large quantity—it was an essential component of his temperament.

Disclosures worthy of notice or quotation are few and far apart. Rarely are they of the depth or number found in Smollett's semi-fictional travel letters [*Travels Through France and Italy*, (1766)], in which he creates a persona not always consistent with the real-life figure. Reading from letter to letter in Knapp's new volume, we see the young Scotsman, for instance, aged twenty-seven and now residing in London, recovering from his first best seller, *The Adventures of Roderick Random*, disclaiming (not altogether truthfully) any personal targets in his novel:

> I am not a little mortified to find the Characters strangely misapplied to Particular Men whom I never had the least Intention to ridicule, by which means I have suffered very much in my moral Capacity, some persons to whom I have been extremely obliged, being weak enough to take Umbrage at many passages of the work, on the Supposition that I myself am the Hero of the Book, and they, of consequence, concerned in the History.

Elsewhere he proclaims to Alexander Carlyle—one of two men to whom he could open whatever heart he had for letters—his fervid, almost obsessed, love of their native land:

> I do not think I could enjoy Life with greater Relish in any part of the world than in Scotland among you and your Friends, and I often amuse my Imagination with schemes for attaining that Degree of Happiness, which, however, is altogether out of my Reach. I am heartily tired of this Land of Indifference [England] and Phlegm where the finer Sensations of the Soul are not felt. and Felicity is held to consist in stupifying Port and overgrown Buttocks of Beef, where Genius is lost, Learning undervalued, and Taste altogether extinguished, and Ignorance prevails to such a

degree that one of our Chelsea Club asked me if the weather was good when I crossed the Sea from Scotland, and another desired to know if there were not more Pope than one, inasmuch as he had heard people mention the Pope of Rome, an expression which seemed to imply that there was a Pope of some other Place. I answered that there was a Pope of Troy, and another of Tartary, and he seemed perfectly well satisfied with the Information, which no person present pretended to contradict.

Wit disguises Smollett's oblique truth: he had many opportunities permanently to return to Scotland and took none; he is writing obviously with Carlyle's own perfervid nationalism in mind. But even in passages like this Smollett the consummate stylist shines through: chiselled sentences, sparkling antitheses, delicate balance, an ear for the music of prose, and just the right amount of well placed levity.

Very rarely does disclosure take the form of self-appraisal. When it does, it is candid and sincere, and often clearly demonstrates the strengths and weaknesses of the man. Here is Smollett in middle age: "I live in the shade of obscurity, neglecting and neglected, and spend my vacant hours among a Set of honest, phlegmatic Englishmen whom I cultivate for their Integrity of Heart and Simplicity of Manners." What touching shyness for a man who was a literary lion of his age! But restraint of an unusual variety lasted to the end. Here are Smollett's last words from Leghorn, his will and testament shrouded in ancient images:

I have nothing to say but that if I can prevail upon my wife to execute my last will, you shall receive my poor carcase in a box, after I am dead, to be placed among your rarities. I am already so dry and emaciated that I may pass for an Egyptian mummy without any other preparation than some pitch and painted linen.

Style conquers content in these letters, in almost every case. It even compensates somewhat for an absence of thought. Even when the disclosure is of paramount interest for students of English culture 1750–1800, Smollett's vivid style outshines his thoughts. Future students, historians especially, will have much recourse to the following statement of purpose in *A History of England*, and many will note how absurd it would be to accuse Smollett of misrepresenting his true aims, but the reader who actually reads these letters and the *History* cannot fail to observe how much of their success is the result of a deft stylist who has since been much maligned and under-rated:

. . . in writing the History of England, I can safely say I had no other view in the Execution of that work than historical Truth,

which I have displayed on all occasions to the best of my Know-
ledge without Fear or affection. I have kept myself independent
of all Connexions which might have affected the Candour of my
Intention. I have flattered no Individual; I have cultivated no
Party. I look upon the Historian who espouses a Faction, who
strains Incidents or willfully suppresses any Circumstances of
Importance that may tend to the Information of the Reader, as
the worst of Prostitutes. I pique myself upon being the only
Historian of this Country who has had Honesty, Temper and
Courage enough to be wholly impartial and disinterested.

The "only Historian?" Not quite. Hume and Robertson, it is true,
sacrificed some objectivity and impartiality to the demands of
writing "philosophical history." But, again, Smollett persuades his
reader more by the clarity and vividness of his style than by the
absolute truth of his assertions.

What does this publication teach us about Smollett that is new?
Some factual observations are perhaps in order. There are approximately a dozen personal disclosures, general in nature, and I have
cited four; nothing, therefore, in the correspondence is going to
assist us significantly in understanding Smollett's personality and
life-style. His self-diagnosis of 1753, "systema nervosum maxime
irritabile" (the most irritable nervous system imaginable), remains
the most profound psychoanalytic statement we have. Nor are these
letters about to fill in lacunae about which students have for so long
been wondering: Smollett's religious opinions, the breadth of his
alleged humanitarian spirit, his various attempts to establish in
England an academy for belles-lettres, the total contribution he made
to the *Critical Review* during its first decade of publication, and most
mysterious of all, his connection with and work done for the Earl of
Bute's administration early in the 1760s [Knapp's biography, *Tobias
Smollett* (1949), reveals almost nothing on the subject]. These and
dozens of other biographical questions remain riddles, unanswered
and at present unanswerable, and students, even after reading the
new Smollett correspondence, will discover themselves returning to
the novels with the hope that the voice narrating them will grow
increasingly more understandable through repeated readings.

Lewis Knapp's notes display erudition and characteristic humility,
and it is a pleasure to have them. His editorial methods are impec-
cable. The most exacting student will find little to carp about,
especially since their author proceeds with such caution and gravity.
Unless a fact can be established beyond a shadow of doubt, Knapp
saves himself and presents his reader with several possibilities.
Personally, I would have preferred heavier annotation, but I do not
wish to suggest that Knapp has not covered his terrain. Certain

advantages would have been gained if the letters Smollett answered were printed as well, but I suppose that would have doubled the cost of production. Very rarely one hits upon an annotation that is questionable. For example, p. 138, "for Theodore B. von Neuhof, King of Corsica, see Frederick A. Pottle, *James Boswell The Earlier Years 1740–1769* (New York, 1966), *passim*," is a curious citation in view of the fact that Pottle's index lists only four passing references and at least four major documents are known to deal exclusively with Theodore, one contemporary [*Histoire des révolutions de l'île de Corse et de l'elévation de Théodore I* (1738); trans. English (1739)] and three modern [André le Glay, *Théodore de Neuhoff* (1907); Valerie Pirie, *His Majesty of Corsica* (1939); Peter Wilding, *Adventures in the Eighteenth Century* (1937)]. Or, p. 36, n. 9 in which Knapp accounts for Smollett's professed dislike in a letter of 1754 of certain emetics: "The bad effects of excessive purges were stressed by Dr. William Fordyce; see his *A Review of Venereal Disease and Its Remedies* (London, 1772), 35–6." It is really unnecessary to resort to a medical work published almost twenty years after Smollett's letter; numerous works published during the early 1750s exist advocating the same views and there are good reasons to believe Smollett had read some; but by 1772 Smollett was dead, and in any case could not have read Fordyce's treatise. Another example is p. 35, n. 4, in which Knapp writes "unidentified" for a Melvil whom Smollett mentions in a letter of March 1754. Would it not be more helpful to a student to have the man who knows more about Smollett's life than any one on this planet hazard a guess? After all, there were several Melvils in London in the early 1750s who might be candidates, to say nothing of the Scottish Melvils (originally from Hungary, but by the late 1600s prominent among Scottish aristocracy), the so-called Earls of Leslie, who also became the Earls of Leven at the turn of the eighteenth century. But any such objections are few and far apart and do not impugn the high standard of factual scholarship of this volume.

The publication of these letters comes at an opportune time, almost at the moment of Smollett's bicentenary, 1771–1971. Undoubtedly, Knapp's volume will form a large part of any celebration of that anniversary. And without his researches of almost five decades such celebration would be much less jubilant. But it is nevertheless to be hoped that Knapp will continue to search for more letters, and to publish them as additions to this excellent volume.

NOTE

1. "Of course, Smollett must have written scores of notes to his associates who helped him prepare issues of the *Critical Review* and the *British Magazine*, as well as to his publishers. Then there must have been letters to his sister Jane, and to his mother, who

lived until 1770. Smollett's available letters are few indeed as contrasted with those of Samuel Richardson, Laurence Sterne, Lady Mary Wortley Montagu, David Garrick, and Dr. Samuel Johnson. They greatly outnumber, however, the amazingly few of Henry Fielding, and amount to about twice as many as those of Oliver Goldsmith." (Preface, p. viii.)

The year 1971 marks the bicentenary of Dr. Smollett's (1721–71) death, and to commemorate this event a definitive Bicentennial Edition of Smollett's Works, is in preparation. This essay comments, in part, on an important step towards such celebration, the appearance of *The Letters of Tobias Smollett*, M.D., edited by L. M. Knapp (Oxford: Clarendon Press, 1970).

VI

Smollett and
the Form of Picaresque Literature

Smollett has never been the best understood writer of English prose, and in at least one aspect—the relation of his imaginative prose works to the so-called "picaresque tradition"—he has been patently misunderstood. In recent years several critics have maintained that all his novels are "picaresque,"[1] and the generalization is so often quoted in college textbooks and secondary works dealing with the English novel that, if not immediately challenged, it threatens soon to solidify into a cliché. The actuality is—and the following remark hopefully will disburden those readers of Smollett who have thus far been unable to decide for themselves—that Smollett's prose works are no more picaresque than his age, held by some to be allegedly "neoclassical," was an "Age of Reason" piously dedicated to rational principles mysteriously governing a supposedly rational group of people.[2] In Smollett's case the confusion has largely arisen as a result of feeble-minded criticism buttressed by wrong-headed historical assumptions, but also because his five prose works, *Roderick Random*, *Peregrine Pickle*, *Ferdinand Count Fathom*, *Sir Launcelot Greaves*, and *Humphry Clinker*, are more than usually anomalous among eighteenth-century prose narratives, and because each is so vastly different from any other.

I. FORM

Nothing has confused the Smollettian picture more than the erroneous belief that "picaresque" is a term describing the form of a prose work. By form I mean the "kinds" of prose (for example, novels, satires, apologues), or to use scientific language, the classes, in the sense of classification, of the prose world.[3] Classes are taxonomically divided into species and sub-species no less than prose kinds divide themselves into sets and subsets of novels, satires, and apologues, and into as yet undiscovered—and this is all important— new forms. Nowhere to my knowledge are the forms of eighteenth-century prose more than lucidly described in Sheldon Sacks' book *Fiction and the Shape of Belief* (1967), and disagree as one may with his reading intuition and his interpretation of individual passages, one must nevertheless in dispassionate fairness credit him with having produced the single most lucid and scientifically tenable work thus far published on the forms of eighteenth-century prose. Sacks' adverse critics have accused him of being Aristotelian, formal, and overly scientific; what they are in fact responding to is a highly logical and organized method of critical procedure that rigorously approaches the problem of literary classification and that insists on defining terms and major assumptions before using them. Without Sacks' book and the variety of criticism it embodies it is unlikely that the recent revaluation of eighteenth-century prose fiction we have witnessed would have taken place. His seemingly rigid separation of form and content and his sharp distinction between coherent and incoherent narratives paved the way towards later exploration, if not comprehension, of some of the precise ways in which an author's ethical beliefs and moral intentions influence the shape of his narrative.

What has this to do with Smollett and the picaresque? More than is evident. If a critic with Sacks' premises rigorously develops a system of classification for prose fictions, other critics have at least two alternatives: refutation of that system on equally rigorous grounds and supplementation of another and hopefully better classification system, or its acceptance. Nothing printed since 1967, or for that matter before 1967, convinces me that a more rigorously determined classification for known prose forms exists. By "known prose forms" I mean those works (for example, *Gulliver's Travels*, *Clarissa*, *Tristram Shandy*) whose forms have been somewhat if not partially or adequately studied and described; unknown forms either have not been partially or adequately studied or, having been studied, are known to be problematic to their subspecies or larger class (that is, the class of novels, the class of satires, the class of apologues) because they resist classification. Smollett's fiction is an example. *Moll Flanders* is another example, and it is at least possible (as the recent controversies over the form of this work abundantly indicate[4]) that Defoe had landed upon a new form that is neither fish nor fowl, flora nor fauna, or, to be more explicit, that *Moll Flanders* is formally neither a novel, a satire, nor an apologue. The point to be gathered, then, is that at the present moment the known forms of eighteenth-century prose are limited to three, while granting that each class has many species and that time will doubtlessly bring others to light.

Where does this classification leave picaresque? Nowhere, because the term describes and always has described the material or content aspect of a literary work. If picaresque had been a denotation of the *form* of a class of eighteenth-century narratives, then doubtlessly it would have included those prose works that are neither novels, satires, nor apologues. And yet those English works traditionally labelled picaresque during the eighteenth century—*Moll Flanders, Jonathan Wild, Roderick Random, Peregrine Pickle, Launcelot Greaves*, to mention only a few—have also been classified as novels, satires, or apologues by the very same critics who use the term picaresque to describe some other aspect of their intrinsic literary nature. Clearly the overlapping is problematic and the precise sphere of each is nowhere stated: a given work (for example, *Roderick Random*) cannot be *both* a novel and a picaresque fiction unless the former refers to one aspect of classification (form) and the latter to another (content). Historically such is precisely the case: by "novel" most critics have loosely meant a fictional prose work in which the fate of individual characters seems more important than any other aspect, and by "picaresque" a cultural milieu or ambiance pervaded by rogues and rascals.[5] But rogues and rascals performing stratagems and tricks pervade many literary works, not only prose works and certainly not only novels, and the rigorous taxonomer queries what mitigates against a picaresque poem, a picaresque ballad, a picaresque play (for example, *Waiting for Godot*)? These and other related questions illustrate that in every classification system, whether of the animal world or of prose narratives, everything depends on the degree of rigor employed by the taxonomer.

Let us therefore recognize that the term picaresque must be restricted to a single dimension of a literary work and exclusively use it to describe the material (that is, contents) of a prose work regardless of its form, observing at the same time the problems it creates if applied to the content aspect of Smollett's prose works.[6]

II. DEFINITIONS OF THE PICARESQUE

Historically, the label has described delinquent and alienated characters wandering through a cross-section of the world. Most scholars have acknowledged that *Guzmán de Alfarache* and *Lazarillo de Tormes* are "Urpicaresques," but this observation, whether implicit or explicit, has not prevented their classification of many works in the category of picaresque which, like *Don Quixote*, bears no more than a slight resemblance to the total attributes of these original works.[7] Critics surveying English prose fiction have spoken of a neo-picaresque or a parodic picaresque, in their attempt to find an all-inclusive label describing many prose works written during

1700–1800. As has been pointed out, both terms remain vague unless the original work or works being parodied are clearly enunciated. If an entire tradition is being parodied, then the difficulty of making a case for neo-picaresque is all the greater, because few students will agree on just which aspects of the tradition are being resuscitated and which ignored, especially if the tradition extends over many centuries.

In an attempt to understand what help the label picaresque can offer us in classifying Smollett's narratives, let us define picaresque content as applicable to those prose works which, regardless of their form—and this last clause is all important—contain a first person narrator, a *picaro*, ~~whose social fluidity is marked,~~ whose perspective towards himself and the external world is demonstrably oblique, and who haphazardly wanders through a variegated natural or mental landscape only to discover that his life is a game from which he ought to and finally does withdraw. The definition will not satisfy everyone, but it is at least a working definition. It derives from *Guzmán* and *Lazarillo* and has been formulated to account for their contents. It says absolutely nothing about the form of these works. Like all definitions it implies several if not many corollaries: for example, the role we may expect love, marriage, sex, childhood, adolescence, parents, friendship, Providence, money, guilt, solitude, stoicism, and chance to play in the *picaro's* world; or—to continue—the *picaro's* sanguinity when confronted with impending calamity, his sense of the individual moment as all important, and the author's aesthetic and comic distance from the *picaro*. A long list of other attributes common to *Guzmán*, *Lazarillo*, *El Buscón* and *Simplicissimus* could be compiled. However, no literary work that fails to meet all the terms of this definition can be classified as picaresque, for every rigorous taxonomer knows he must first decide whether a given specimen is flora or fauna before worrying about its further classification as mammalian, reptilian, amphibian, etc. The essential thing for all classification is establishment of a definition and rigorous adherence to its requirements.

Only *Roderick Random* among Smollett's five prose fictions meets *some* of the requirements of the definition. Roderick's perspective is often but not always oblique and yet the work at large meets the other requirements of our definition so that it is probably valid to call its material picaresque. Smollett's other four fictions are eliminated from the picaresque kingdom on grounds that they are not first-person narratives.[8] If this requirement is dropped or even slightly relaxed to include, for example, first-person authors of letters in epistolary novels, notice how many prose fictions must suddenly be categorized as picaresque: all prose works written in third-person narrative displaying an alienated and roguish protagonist who wanders through different strata of society and who finally retreats from his previous life. What prevents *Tom Jones* from being classified as picaresque?[9] He wanders through low life permeated by rogues, and a case could be made for his oblique angle of vision. Enough problems exist (that is, a definition of every term in the original definition) even if the above definition is mercilessly adhered to without softening it, exploiting it, or cunningly twisting whatever little virtue it possesses by affirming that some prose works are "more picaresque" and some "less picaresque," or some "hard picaresques" and others "soft picareques."

How, then, can Smollett be classified as a picaresque novelist? One out of five does not constitute a strong case and if the definition is relaxed, a possibility already entertained, then *Guzmán* and *Lazarillo*, works from which the definition was originally constructed, must be thrown out of court. At this point critics who want their cake and also want to eat it will retort that Smollett's narratives are not "proper picaresques," but are related and derivative members of the class; that is, they ape, or parody, elements of genuine picaresques. This may be true, but they also parody elements of genuine satires (for example, *Gulliver's Travels*). Why seize upon picaresque elements to the exclusion of other elements? Why not then classify Smollett's works as "satires"? After all, they also parody and burlesque genuine romances, and at other times genuine low-life realism. Why classify them as parodic picaresques rather than as parodic satires, parodic romances or works parodic of realism? That is, why make one attribute among many the *determining* factor of an entire class unless it can be demonstrated that this, and no other, attribute is somehow more intrinsic or essential to the class than all others? Even if the singular significance of this attribute could be unequivocally demonstrated, we would still need to exert extreme caution, since visible signs of a class are often deceptive. Worms, which hardly resemble mammals, breed by live birth just as mammals do. Many other creatures, on the other hand, resemble mammals, especially in their hair-like qualities, yet have nothing whatsoever in common with them. Other critics will argue that Smollett's fictions are indebted to Fielding's novels and contain attributes such as plot, realism, and character that are similar to, and occasionally actually modelled upon, his works. Again, this may be true. All these theories may contain some truth, but for the purpose of classification—if one is seriously interested in classifying Smollett's five works—far greater rigor than has previously been exercised must now be summoned. Smollett's fictions, if loosely discussed, are everything and nothing—so the argument goes—are picaresques, satires, and novels at the same time, or are mutated combinations of the three such as "more picaresque, less satiric, and somewhat resembling a novel."[10]

III. ON THE FORM AND CONTENT OF SMOLLETT'S WORKS

The methodological weakness of criticism that classifies works without rigor is perhaps most readily apparent in its conclusions. It eventually flounders in chaos because of a refusal to define terms, and at later stages, when presented with the logical deductions of its unstated but implied initial hypotheses, sorely complains of never having intended to allege that Smollett, for example, wrote in forms that are at once all the forms. Such critics—and recently there have been several in Smollett's case—sometimes argue that labels (that is, picaresque) are a necessary evil if a man's works are to be presented to a reading audience. Granting that these writers are not essentially concerned with problems of literary taxonomy, I nevertheless doubt the validity of the assumption as much as I question the assertion that Smollett's age was "rational," his contemporary writers "neo-classical," and his fellow thinkers (not individually but as a group) "enlightened." What difference, after all, is there between a literary tag employed in the name of facility, and an historical label used on grounds of expedition and palatability?

Space does not here permit me to discuss in detail the contents of Smollett's other four novels and the precise reasons for which each should be eliminated from the picaresque category, but something must be said about each, however perfunctory.[11] As a prolegomenon, I must unequivocally say that I am only describing this author's materials (that is, sources, influences, ethical assumptions, intellectual allegiances, etc.) and not the form he gave to these materials. If I am dubious of the status of all five as formal novels, I am nonetheless reasonably convinced that not one of the five is formally a genuine satire (such as *Gulliver's Travels*) in which is meant a prose work whose chief attribute is excoriation of identifiable objects external to the fictive world of the satire itself.[12] This leaves the apologue form and possibly forms as yet unidentified but worked out by Smollett. If his fictions are formally apologues they are observably different kinds of apologues from *Rasselas* or *Candide*. This empirical difference could well lead a critic interested in prose classification to conclude that Smollett's fictions are shaped into undiscovered and as yet undefined forms.

Peregrine Pickle (1751), his second prose work, is a third-person episodic narrative, relating the adventures of Peregrine, the main character, from birth to marriage. The work is a loose, sprawling narrative displaying little if any observable coherence whatsoever, and contains elements of almost every known type of previous prose material:[13] satirical (the "College of Authors"), novelistic (particularly showing influences of Fielding in Peregrine's relation to his parents, aunt and uncle), picaresque (Peregrine's stratagems, games, and flexible mobility), quixotic (his delusive attempts to change the world by indulging his bizarre imagination in stratagems), realistic ("The Memoirs of a Lady of Quality"), romantic (the atmospherics and imagery employed in parting scenes with Emilia), didactic (English versus foreign manners and customs), farcical and burlesque ("The Doctor Prepares an Entertainment in the Manner of the Ancients"), grotesque (many of the actions of Grizzle, Trunnion, Keypstick), and so forth. One wonders why one of these tags (let us say picaresque) ought to be grasped to the exclusion of another (for example, grotesque)? The total materials of *Peregrine Pickle* are doubtlessly as grotesque as they are picaresque, and as satiric as they are grotesque; it makes little logical sense to isolate one out of the grab bag as a proper label describing the work at large. Even if it could be demonstrated beyond a shadow of doubt—supposing this could be ascertained on some contrived statistical basis, which to my knowledge it cannot—that the picaresque materials in *Peregrine Pickle* outweigh all other materials, some of which (but not all) have been mentioned, this fact in itself would prove nothing about its form. Its shape is not visibly unified in the sense that *Gulliver's Travels*, *Clarissa*, *Tom Jones*, and *Rasselas* are;[14] its beginning has little relation to its middle, and the entire thrust of the work, like its predecessor *Roderick Random*, does not tend toward the ending Smollett gives it. If it were coherent it would not contain "The Memoirs of a Lady of Quality" or many other episodes (for example, Chapters ci–ciii) that have perplexed discerning critics for decades.

Ferdinand Count Fathom (1753), Smollett's third fiction, is also a third-person narrative containing even fewer picaresque elements than either of its predecessors. Other than Fathom's social mobility and an array of roguish characters, the fiction meets none of the requirements of the definition stated above. Neither Fathom nor the less important Renaldo are *picaros*. Fathom bears little resemblance to the typical *picaros* in *Guzmán*, *Lazarillo*, or *Gil Blas*, who view the world askance through a double vision of caring and not caring. He is instead an incorrigible villain—hardly a salient characteristic of earlier *picaros*—who wanders as much as Odysseus and Tom Jones, and who is saved by the quirks of an unpredictable Fate, a timely Providence, and an inexplicably lenient Deity in a work otherwise demonstrating, unlike Tom Jones, no Christian humanism and symbolism. In addition to these objections, the reader's intuition informs him that Smollett's intentions and mood are different from those in his two former works.[15] He experiments with new materials, especially in the realms of human nature and natural landscape, aspects untouched earlier, but also fuses several disparate worlds within the confines of a single book.[16] His achievement or lack of it has never been agreed upon. But whether or not we like it is another matter unrelated to the few picaresque elements among its *total* materials contained in a shape that is, if not incoherent in comparison to the best eighteenth-century fictive shapes, at least unclassified at the present time.

Sir Launcelot Greaves (1760–61), Smollett's fourth work, is again a third-person narrative, this time professing to be written in a manner parodic of Cervantes' *Don Quixote:*

> "What (said Ferret) you set up for a modern Don Quixote?—The scheme is rather too stale and extravagant. What was an humorous romance and well-timed satire in Spain, near two hundred years ago, will make but a sorry jest, and appear equally insipid and absurd when really acted from affectation, at this time of day, in a country like England."[17]

That the entire work glances at the quixotism of Don Quixote and attempts to find equivalent English themes is unquestionably true, but the concerns of quixotism, as every historian of Spanish literature knows, have little to do with those of picaresque. No respectable Hispanist would confuse them and most would sorely chide those critics who did.[18] Practically nothing in *Greaves* depicts a picaresque world: neither the main characters nor minor ones, not Launcelot's angle of vision, nor his sense of existence in the world about him; and nothing in his very limited wanderings suggests the roguish games and stratagems typical of *picaros*. A case for classifying the material of *Greaves* as picaresque to the exclusion of other types of content matter presents so many insurmountable difficulties that it need not be seriously considered.

Humphry Clinker (1771) remains—Smollett's last work—an epistolary prose narrative divided into five different correspondences displaying at least five different points of view. Matthew Bramble, a fifty-five year old invalid composed of a tough exterior and tender interior (a heart of gold) is ostensibly the main character although the book is titled *Humphry Clinker*. Less important characters—Jery and Lydia Melford, Win Jenkins, Tabitha Bramble, Clinker himself —comment on many of the same incidents that impel Bramble to write to Dr. Lewis; but Smollett is fascinated by the multiplicity of viewpoints he has created and makes it clear that no two correspondents see the mundane things of this world through similar eyes.

While the minor characters range from comic to stupid, and from grotesque to uninviting, Bramble, the character to whom Smollett gives almost twice as many letters as any other, is more multidimensional and psychologically complex. His origins lie in the sensibility movement that during the 1750s and 1760s had gripped England generally and Smollett particularly and, to a lesser extent, in the author's own life: both are ailing, moving into old age, and on journeys in search of health. Bramble's letters deal with social customs, economic problems, medical observations on his own case, and a host of other public areas. Smollett arouses our interest in the relation of Bramble's psychology and physiology, especially the disparity between his exterior and interior, and his momentary state of mind as determining the immediate direction of an illness. Jery's letters are largely comments on his uncle's. If a minor character travelling amidst this entourage were unmistakably identified by a critic as a *picaro* clearly showing the traits of a Guzmán or Lazarillo, it would be of little consequence to our sense of the author's intentions at large. We may not be able to state what the form of *Humphry Clinker* is—if it is formally not a novel, it nevertheless comes closest among Smollett's five fictions to approaching that form—but its deepest materials are remarkably contemporary. Likewise, if Bramble is a *picaro*—as Spector insists[19]—then he is one of the few *picaros* in European literature who does not narrate his early years and manhood; who has little social flexibility and whose stance and perspective appear incredibly irascible and intemperately severe in comparison to the cunning devil-may-care perspective of a Lazarillo, for example; and the only *picaro* to my knowledge who possesses little if any of demonstrably utilitarian ethic evident in works like *Guzmán*—that whatever works for the *picaro* is always best. If Bramble, then, is a *picaro*, he is indeed a mutant member of the family.[20]

IV. SOME INTIMATIONS ABOUT THE FUTURE

Indications exist that the notion of Smollett's supposed indebtedness to the picaresque tradition is coming under fire, but the battle is far from having been won. The most recent book on Smollett in English, Robert Spector's *Tobias Smollett* (1968), argues, "contrary to most critical opinion, that Smollett maintained the picaresque form throughout his five novels, that *Humphry Clinker*, no less than *Roderick Random*, belongs to that genre."[21] Contrary to most critical opinion? If that were true, the debate presently raging among Smollettians and other students of the eighteenth-century novel would be supererogatory, as a sensible review of Spector's book has

noted in this journal. "As far as I can determine . . . no substantial
criticism of Smollett's novels has ever suggested that he completely
escaped from the picaresque (or satiric) mode."[22] This reviewer's
equation of picaresque and satiric modes—could he have confused
his syntax and meant by "or" merely the two in apposition?—must
give pause to every reader of eighteenth-century English fiction
interested in problems of classification. It impels me to wonder if his
review can be trusted; but his objection to Spector's thesis on grounds
that scholars have never "completely escaped," any more than did
Smollett, from picaresque material is tenable and historically
defensible.

Questions about the meaning of the label "picaresque" are being
asked to the embarrassment of its many users. Some critical theorists
no longer are satisfied to be bludgeoned or cajoled into believing that
picaresque material was Smollett's guiding force. Philip Stevick, in a
very recent essay on "Smollett's Picaresque Games," takes Spector to
task for arguing what to him appears an untenable thesis:

> Spector's *Tobias George Smollett* . . . seems to me an interesting
> attempt to make sense of the Smollett canon as a unified whole.
> But is it not procrustean in its insistence that *all* the fiction is pica-
> resque? For example, Spector describes Matt Bramble as "a
> picaro in the sense that Smollett uses him as an observer of society
> and that his observations are carried on as a result of the typical
> picaresque journey device" (p. 130), a use of literary category that
> strikes me as being imprecise and unpersuasive. I find neither Sir
> *Launcelot Greaves* nor *Humphry Clinker* picaresque . . . *Ferdinand
> Count Fathom* is a difficult case, for its first two-thirds are as
> picaresque as the earlier two novels.[23]

This does not imply, of course, that Smollett's first two novels are
"very much" picaresque but merely, as Stevick says, that they are "as
picaresque." Stevick's method distinguishes between Smollett's early
and late works, and he is doubtlessly correct to be interested in the
precise ways that prose works are related to and derivative from
earlier prose works. But ultimately I wonder if he does not entrap
himself (although to a far lesser degree than Spector) by using the
term without defining it, and by amassing Smollett's earlier fiction
into a picaresque mold to the exclusion of many other possible
molds—this despite his having just asserted that at least one half of
Smollett's five prose works are demonstrably *not* picaresque, an
assertion that might well have led him to entertain the possibility
that not even the first two works are:

> Every book on picaresque fiction I have seen defines its canon in
> somewhat different ways. But no one, to my knowledge, has ever
> excluded Smollett. By speaking of Smollett's place in relation to

the tradition that precedes him and the one that follows him, I do not wish to imply that the precise shapes of these two traditions are not highly problematical. They are, of course. Robert Giddings's *The Tradition of Smollett* (London, 1967) attempts to connect Smollett with these two traditions, with uneven success. It is enough for my purposes that the readers share my assumption that Smollett's early work contains sufficient qualities in common with earlier indisputable exemplars of the genre, *Guzmán de Alfarache* say, so that it is legitimate to speak of Smollett's fiction as picaresque.[24]

Stevick's last sentence is everything: "that the readers share my assumption." Readers are willing to indulge an assumption even if they are in wholehearted disagreement with it, if a critic's reading intuition and exposition of the deductions of that intuition demonstrate that it leads to a perceptive and possibly accurate description of a work of art.[25] The opposite has been true of many of Smollett's critics. One cannot help but believe that their willingness to be imperiled by a problematical, although appealing, label is in great part responsible for this development. Sir Walter Scott, author of an essay on Smollett's works that is still read and to this day remains one of the best, barely uses the word.[26] By contrast, the critical appreciations of such critics as Saintsbury, Baker, Childs, and, more recently, Giddings suffer from a myopia caused by their proclivity to accept a traditional critical tag without questioning its authenticity and tyranny. The first sentence of Saintsbury's section on Smollett in *A Short History of English Literature* reads: "The novels of Tobias George Smollett relapse in appearance and general plan upon a form—that of the 'picaresque' or adventure-novel—older than that of Fielding or even of Richardson; but in reality they contributed largely to the development of the new fiction."[27] Saintsbury's dichotomy between the actual contents of Smollett's novels and their influence is understandable enough, but his theory of a regression and relapse is tenuous. Whether Smollett himself thought it was a "relapse" is beside the point. What counts is the path Saintsbury is compelled to tread because he is blindfolded by a tyrannical tag he somehow thinks he must uphold, and it greatly impedes his freedom in exploring Smollett's fiction. Critics interested in genre theory and in rigorous literary classification must resort to labels (romance, realism, picaresque, etc.), but readers whose concern is primarily with the enjoyment they derive from an author ought to avoid them. The same problem beset E. A. Baker, who measured all of Smollett's novels by a picaresque standard: "*Ferdinand Count Fathom* may be described as a sort of picaresque novel having a thoroughgoing miscreant instead of a genial rogue as its central figure, and an intricate plot superimposed, in order to produce a contrast with the behaviour and happier fortunes of the virtuous people."[28] And yet Smollett, according to Baker, "confounds the tale of picaresque adventure with the criminal biography," which leads Baker to conclude that "Smollett was neither a thinker on life and art nor a serious novelist." If that is true, then why bother with him at all? If he was not serious about the works he was writing, why must all this effort be wasted on him? Such questions seem not to have fazed Saintsbury and Baker. Baker's estimates of Smollett are not surprising, in view of the fact that his most precise location of Smollett's material is merely "a sort of picaresque novel."

Long lists of similar appraisals could be collected, all demonstrating the critical despotism this term has exercised;[29] and while it is obviously impossible to prove that such critics as Saintsbury and his followers would have creatively explored this novelist's *oeuvre* if the label were dropped altogether, the fact that Smollett's "picaresque interpreters" have uniformly uttered the least profound pronouncements about his achievement is too striking to be dismissed as purely coincidental.

In fact, the history of criticism on Smollett underscores the validity of Stevick's point—that Smollett's relation to original picaresques and to an intervening picaresque tradition is indeed "highly problematical." This relationship must remain problematical so long as impressionistic criticism of Baker's variety ("a sort of picaresque novel") makes an impact on scholars interested in classification; nor will clarification issue while confusion persists about the status of picaresque as a form or material. Literary history, particularly the writings of eighteenth-century critics, affords not much help here. The term picaresque was in Smollett's era much more inclusive than it has been at almost any time since then: a catchall for literally any variety of literature depicting low-life characters and characters as they are rather than as they ought to be, and more often than not merely a muddled synonym for romance. This fact of literary history has been sufficiently documented and requires no further amplification at this time of day. The label, not altogether unlike satire, was so overwhelmingly muddled and inclusive that upon occasion it accommodated most prose works, except Richardson's; not even the non-exacting exegetes of the eighteenth century could render *Pamela* and *Clarissa* picaresque. But whereas the label satire at least found a handful of eighteenth-century critics who were willing to discriminate among its many muddled meanings, the term picaresque was not so fortunate. Therefore, when George Kahrl summons Smollettians to consult a review printed in the *Critical Review*[30] which may or may not have been written by Smollett, he heralds our attention to a commonplace statement that is of limited historical interest only.[31] Dozens of similar formulations exist demonstrating over and again that Smollett's contemporaries were not a discriminating lot so far as critical labels are concerned; were indeed perfectly happy and seemed to understand each other very well when using interchangeably such terms as picaresque, quixotic, satiric, roguish, romantic, and numerous other labels. But the theory of genres, and criticism interested in rigorous classification, has advanced in two centuries. The skeptical taxonomer who proceeds with caution and gravity will wonder why he should return to the writings of men who not only indiscriminately lumped together Defoe, Fielding, and Smollett (as different in their fictions as in the techniques influencing the shape these fictions took) but also *Guzmán, Lazarillo, El Buscón, Don Quixote, Gil Blas, Pilgrim's Progress, Moll Flanders, Joseph Andrews, Tom Jones, Clarissa, Roderick Random, Peregrine Pickle, Count Fathom, Memoirs of Vidocq, Jeremiah Grant, Chrysal; or The Adventures of a Banknote,* and many others.[32] His skepticism will be apparent whether he is interested in the classification of forms or materials. It is doubtful that any critic concerned with classifying prose work of Smollett's age can bury himself in the writings of the period itself on grounds of historical fidelity. On this matter—Linnaeus' ideas, we must remember, were unknown in England before the 1750s, and took two decades to disseminate—Smollett and his contemporaries afford little help to Stevick's "highly problematical" dilemma.

Smollett's five works differ in so many aspects from these books that even the common sense of calling him related and derivative is questionable. If a *picaro's* tale, after all, is to be equated with the altogether different world of knight-errantry, then anything in literature may as well be likened to anything else. Imagining windmills and winebags as creatures, or flocks of sheep as armies, might as well describe the stuff of psychological realism or Gothic horror. The proof is in the pudding for no two "picaresque critics" agree on which of Smollett's novels is picaresque. I have already cited Spector, whose book attempts to show, "that Smollett maintained the picaresque throughout his five novels," and Stevick, for whom *only Roderick Random* and *Peregrine Pickle* are somewhat picaresque. Yet here is a third reputable student of picaresque literature who is additionally a Hispanist with considerable knowledge of Spanish literature: "*The Adventures of Ferdinand Count Fathom* (1753) is not one of Smollett's successful novels, [but] it is the *only one* that is fully picaresque—the last European novel of any consequence that is directly within the tradition started by *Guzmán de Alfarache*."[33] Precisely why any of these scholars believes that one or another of these works is picaresque to the exclusion of the others is beyond me, but the evidence speaks for itself: Stevick for Smollett's first two works, Parker for the third, and Spector for all five. A fourth scholar, who has written an entire book on the picaresque tradition, *The Picaresque Novel*, maintains a very different belief. "A careful examination of Roderick's character reveals that it is neither picaresque nor wholly nonpicaresque. The confusion in characterization is symptomatic of a deeper confusion throughout the book."[34] Miller never tells his readers what *Roderick Random* is, only what it is *not*. But the greater question, far more consequential than problems relating to the content of a particular prose work, remains. On what grounds are these works being classified as picaresque? If the disagreement among these four critics is an indication, the criteria are very arbitrary indeed. No resolution to this development will take place until the term is defined and until these scholars, as well as their reading audiences, speak a common language, if not for appreciative purposes at least for taxonomical ones.

When that day arrives, even a common language will not solve the largest dilemmas about Smollett's fiction: (1) the form of his narratives which, so far as I can tell, operate on almost entirely different principles from those of Richardson, Fielding, and Sterne;[35] (2) his particular variety of realism, which practically defies classification among the patterns of known literary realism in eighteenth-century prose; and (3) his idiosyncratic brand of morality.

The last aspect may hold a partial key to Smollett's lock and will, in any case, advance our understanding of his art much more so than such amorphous labels as picaresque. Smollett had been stung, as he tells us several times in *Count Fathom*,[36] by critics who trounced over his first two novels and thrashed him because of low-life characters whose apparent morality was nil; thereafter, he dedicated himself to the "instruction of mankind," his phrase, by consciously or unconsciously devising radically different prose forms that lent themselves to didactic ends without wandering in quite the same gutters and dipping into the same sewers his critics had accused him of stooping to in *Roderick Random* and *Peregrine Pickle*. A quarter of a century ago, Louis Martz demonstrated how Smollett's hack writing influenced the intrinsic style (sentences, diction, metaphor, prose rhythm) of his later works.[37] Smollett's extrinsic form, however, the actual shape of his plots, has remained unexplored territory.[38] If this virgin terrain can be investigated, it may account not only for the marked disparity of opinion so obvious in the critical writings of Stevick, Spector, Miller, and Parker, to mention only four,[39] but also for the dearth of incisive critical writing about Smollett's works.

Signs exist that a revaluation is taking place and that the now age-old claptrap—Smollett's novels are picaresque—may soon be coming under serious attack. Hopefully it will soon be rendered as antediluvian as the notion of "an Age of Reason." A single comment by Martin Battestin in an essay otherwise devoted to Fielding's Christian vision of life in *Tom Jones* further indicates that critic-scholars will not forever remain silent on the matter of the anomalous shape of Smollett's narratives. Battestin, writing about the essentially nontragic universe imitated by some eighteenth-century comic novelists, comments: "A similar rationale, I believe, underlies that extraordinary series of calamities and fortunate restorations which modern critics have deplored in the plot of Goldsmith's Christian fable, *The Vicar of Wakefield;* and Smollett, too—though in a much more arbitrary and perfunctory fashion—attempts to justify the preposterous turns and discoveries of *Roderick Random* by attributing them all to the marvellous workings of Providence."[40] The phrase, "though in a much more arbitrary and perfunctory fashion," expresses the direction of the current trend. If Smollett's episodic fictions have little observable coherence, and if he indeed is an amateur who never learned how to give shape to his stories, these are pressing matters to which we should be addressing ourselves, together with more rudimentary taxonomical questions about "more or less picaresque." Sooner or later serious students of the eighteenth-century novel are going to face up to the charge uttered (perhaps reticently but nevertheless perceptibly) by Battestin: namely, that Smollett, unlike Richardson and Fielding, was an amateur when it came to form, to the artistic and architectural shaping of his fictive work. At the time it will be of little avail to retort that he wrote in a picaresque tradition, or that one, two, three, or all of his prose works are somewhat picaresque. Future readers will naturally dismiss these questions as pedantic, and demand merely to know why they should read Smollett and what kind of sense can be made out of his fictional works. But serious theorists and Smollettian defenders who care about passing on his works from century to century will turn for help to such a discriminating work as Paul Gabriel Boucé's *Les Romans de Smollett*[41] extensive *explication de texte* sensibly arguing for another kind of classification than picaresque. Such critics as Boucé, and to a lesser extent Sacks and Battestin (lesser because they are not primarily concerned with Smollett), may not possess the answers about Smollett's form and content, but the kinds of questions they explicitly ask or imply bring us closer to the literary truth and, more importantly, provide a framework in which we can begin to talk sensibly about this misunderstood writer of the eighteenth century.

While the aesthetic aspect of Smollett's achievement is independent of the problem of rigorous classification of his prose, the two are related and not as disparate as may first appear. For it may be that the anomalies of his form and material have clouded his artistic achievement and vice versa, and that clarification in one realm will bring light and enlightenment to the other.

NOTES

1. Robert D. Spector, *Tobias Smollett* (New York, 1968).

2. The eighteenth century, prone for a number of reasons to labelization, has been called an age of almost everything, but never, to my knowledge, an "Age of the Picaresque."

3. Throughout this essay I use the term "form" in this restricted sense only; nowhere is it used in the common literary sense as denoting a structure or pattern of some kind as, for example, in Tuvia Bloch's article, "Smollett's Quest for Form," *Modern Philology*, LXV (1967), pp. 103–113, in which form is merely a synonym for shape. As will soon be evident to the reader, much of my argument rests on the writings of Ronald S. Crane and Sheldon Sacks, and to the school of thought they embrace. It would take another essay, at least doubly long, to explain why my debt to them, at least in the case of Smollett, is greater than to the works of any other single group. I am also indebted to Walter Anderson and Ralph Rader for clarifying matters about the form of prose works. Throughout this essay I assume that the reader is familiar with Sheldon Sacks' book *Fiction and the Shape of Belief* (Berkeley and Los Angeles, 1967) and for this reason have not discussed its basic assumptions and method of procedure, with which I am in agreement.

4. See Paul J. Hunter's casebook on *Moll Flanders* (New York, 1970) and Ian Watt, "The Recent Critical Fortunes of Moll Flanders," *Eighteenth-Century Studies*, I (1967), pp. 109–126.

5. This has been abundantly demonstrated by Joseph Virgil Recapito's doctoral dissertation, "Towards a Definition of the Picaresque," University of California, Los Angeles, 1967. 2 volumes. Department of Spanish and Comparative Literature. See also, although their success is uneven: H. W. Streeter, *The Eighteenth Century English Novel in French Translation* (New York, 1936); A. B. Shepperson, *The Novel in Motley* (Cambridge, Mass., 1936); Robert Alter, *The Rogue's Progress* (Berkeley and Los Angeles, 1964); Stuart Miller, *The Picaresque Novel* (Cleveland, 1967).

6. The dangers of failing to define this loose term before applying it are clearly delineated by Claudio Guillén in "Toward a Definition of the Picaresque," *Proceedings of the IIIrd Congress of the International Comparative Literature Association* (The Hague, 1962), pp. 252–266.

7. Eighteenth-century critics (of which Smollett was one) were themselves mostly guilty of this but moderns commit the same error. It matters not, however, whether Smollett *thought* he wrote or did not write picaresque: imagine an ill patient who argues to his physician that as the patient he ought best to know the nature of his ailment because his body is his and not the physician's. In criticism the trained and judicious critic often sees far more than the author. See E. D. Hirsch, *Validity in Interpretation* (New Haven, 1966).

8. Some critics will argue that picaresque material need not be confined to first-person narratives and yet the most astute writers on the subject (Guillén, Levin, Alter, Miller, Parker, Castro, Flores, Gilman, Valdés, Valbuena-Prat) emphasize the singular importance of the *picaro's* first-person point of view through whose eyes the readers view the entire world. I am willing to entertain the possibility of third-person picaresque works if those critics who wish to broaden the class can justify the wisdom of framing a definition in which almost every prose work dealing with travels and low life is admitted. The great advantage of a first-person narrative requirement, in addition to its historical advantages (*Guzmán, Lazarillo, El Buscón, Gil Blas, Simplicissimus*, are all first person narratives), is that it enables the critic to discuss a fairly manageable number of works. One could, for example, organize a book entitled "The Picaresque Tradition" around such works as Smollett's *Roderick Random*, Marivaux's *La Vie de Marianne*, Mann's *Felix Krull*, Eillison's *Invisible Man*, Svevo's *Confessions of Zeno*, and Bellow's *Adventures of Augie Marsh*, while it would probably persuade few critics of its critical acumen.

9. Nothing. In fact many of the "picaresque critics" admit all works that deal with travel. For example, Sir Walter Scott, *Miscellaneous Prose Works: Biographies* (London, 1850), 1, 264, and Harold Child in A. W. Ward and A. R. Waller (eds.), *Cambridge History of English Literature, The Age of Johnson* (Cambridge, 1913), X, 47: "In its way, this [*Humphry Clinker*] is another picaresque story, insomuch as, during its progress, the characters . . . pursue their travels in England and Scotland." If travel is the determining factor, then the massive bulk of eighteenth-century travel literature is picaresque.

10. See D. J. Dooley, "Some Uses and Mutations of the Picaresque," *Dalhousie Review*, XXXVII (1957), pp. 363–377, whose distinction between original and derivative picaresque material leads him into byways of criticism, never to the heart of a writer and his work; Smollett is a fair example: "The real follower of the picaresque tradition in eighteenth-century England was Smollett, but the Spanish form came to him through a French intermediary: he imitated, and indeed translated, Le Sage's *Gil Blas*. . . . Smollett's heroes are not quite so characterless; when he describes the early career of *Roderick Random*, for example, he is remembering his own state of mind as a young Scotsman newly arrived in London and as a surgeon's mate in the Navy. The Smollett hero is not a servant, but he is still a rascally adventurer—likely to be rewarded with a bride much too good for him (Peregrine Pickle wins a young lady whom he has previously tried to seduce with the aid of drugs). The adventurous career of the hero, however, is of less importance than the exposure of various types of people which is made possible by the adventures—the London sharpers who impose on young Scotsmen, the naval officers who make the life of the British sailor worse than that of a condemned felon, and so on. In fact, Smollett's declared intention was to promote 'that generous indignation which ought to animate the reader against the sordid and vicious disposition of the world.' *Humphry Clinker*, his last novel, showed that there was another side to him besides irascibility, but even there he showed himself as a man reacting violently against the injustices he saw around him" (pp. 367–368).

11. See note 3. Lest I am misunderstood, I must repeat that by "form" I mean the rigid classification of Smollett's fictions in relation to other fictions. Recent explicators—M. A. Goldberg, Robert Giddings, Wayne Booth, Ronald Paulson, Wayne Shumaker, R. D. Spector—say little about this aspect of Smollett's prose. Again, Sacks makes the single most perceptive remark on the subject—his only comment on Smollett in *Fiction and the Shape of Belief* (Berkeley and Los Angeles, 1967), pp. 270–271: ". . . we should not need to justify our pleasure in the work [*Humphry Clinker*] by trying to find for it a new principle of coherence. If we were to consider it as a work organized as an action with so many digressions of one kind and another that its total effect was somewhat vitiated, and if we then described the relatively clear relation between the elements which do tend to vitiate a single coherent effect and Smollett's ethical (and other) intentions, it would not be difficult to explain why so many readers have greater pleasure from the work's parts than from the accomplishment of its artistic end."

12. For example, if *Humphry Clinker* is formally a satire organized by principles different from those governing the organization of novels and apologues, then *Gulliver's Travels* cannot also be a satire; and I know of no responsible critic of eighteenth-century prose who would classify the form of Swift's work as anything but a satire.

13. The title as well as the inner contents of Rufus Putney's article, "The Plan of Peregrine Pickle," *Publications of the Modern Language Association*, LX (1945), 1051–1065, is misleading because it suggests organizational coherence nowhere to be found in Smollett's work. Putney's most profound point is that Smollett's plot embodies moral lessons. So do all plots. For Putney's failure to discover organizational coherence, see especially p. 1053.

14. This does not mean, of course, that our enjoyment of the work is diminished; it only implies that Smollett organized his material in a totally different manner from that of Swift, Fielding, Johnson, and Sterne.

15. Part of the reason, I believe, is not strictly literary as I have attempted to show in a psychoanalytic analysis of his life at this time: see *Journal of the American Medical Association*, CCXVI (1971), 85–89.

16. The best essay I have read on the composition of this prose work never mentions picaresque at all and despite this lack manages to gain deep insight into its construc-

tion; see T. O. Treadwell, "The Two Worlds of *Ferdinand Count Fathom*," in G. S. Rousseau and P. G. Boucé (eds.), *Tobias Smollett: Bicentennial Essays Presented to Lewis M.. Knapp* (Oxford, 1971), pp. 131–154.

17. Tobias Smollett, *Sir Launcelot Greaves* (London, 1760–61), Ch. xiv.

18. And yet the distinction is constantly being blurred on the tenuous grounds that eighteenth-century writers themselves failed to distinguish the two. See, for example, Ronald Paulson, *Satire and the Novel in Eighteenth-Century England* (New Haven and London, 1967), p. 167. At this rate there never would be much critical progress. See n. 7 above. A. D. McKillop, a knowledgeable student of Smollett's works, is puzzled by *Launcelot Greaves*, "an oddity" as he calls it, and comments in *The Early Masters of English Fiction* (Lawrence, 1956), p. 169, that "though the book is not well organized, it has some fine sketches of humorous characters and some remarkable genre pieces, notably the inn interior, a high visualization of a type of scene much used from Fielding to Dickens." The problem is that such a critic as Paulson, for example, is not seriously interested in the classification of prose narratives but rather, as he explicitly states in the Preface of his *Satire and the Novel*, in the ways that satiric elements gradually crept into and became a significant aspect of eighteenth-century novels. While this is certainly a worthwhile enterprise it contributes little to illuminating the problem of classification of Smollett's prose narratives.

19. Spector, *Tobias Smollett*, p. 130.

20. How many mutations can a literary figure have and still retain his identity within a class? While the question appears ridiculously pedantic and overly rigid, it is nevertheless important when classifying prose forms and their materials.

21. Spector, *Tobias Smollett*, Preface, n. p.

22. Philip Mahone Griffith, review of Robert D. Spector, *Tobias Smollett, Studies in Burke and His Time*, XII (1970), 1736–1737.

23. Rousseau and Boucé, *Tobias Smollett*, p. 115.

24. Ibid., p. 112.

23. The same is true of scientific hypothesization in which models are valued less for their absolute truth and mathematical validity than for their ability to illuminate unexplored territory. See Karl Popper, *The Logic of Scientific Discovery* (London, 1959).

26. Scott, *Miscellaneous Prose Works: Biographies*, pp. 252–286.

27. George Saintsbury, *A Short History of English Literature* (New York, 1910) [originally published 1898], p. 605. See also the same idea in Saintsbury's *The English Novel* (New York, 1919) [originally published 1913], p. 116.

28. E. A. Baker, *The History of the English Novel: Intellectual Realism from Richardson to Sterne* (2nd ed.; London, 1937), IV, 216.

29. See, for example, how little it enabled Harold Child, *Cambridge History of English Literature*, X, p. 40, to say about Smollett's fiction.

30. George M. Kahrl, *Tobias Smollett Traveler-Novelist* (Chicago, 1945), p. 57, n. 16. [*Critical Review*, XV (1763), 13–21.]

31. Naturally the point is unnecessary if the critic is uninterested in classification of narratives, as, for example, J. M. S. Tompkins, *The Popular Novel in England 1770–1800* (London, 1932).

32. Such critics as E. D. Hirsch in *Validity in Interpretation* (New Haven, 1966) and the contributors to a symposium on periodization that appeared in *New Literary History*, II (1969), reveal the dangers of such loose methodology.

33. Alexander A. Parker, *Literature and the Delinquent: The Picaresque Novel in Spain and Europe 1599–1753* (Edinburgh, 1967), p. 127. My italics.

34. Stuart Miller, *The Picaresque Novel* (Cleveland, 1967), p. 54.

35. I have tried to explain some of the differences in G. S. Rousseau, "Smollett and Sterne: A Revaluation, "*Archiv für das Studium der Neuren Sprachen und Literaturen*, CCVII (1971), 1–12.

36. Tobias Smollett, *Ferdinand Count Fathom* (Oxford, 1925), 1, Chapter i, pp. 10, 12.

37. Louis Martz, *The Later Career of Tobias Smollett* (New Haven, 1942).

38. Especially exploration of the variety given to the plot of *Tom Jones* by R. S. Crane. Before me is a list of all Smollett doctoral dissertations in America of the last twenty years, not one of which is devoted to a serious study of Smollett's plots.

39. Ian Watt, *The Rise of the Novel* (Berkeley and Los Angeles, 1956) says very little

about Smollett and clearly views his fictions as irrelevant to the concerns of formal realism.

40. Martin Battestin, *"Tom Jones:* The Argument of Design," in H. K. Miller, E. Rothstein, and G. S. Rousseau (eds.), *The Augustan Milieu* (Oxford, 1970), p. 318.

41. Paul Gabriel Boucé, *Les Romans de Smollett* (Paris, 1971).

Note: The above essay elicited the below reply from Professor P. G. Boucé of the Sorbonne in Paris. It appeared in *Studies in Burke and his Time*, XIV (Fall 1972), pp. 73–80 and appears by kind permission of the editors.

Smollett's Pseudo-picaresque: A Response to Rousseau's Smollett and the Picaresque

Over the last five years or so, there has been a marked upsurge of interest in the picaresque, one of the most difficult and elusive genres—if it is a genre at all—to define historically and critically. The term "picaresque" was—and still is—in some danger of becoming a loose and flabby critical monster. Into its ever-gaping and ravenous jaws, critics—hard-pressed for time and with little concern for the rigorous niceties of taxonomical classification—would cram works by such widely different authors as Alemán, Quevedo, Swift, Le Sage, Smollett, Surtees, Dickens, Céline, Saul Bellow, and Ralph Ellison, to give but a sample of a nauseating and most uncritical hodgepodge. It must be acknowledged, to put in a few words of excuse for such muddled practices, that most scholars or critics of English literature are unfortunately little familiar with the so-called "picaresque" novels of sixteenth-century Spain, and that the Hispanists themselves seem by no means to agree about a firm definition of the picaresque. But there are welcome and unmistakable signs that this critical use and abuse of the term—and concept—of "picaresque" may be coming to an end, although the struggle towards a clearer and more critically helpful definition is by no means over. Such critics as Ronald Paulson in *The Fictions of Satire* (1967) still speak of "Swiftean picaresque"—at best a most unilluminating and confusing label; and in the realm of Smollettian studies more specifically under consideration here, Robert Giddings in *The Tradition of Smollett* (1967) and Robert D. Spector in his *Tobias Smollett* (1968) still make cogent, if notoriously mistaken, claims for the classification of Smollett as a "picaresque" novelist.

Apart from the books and articles quoted or referred to in G. S. Rousseau's "Smollett and the Picaresque: Some Questions about a Label,"[1] such studies as W. M. Frohock's "The Failing Centre: Recent Fiction and the Picaresque Tradition,"[2] and the publication of Helmut Heidenreich's *Pikarische Welt* and of Bruno Schleussner's

Der neopikareske Roman: Pikareske Elemente in der Struktur moderner englischer Romane 1950–1960[3] should help to clear the atmosphere of the murky vagueness that has for too long obscured the analysis of picaresque novels. Rousseau's article thus crystallizes a current concern both of literary critics at large and of specialists of the English novel as well. His attempt to clarify the critical issues at stake is a most courageous and rewarding one. Clearly written and forcefully argued, his article displays a sound grasp of the picaresque tradition and of the critical studies devoted to it. Influenced by the highly precise approach of such formalist critics as Walter Anderson, Ralph Rader, and Sheldon Sacks, Rousseau brings to bear a scalpel-sharp conceptual tool on the tangled mass of Smollettian criticism. Although his attempt is the most fruitful one I have encountered so far, it is but fair to acknowledge that other Smollettians besides him have also concerned themselves with the much vexed question of Smollett's picaresque. Apart from Philip Stevick's provocative "Smollett's Picaresque Games,"[4] Alice Green Fredman's "The Picaresque in Decline: Smollett's First Novel"[5] and Angus Ross's "The Show of Violence in Smollett's Novels"[6] both display the same healthy concern for a more refined analysis of the picaresque elements at play in Smollett's novels; the existence of such sundry *elements*, in varying proportion, does not imply that he should automatically be labelled as a "picaresque" writer.

Although I agree wholeheartedly with the general thrust of Rousseau's article, I should like to offer a few brief remarks and suggestions which may prove helpful to those who wish to take further the analysis of the picaresque in general and its particular critical relevance to the study of Smollett's novels. Rousseau sets out to give a working definition of picaresque content

> as applicable to those works which, regardless of their form— and this last clause is all important—contain a first person narrator, *a picaro*, whose social fluidity is marked, whose perspective towards himself and the external world is demonstrably oblique, and who haphazardly wanders through a variegated natural or mental landscape only to discover that his life is a game from which he ought to and finally does withdraw.[7]

With commendable critical foresight, however, Rousseau states that this "definition will not satisfy everyone."[8] From my own reading of the Spanish picaresque novels, of *Gil Blas*, and of Marcel Bataillon's seminal studies of the genre,[9] I could not help noticing the importance of the picaro's humble, even—in modern parlance—proletarian origins. Both for Lazarillo and for his French descendent, Scipio, Gil Blas' shifty valet, there exists a problem of misgeneration and/or of miscegenation. Scipio, for instance, is the son of an honest soldier of the Holy Brotherhood and of a handsome young gipsy wench who tells fortunes, called Coscolina. Neither Roderick nor Peregrine stems from such lowly stock, but Ferdinand Count Fathom is a sort of living Gordian knot of matrimonial uncertainties, the offspring of a murderous and amorous camp follower and of a soldier—several sons of Mars secretly contending at the same time for the paternity of young Fathom. It is interesting also to note that poor Humphry Clinker's existence is also the long-forgotten result of a dallying misalliance between young Matthew Bramble and an unfortunate maid at a roadside inn. This does not mean, of course, that such origins, or the bar sinister, are enough to brand a character as a picaro—far from it—especially in the case of Humphry Clinker, who, in spite of the picaresque visceral struggle he has to fight to keep alive, is the moral and religious antipode of the picaro as such.

Another point which Rousseau fails to stress in his working definition of the picaresque is the picaro's cheerful but total amorality. Lazarillo has no time for subtle distinctions between good and evil, *meum* and *tuum*, because first and foremost he has to keep alive. Hunger, which "commonly maketh men have ready wittes,"[10] as is well known, has no ears attuned to the finer points of morality, and hungry picaro will eat dirty puddings of more than dubious provenance. In fact, the genuine picaro has little or no choice between right and wrong, for if he wishes to survive he has to obey the clamorous visceral urges of an empty belly. Such is very rarely the case of Roderick, Peregrine, or even of Ferdinand Count Fathom, although these characters may, in the course of their ups and downs, briefly come close to starvation.

The final point I would like to query in Rousseau's definition of the picaresque is the *withdrawal* from life as a *game*. The withdrawal, at least in the case of Lazarillo, is far from obvious, or it is more of a much sought after social elevation and integration, even at the price of implicit, but smugly accepted dishonour. Such is Lazarillo's happy (?) triangular matrimonial arrangement by the end of the book: he is a knowing and self-complacent cuckold who has clambered to the top of his shaky, pitiful social ladder and there rests contentedly to the end of his days. Whether life is a "game" to a genuine picaro, I am much inclined to doubt, but if so, it is a cruel game, with more blows, knocks, and buffets to be gained than from the exhilarating thrills of a purely gratuitous sporting activity. Among Smollett's eponymous heroes, only Peregrine would tend to consider life as an endless game of satirical pranks or practical jokes, but even he, the well-endowed offspring of a bourgeois family, has at last some rough common sense knocked into his fun-loving carcase.

Rousseau's emphatic statement that "Only *Roderick Random* among Smollett's five prose fictions meets *some* of the requirements of the definition"[11] appears to me as rather too categorical, as well as his critical corollary that "*Ferdinand Count Fathom* (1753), Smollett's third fiction, is also a third-person narrative containing even fewer picaresque elements than either of its predecessors."[12] In fact, as I have tried to show in my own study of Smollett's fiction,[13] I think that *Ferdinand Count Fathom*, although a failure—because of the impossible coexistence of picaresque elements side by side with the avowed didactic aim of a moralizing sentimental romance[14]—comes closest to the literary presentation of a picaro in the person of Fathom himself. Roderick can hardly be assimilated, even remotely, with a picaro. His origins—of which, as a fiery-tempered Scotsman, he is inordinately proud—are far too respectable, and although more than once—especially when involved in matrimonial cynegetics—he does not hesitate to launch himself headlong into shady dealings, he is no true picaro at heart. At best—or worst—Roderick is but a temporary rogue, *forced* to deport himself so by the sheer pressures of circumstances over which he has no control and by his own foolish indiscretions in sentimental or financial matters.

Perhaps Rousseau puts too much stress on the first-person narrative as a basic requirement of the picaresque genre. Although historically this is largely true, to deny the possibility of any third-person picaresque, even for sound taxonomical reasons, appears to me as somewhat of a crippling *petitio principii*. Couldn't the third-person picaresque exist as a well-attested avatar or mutation of the first person autobiographical picaresque confession? Surely, no genre in its lifelike protean fluidity can be lopped off and maimed to conform to the procrustean requirements of an arbitrary taxonomy. Although I fully realize the dangers of relaxing somewhat the requirements of Rousseau's working definition of the picaresque, it seems to me by no means impossible to define a form of third-person picaresque as a sub-category of first-person picaresque. Much of the confusion about the picaresque—and hence Rousseau's legitimate desire for a clear, sharply delineated, and limited concept of the picaresque— stems from the usual lack of distinction between the fictional use of the *episode* and of the *road* as the axiomatic vector of many narratives of adventure. The interaction of these two elements, as for instance in *Joseph Andrews*, is so fused and subtle as to become the fictional core of a type of novel which might be called "peripatetic" in contradistinction to the "picaresque," the latter genre displaying the life, adventures, experiences, and occasional thoughts thereon of low-born, usually hungry, resourceful, and amoral characters in search of decent social integration.

But to return to *Ferdinand Count Fathom* and the picaresque, I certainly wish to make no claim for the classification of the novel as "picaresque," but Fathom, the hero, or rather anti-hero, does possess the highest number of picaresque traits among Smollett's characters. As has already been suggested, Ferdinand's obscure birth is branded, like Lazarillo's or Le Sage's Scipio's, with genealogical infamy. Smollett dwells at length on the alcoholic, amorous, and thieving heredity of Fathom, a notion he sums up with the help of the proverb "What's bred in the Bone will never come out of the Flesh," which he uses as the appropriate epigraph of Chapter forty-three in his novel. Could heredity be considered as a sort of picaresque determinism ruling the deportment of Scipio—who was naturally inclined to larceny—and of Fathom? During his formative years, spent in the house of the generous but easily beguiled Count Melvil, Ferdinand displays the sagacious psychological, moral, and intellectual suppleness of a picaro in service. "Sagacity" and "pliant" are words that crop up time and time again in the early chapters of the novel to qualify Fathom. As Ferdinand is more or less consciously training himself from the start to be an upper-class picaro, Smollett endows him with special musical and artistic gifts seldom to be found among the Spanish picaros. Finally, Fathom's Hobbesian cynicism is best summed up by his staunch creed: "Homo homini lupus," a harsh lesson soon knocked—and painfully so—into the head of the young Lazarillo.

But it is only fair to stress that if such are the most noteworthy picaresque traits of Fathom, they fail to turn Fathom into a genuine picaro. First and foremost, he lacks Lazarillo's or Scipio's cheerful and light-hearted optimism. *Ferdinand Count Fathom* is Smollett's least comic novel, and its general atmosphere is one of drab, grim misery, briefly dispelled by short-lived flashes of coruscating, glittering, sentimental pinchbeck. As early as the preface of *Roderick Random* (1748), Smollett showed that he felt little or no empathy for Le Sage's laughing—and laughable—Gil Blas. Smollett's overtly moral outlook prevents him from grasping the subtle lesson contained in Gil Blas' warning to his reader—the translation is Smollett's own—"if thou perusest my adventures, without perceiving the moral instructions they contain, thou wilt reap no harvest from thy labour; but if thou readest with attention, thou wilt find in them, according to the precept of Horace, profit mingled with pleasure."[15] Whereas Le Sage in *Gil Blas* seeks to laugh people out of their besetting follies, Smollett in *Ferdinand Count Fathom*—both in the self-dedication and in the novel itself—displays a grim puritanical urge to write "in terrorem." Nothing could be more opposed and foreign to Le Sage's lighter, more human and humane implicit morality. Finally, Fathom is a failed picaro because Smollett set out to use him as an exemplary amoral monster. *Ferdinand Count Fathom* is an unfortunate exercise in moral teratogenesis, where the "good" characters, Monimia and young Melvil, never come to life long and powerfully enough to counterbalance effectively the harrowing tale of Fathom's uninterrupted and dreary villainy. Fathom's sudden and unconvincing sickbed repentance is a most unpicaresque trait, a fault Le Sage was clever enough to avoid in Gil Blas, where his two most notorious picaros—Don Raphael and Lamela—are finally burnt at the stake. Obviously Smollett himself must have felt embarrassed by Fathom's all too sudden conversion, as eighteen years later in *Humphry Clinker* (1771) the penitent Fathom turns up under the guise of a dedicated and benevolent country apothecary renowned for his charitable devotion to his patients and the near-saintly austerity of his life. In his last novel, Smollett must have wanted to comfort himself, perversely, with the thought that it is possible to convert a picaro into a saint. But unfortunately, neither Fathom's picaresque exploits, nor his saintly activities come off very well; in the end, Fathom is one of Smollett's most fascinating literary failures, a pseudo-picaro.

The picaresque battle—or rather anti-picaresque battle—is far from over as far as Smollettian studies are concerned. In spite of such sensible and valuable efforts as Rousseau's important article, critics still continue to fling about carelessly the "picaresque" epithet with little regard for the requirements of a useful critical taxonomy. Thus John M. Warner in a recent article on "Smollett's Development as a Novelist" does not hesitate to write that "Smollett, *like the other English picaresque writers of his time*, was attracted to satire for several reasons."[16] This vague and unsubstantiated statement will in no way help the readers of Smollett's fiction to gain a firmer grasp of the picaresque elements actually at play in his novels but hardly potent or important enough to earn their author the dubious label of "picaresque." Much work then remains to be done, in connection with specialists of Spanish, French, and German literature, but I do hope that whatever the solutions put forward, the critics and scholars devoting their theoretical and historical skills to the vexed problem of Smollettian pseudo-picaresque will not turn the issue, as Rabelais has put it ironically, into a "Questio subtilissima, utrum chimera in vacuo bombinans possit comedere secundas intentiones."

NOTES

1. G. S. Rousseau, "Smollett and the Picaresque: Some Questions About a Label," *Studies in Burke and His Time*, XII (1971), 1886–1904.
2. W. M. Frohock, "The Failing Center: Recent Fiction and the Picaresque Tradition," *Novel*, III (1969), 62–69.

3. Helmut Heidenreich, *Pikarische Welt* (Darmstadt, 1969); Bruno Schleussner, *Der neopikareske Roman: Pikareske Elemente in der Struktur moderner englischer Romane 1950–1960* (Bonn, 1969). Both of these works have been perceptively reviewed by Ulrich Wicks in *Novel*, V (1971), 71–74.

4. Philip Stevick, "Smollett's Picaresque Games;" in G. S. Rousseau and P. G. Boucé (eds.), *Tobias Smollett* (New York, 1971), pp. 111–130.

5. Alice Green Fredman, "The Picaresque in Decline: Smollett's First Novel," in John H. Middendorf (ed.), *English Writers of the Eighteenth Century* (New York and London, 1971), pp. 189–207.

6. Angus Ross, "The Show of Violence in Smollett's Novels," *Yearbook of English Studies*, II (1972), 118–129.

7. Rousseau, "Smollett and the Picaresque," *Studies in Burke and His Time*, XII, 1889.

8. Ibid.

9. See, for instance, Marcel Bataillon, *Le Roman Picaresque* (Paris, 1931), p. 155; see also Bataillon's introduction to A. Morel-Fatio's translation of *Lazarillo de Tormes* (Paris, 1958), pp. 7–82, as well as his series of lectures on "L'honneur et la matière picaresque" summed up in the *Annuaire du Collège de France*, (1963), 485–491.

10. J. E. V. Crofts (ed.), *The Pleasant Historie of Lazarillo de Tormes*, trans. David Rouland of Anglesey [1586], Percy Reprints (Oxford, 1924), p. 31.

11. Rousseau, "Smollett and the Picaresque," *Studies in Burke and His Time*, XII, 1890.

12. Ibid., 1894.

13. Paul-Gabriel Boucé, *Les Romans de Smollett* (Paris, 1971); on *Ferdinand Count Fathom* and the picaresque, see pp. 138–144 and the chapter devoted to *Ferdinand Count Fathom* and *Launcelot Greaves*, pp. 198–242.

14. For a sound analysis of *Ferdinand Count Fathom* and its failure as a novel, see T. O. Treadwell, "The Two Worlds of Ferdinand Count Fathom," in Rousseau and Boucé, *Tobias Smollett*, pp. 131–153.

15. Alain René Le Sage, *Gil Blas*, trans. Tobias Smollett (London, 1778), I, x.

16. John M. Warner, "Smollett's Development as a Novelist," *Novel*, IV (1972), 148–161; italics added.

VII
Beef and Bouillon:
Smollett's Achievement as a Thinker

For to what purpose is all the toil and bustle of this world? What is the end of avarice and ambition, of pursuit of wealth, of power, and pre-eminence? The wages of the meanest labourer can supply them. We see that they can afford him food and clothing, the comfort of a house and of a family. If we examine his oeconomy with rigour, we should find that he spends a great part of them upon conveniences, which may be regarded as superfluities, and that, upon occasions, he can give something even to vanity and distinction. What then is the cause of our aversion to his situation, and why should those who have been educated in the higher ranks of life, regard it as worse than death, to be reduced to live, even without labour, upon the simple fare with him, to dwell under the same lowly roof, and to be clothed in the same humble attire? Do they imagine that their stomach is better or they sleep sounder in a palace than in a cottage?
> (Adam Smith, *Theory of Moral Sentiments*, London, 1759, p. 73)

The novels of Smollett show money being made and lost in rational and technical ways.
> (George Steiner, *The Death of Tragedy*, New York, 1961, p. 264)

I have seen nothing great in life except cruelty and stupidity.
> (Paul Leautaud, *Lost Illusions*, London, 1974, frontispiece)

1. Homage to Pope

Smollett's greatest debt to a literary figure is not to Chaucer, Shakespeare, Cervantes, or to "brother Fielding," his contemporary, but to a poet who died just as Smollett was making his way toward London, the centre of the world's literary activity. In Alexander Pope Smollett found the model and proper image of a satirist he could unflinchingly imitate. Temperamentally, psychologically, and even intellectually, the two men were dissimilar. Although the product of a full generation preceding Smollett's own, Pope nevertheless represented for Smollett all things good: courage, intelligence, talent, knowledge, and—most of all—truth.

After his death in 1744 Pope became more or less a national legend, a monument of winged Virtue; this exaltation enhanced Smollett's admiration for the satirist. The evidence is so weighty that there can be little or no question about the degree of Smollett's worship, before and after 1744. He lost few opportunities—even in the notes to his early satires, *Advice and Reproof* (1746–1747)—to praise the great poet.[1] And almost thirty years later, obviously cognizant that he had none of Pope's sheer talent for verse, he continued to extol Pope. "The Ode to Solitude," Smollett wrote in *Humphry Clinker* (1771), "is the first fruit now extant of Pope's genius,"[2] and a decade before that, in *Sir Launcelot Greaves* (1760–1761), he affirmed, speaking through the voice of Dick Distich, that "of all those whom Pope lashed in his *Dunciad*, there is not one who did not richly deserve the imputation of dullness; and everyone of them had provoked the satire by a personal attack. In this respect the English poet was much more honest than Boileau."[3] In Pope, the poet *and* the man, Smollett found the apex of integrity and an unparalleled ethical courage. Swift, too, had been brave, and Smollett had learned a great deal from his prose. But for Smollett, Pope was the braver; the more reliable through unquestioned "honesty."

Actually, it was *The Dunciad*, more than any other work, that permitted Smollett to glow with admiration for Pope's courage, and virtually to revel in the poet's discovery of a vehicle (the extensive, almost "epic," lampoon) by which to convey Herculean bravery. While there is evidence in the concluding letters of *Humphry Clinker* (the scenes at the Baynard and Dennison properties) that Smollett also thought highly of the rendition of the "Augustan Myth" found in Pope's *Imitations of Horace*, this is not the "Pope" who profoundly moves Smollett. In the *Dunciad* of 1728 and the *New Dunciad* of 1742, Smollett located a kindred voice; there he discovered relief of his own skeptic propensities and psychological energies. These works encouraged him during his early career to grasp at qualities that were even vaguely "Popean"—to lose no chance, for example, to review Warton's *Essay on the Genius of Mr. Pope*, not out of interest in it but concern for Pope.[4]

Why open with such a preamble, and dwell on this fact of literary history? It would be unnecessary if Smollett's *literary* origins had not recently become obscured, and if the prolonged controversy

concerning his debt to picaresque fiction had not muddied the waters
even further.[5] Whatever his later allegiances to prose romance in all
its under- and overgrowth in three centuries, to picaresque and
quixotic fiction, Smollett's largest debt was to an English poetic
satirist whom he read again and again. Especially in *Roderick
Random*, Smollett's first novel, he conceived himself a satirist and his
narrative vehicle, prose satire. He even worried that readers would
interpret his attack as specific and pointed—and they did! Thus the
much-discussed "Apologue" appended to the fourth edition of
Roderick Random answering these critics with an allegory of animals
and an unequivocal conclusion extricating the author:

> Christian reader, I beseech thee, in the bowels of the Lord,
> remember this example while thou art employed in the perusal of
> the following sheets; and seek not to appropriate to thyself that
> which equally belongs to five hundred different people. If thou
> shouldst meet with a character that reflects thee in some ungracious
> particular, keep thy own counsel; consider that one feature makes
> not a face, and that, though thou art, perhaps, distinguished by a
> bottle-nose, twenty of thy neighbors may be in the same predica-
> ment."[6]

There is hardly anything startling nowadays in the notion that
the young Smollett thought of himself pre-eminently as a satirist. It
is an idea discussed in dozens of recent essays and books, perhaps
most forcefully by Ronald Paulson in *Satire and the Novel in Eighteenth-Century England*.[7] But from Paulson one gains the impression,
perhaps unintended, that Smollett *remained* a satirist—that there was
only insignificant transformation of his satiric vehicle in *Humphry
Clinker*, his last novel. Moreover, there is hardly a hint about his
literary origins and subsequent innovation: why Smollett would have
modelled his career after Pope, for example, and not Swift, Dryden,
or any number of other satirists; or any inference, in conjunction
with this "imitation" of Pope, of Smollett's conviction in the 1740s
that he was cut out to be a poet rather than a novelist. It was later, at
the end of the decade, that he veered.

Some of the clues are not difficult to find, and, as might be sur-
mised, they lie in *The New Dunciad*. Here Pope, Smollett thought,
brought off what no one else would dare: personal, direct and
abusive satire, embedded in a visionary vehicle revealing the apocalypse of human culture. Smollett himself, from his earliest imaginative
writings—*The Regicide*, *Advice* and *Reproof*, *Roderick Random*,
various odes and English lyrics—had been keenly interested in the
endings of works. He heard the thunder in the last two hundred lines
of Pope's poem. Pope's bravery in combining excoriation and
apocalypse (it takes courage to predict the end of the world when one

has already attacked one's critics) was as noteworthy as the final product itself. That Smollett should have thought each and every one of the personal attacks as "richly deserved"—as he says in *Launcelot Greaves* of the way he "read" his own culture—is abundant testimony.

But above all Smollett was awed by Pope's courage: by his willingness to stand alone; to take on a whole epoch. Other capable poets had written lampoons; Smollett knew this very well. But no one else in England had been willing to stand his ground so firmly: not the Scriblerians, not Swift who attacked "segments" only, and certainly not "cater-cousin Johnson" who was, in the admirable phrase of W. J. Bate, a "satirist manqué."[8] If more of Smollett's letters had survived—only two or three are extant from these years (1740–1748)—Smollett himself would no doubt have commented on some of these matters. *Roderick Random*, a "satyr on Mankind," almost serves as a substitute. Swift had been a great writer, but he seemed in Smollett's estimate to have lived in another age and another social world. He dealt with problems that had been replaced or with problems no longer, by virtue of social and political change, urgent—problems that now, the 1740s, were of little consequence. The fact that there are not more than one or two references to Swift in the corpus of Smollett's writings (except, of course, the catalogue of writers in the *History of England* and *Present State of All Nations*) counts, in actuality, for little. Smollett had learned much about the art of prose from Swift; but the author of *The Dunciad* was his idol and greatest teacher. "We are now happily housed with that gentleman, who has really attained to that pitch of rural felicity at which I have been aspiring these twenty years in vain."[9] The sentence could have described Pope.

II. Formal and Fictive Experimentalist

If Smollett had continued to write prose "satyres on Mankind" or if his parodic tendencies were greater, his debt to Pope would be the subject of more formal inquiry and far more worthy of close scrutiny than it has thus far been. He did not continue—and this also is common knowledge. Readers of his novels from the early *Roderick Random* (1748) and *Peregrine Pickle* (1751) to *Humphry Clinker* (1771) know very well that none of his works after *Roderick Random* can be called "essentially satiric," not if by this term one designates the primary thrust of a work. And this matter has nothing to do with definitions of satire, or with subtle distinctions between harsh ("Juvenalian") and soft ("Horatian") satiric modes (Smollett himself continued to insist that in his early novels he had no specific targets in mind but was addressing himself to human conditions at large). As early as his second novel, *Peregrine Pickle* (1751), other elements began to enter the core of the narrative in an essential way: a notion of plot so loose it could even accommodate the allegedly authentic "Memoirs of a Lady of Quality"; satire even less specific and pointed than in *Roderick Random;* the inclusion of grotesque landscapes and grotesque characters; a new kind of "comic painting" in a new and original way (as in the blending of the world of the Garrison with that of Perry's travels abroad); comic "humour" types that are much less Jonsonian in origin; slower pace and tempo; and, of course, the use of such current and fashionable *topoi* as the Grand Tour, moral vice, corruption, the dissipation of the wealthy, and, in general, the appalling manners and morals of the times. And the discerning reader begins to suspect all his experimentation in the name of realism—the author's imagined world of ugliness.

From this chronological moment onward, Smollett continued to innovate. The extent of his innovation is so great, in fact, that no two successive novels—whether *Peregrine Pickle* and *Count Fathom*, or *Count Fathom* and *Launcelot Greaves*—read alike. This further observation has been the source of some of Smollett's critical woes in recent times. The reading imagination is programmed to categorize and label, and readers of novels often wish to capsule their impressions in a unified description: they may allow exceptions here and variations there; but what to do with an author who has no consistent voice or plot, or types of characters, or genre at all? It is usually too much trouble to insist that one refer to "the Smollett in *Roderick Random*" or "the Smollett in *Humphry Clinker.*" Readers of an anonymous *Peregrine Pickle* and *Count Fathom*—whether in 1753 or today—would never deduce a common author. How could they? Whatever similarities exist between Smollett's second work, *Peregrine Pickle*, and his last, *Humphry Clinker* (an epistolary narrative with less satire in it than almost any other ingredient), are almost accidental and certainly do not exist in the realm of form.

Such an oeuvre has impelled certain critics—and every good author must have "critics" whether he wills it or not—toward exaggeration. Those (the majority) insistent on neat categorization labeling have to strain plots and characters and contort details to make the novels fit a general theory of *all* the novels.[10] Thus Smollett is depicted as transforming the picaresque in one way or another in each of the novels. More cautious critics, those willing to tackle one novel at a time, have tended to produce "readings" of individual works.[11]

The results of both approaches have not enhanced appreciation of Smollett's talents, nor has either approach produced any satisfactory estimate of his contribution to the development of English fiction. The former class, those speaking and writing about Smollett as if *Roderick Random* and *Humphry Clinker* were similar prose artifacts, generally hang the weight of their generalizations on the first and last novels, and one often wonders if they ever troubled to read the middle works. Generally they write the least critically sophisticated books and are chided by reviewers for lack of discrimination. On the other hand, the latter group—generally more erudite and critically sophisticated—has been unable to do anything to fix Smollett's position within the development of English fiction from Defoe and Richardson to the present. This group often makes a brilliant *aperçu* about a particular novel, but one not striking enough or published in such a way as to make a difference in Smollett's ultimate achievement as a novelist.

Since my sympathies are exclusively with the second group (I cannot imagine that the first group will ever do anything except destroy Smollett's reputation forever), I believe that questions about his ultimate achievement are profoundly related to his formal experimentation. But something of a logical dilemma presents itself here. How to comment on this experimentation without making value judgements of the type: "Smollett in this mode" is better than "Smollett in that mode"—ostensibly in the name of singling out his achievement. Incidentally, this is exactly the trap into which John Butt sauntered, although he thought he was merely describing what Smollett had written.[12] For example, *Roderick Random* is in every formal sense a better book than *Count Fathom:* its characters more credible, its plot more interesting, its realism more engaging (and specific), its morality clearer; its readers praised it more in its time and it continues to be read today. How is one to speak about "Smollett's achievement" when confronted with such blatant disparities of accomplishment? On the other hand, to assume the role of the objective historian who merely reports is intolerable in Smollett's case, precisely because he has become such a minor and neglected novelist today.

Other authors offer useful comparison here. The quality of Fielding's fiction, for example, is more uniform. Even if readers of *Amelia* and *Jonathan Wild* have not been as enthusiastic as readers of *Joseph Andrews* and *Tom Jones*—both unquestioned masterpieces— Fielding's works, considered as a whole, reveal sufficient uniformity of quality, and similarity of imagined world and authorial voice (even *Tom Jones* and *Jonathan Wild*) to permit one to speak of a composite Fielding.[13] The same is even true of Sterne and Jane Austen, novelists whose indelible mark is evident in every novel. As opposed to the case of Defoe, Smollett did not contribute enough metaliterary writing to his culture to warrant talk about an achievement without consideration of his novels. Thus, if one removed *Moll Flanders* and *Robinson Crusoe* from Defoe's oeuvres, there is still enough, in quantity and quality, to consider Defoe a prodigy of literature—a kind of unparalleled professional writer without consideration to historical era. Smollett was no such thing. He stands on his six novels, or on very little else. The rest, as a matter of fact, is ephemeral hackwork.

These six novels have engaged some important formalist critics; but precisely because Smollett's form of the novel is so defective, they have been toiling, as it were, with a mutant species. And this is why I have begun with an emphatic statement about Pope's symbolic importance to Smollett. The formalists who have studied Smollett's novels have concluded what their intuition could have told them all along: first that Smollett's sense of form (let alone his actual forms) is defective, and second that his forms are structurally so dissimilar that it is not possible to talk about more than one at a time. At this point, the progress of modern Smollett criticism grows tedious, even painfully vertiginous. Willy-nilly the formalists (Aristotelians, New Critics, organicists, Humeans, structuralists, linguists) find themselves in a precarious position from which to make persuasive pronouncements; the nonformalists (biographers, historians of literature, students of eighteenth-century culture in general), uninterested in their writings on questions concerning literary worth, do not understand what the fuss is all about in the first place.

And yet surely one of the appointed tasks of literary criticism is demonstration of excellence. Why read a given novel or poem? Why is *Hamlet* a universally great work while hundreds of other plays are not? The same questions are asked about Smollett's novels (especially today when his books are rarely read), and for reasons already given it has not been possible to provide satisfactory answers. For those who never saw merit, the matter is straightforward—and capable of speedy resolution. Smollett the novelist is a bore, an author on whom it is hardly worth expending any energy or effort. But for the others who sense merit and achievement—some explanation and demonstration are necessary.

Yet the formalists disagree among themselves about Smollett. In America since the 1930s, the "New Critics" and "Chicago Aristotelians" have carried on the bulk of exegesis regarding literary forms and genres in fiction. Neither group has pronounced about Smollett at great length, partly out of neglect, and partly because both schools have tried and failed. The typical formalist utterance is made *en passant* in a work about writers other than Smollett—not because the formalists have not tried but rather because it has not seemed possible as yet for anyone to write a single good and persuasive book about Smollett's fiction. A leading Chicagoan, in a lengthy work, *Fiction and the Shape of Belief*, had only this to say about Smollett:

> The flexibility of the apparently rigid terminology employed in the present work might also be seen, I think, in considering works like *Humphry Clinker*; for here again we should not need to justify our pleasure in the work by trying to find for it a new principle of coherence. If we were to consider it as a work organized as an action with so many digressions of one kind and another that its total effect was somewhat vitiated, and if we then described the relatively clear relation between the elements which do tend to vitiate a single coherent effect and Smollett's ethical (and other) intentions it would not be difficult to explain why so many readers have felt greater pleasure from the work's parts than from the accomplishment of its artistic end.[14]

Although rigid, it is a perceptive point, certainly one worth making. But it could not sustain an entire essay, let alone a book; and the rest of the author's writings do not suggest he is sufficiently interested to explore the matter further, though he is certainly capable.

The fault must lie elsewhere—in matters pertaining to an author's pangs in formal experimentation. Smollett's novels—partly neglected, partly not conducive to logical and intelligent criticism, and generally so uneven that it makes no sense to discuss them *ensemble*—have come to occupy a rather minor position in a library of criticism of the novel because they will not yield to facile generalization. Take Sacks's above *apercu:* even if he were to write an essay proving his point about the relation of parts to whole, his results would be negative in that they prove what the book is *not*, and not what it *is*. And negative results, though created in the name of scholarship, fail to impress. Academics, understandably interested in promotions, continue to churn out details about this or that aspect of Smollett's life. But it is material that proves tedious to the average, intelligent reader. Certainly it does not have an iota of bearing on the excitement (or the lack of it) in Smollett's novels. As Edmund Wilson has suggested, novels ultimately stand on their own. Novels, after enough time has elapsed—one or two centuries—tend to absorb their culture, not *vice versa*, and in the end they prove more interesting to the readers than the culture which may have had a considerable role in shaping them.[15]

Exactly this has happened to Smollett. Every critical commentary on his fiction finally reverts to questions about his culture. Because Smollett, like Pope (though a different realm, and with differing results), was willing to experiment, he forfeited much of his reputation. Had he written six versions of *Roderick Random*, with its proper dosage of realism, squalour, and descriptions of the exotic, he would be more widely read today. But destiny dealt Smollett a losing literary card.

III. The Critic Wanders

This much said—Smollett's impulse to emulate Pope and his courage to experiment formally—some personal disclosures may further assure the reader of my intentions in this essay. No breach of faith or of purpose dissuades me from this position. Though Smollett is not my favourite novelist, I enjoy him immensely; I have been reading him for over a decade and shall continue to do so. I have also an "academic investment" in his welfare in that I am assisting in the preparations of the Bicentennial Edition of his works to be published by the University of Iowa Press. As I stated elsewhere, I prefer Sterne, partly because there isn't enough leaven in Smollett's comedies.[16] I laugh when I read Sterne; I rarely laugh when reading Smollett. For each funny, not to say hilarious, moment in Smollett— such amazingly bizarre scenes as that in which Mrs. Grizzle urinates in her bed or Commodore Trunnion tacks up the road on the way to his wedding—there are dozens more in *Tristram Shandy*, usually more ribald and generally more lascivious. Although Smollett is often masterful at "comic painting" in narrative, another more potent sentiment sustains me when reading him—the rawness, cruelty, and savagery that pervade his world.

Here, again, one cannot, unfortunately, speak about the total oeuvre. There are soft elements too: rustic scenes in rural England and the Scottish highlands; moments of exquisite and delicate sensibility in such disparate places as jails and castles; even attempts at love scenes (although, as one critic has pointed out, Smollett rarely brings these off).[17] But still, rawness, crudity, ugliness and squalour outweigh any genial laughter sometimes encountered in Smollett's fiction. My reading intuition senses in the narrator of his novels (they are all written in the distant third person, with the exception of *Roderick Random*) a voice altogether different from either that of Sterne or Fielding, Richardson or Johnson—but not so different from Pope in certain of his exasperated moods:

> Stuck o'er with titles and hung round with strings,
> That thou may'st be by kings, or whores of kings.
> Boast the pure blood of an illustrious race,
> In quiet flow from Lucrece to Lucrece;
> But by your father's worth if yours you rate,
> Count me those only who were good and great.
> Go! if your ancient, but ignoble blood

> Has crept thro' scoundrels even since the flood,
> Go! and pretend your family is young:
> Nor own, your fathers have been fools so long.
> What can ennoble sots, or slaves, or cowards.
> Alas! not all the blood of all the HOWARDS.[18]

Smollett's attention, however, was not focused on powerful families like the Howards; he studied vice in low- or middle-class villains and knaves. In fact he scrutinized them in such detail in his fiction that general readers—not just critics—have been scared off.

Recently I received this appraisal from a critic who prefers to remain anonymous. He is a distinguished eighteenth-century scholar, however, whose name would immediately be recognized by readers of this volume:

> I cannot read Smollett anymore. I have heard about the making of a definitive text of his work and I can't see how it makes any difference considering the depravity of his rotted mind. After reading these novels I wander through the titles of the chapters of his books and see nothing but revenge, revenge, revenge. For no reason at all people are hurt and humiliated, even skinned; even those who help him to perpetrate fun. Jokes about hunchbacked people and lame matrons. Pissing for no reason at all (I would prefer the honest crudity of *The English Rogue*). Can you really call him a novelist of amusement? Can you honestly say there is one moment of pleasure in the whole of Smollett? Peregrine determined to punish Pallet with some new infliction in the management of which he promised himself a store of entertainment. Ultimately the poor reader is in the midst of a totally unpleasant and nasty neurotic mind who learned nothing from *Gil Blas* and, quite frankly, has not even the imagination of *Peter Wilkins* or *Joe Thompson*.[19] Any argument that Smollett's is an absurd, existential world is rubbish: there is no connection between his thoughts and cruel characters and those of Godot: and to beatify this garbage by titling it "black humour" is deception and folly. At least *Fanny Hill* is straight-forward. Latroon vomiting up his evening meal because he is so hungry, and then having the landlady scoop it up and recook it because he is so hungry—that is *credible* poverty! But there is no such design or purpose in Smollett's books: just random and perverse human indecency.

Although I do not completely agree with this shrewd estimate, my sympathies with it are great—great enough to reflect that I react to Smollett not too differently from our anonymous reader. But what disgusts him, thrills me. Squalour and grotesquerie are parts of life, and although unpleasant, must be faced. Moreover, I suspect that our sense of literary criticism varies: our anonymous critic would have written this essay differently, or not at all. I have not (like Smollett) taken the "safe route," in large part because academic criticism is of limited value in the resuscitation of a minor novelist. Even a "touchstone" would do more for Smollett than pedantic, albeit accurate, detective work. Every critical essay is of course itself an act of courage—as is this one—and courage, at least in criticism, is the quality of mind that distinguishes leaders from mere followers and enables them to take daring steps. The courageous critic must look after himself, not after his brothers or their values. And courage in this case, reviving Smollett, allows me, indeed entices me, to admit that Smollett, although a novelist I enjoy, is imperfect in almost every conceivable stylistic aspect: not least in the credibility of his characters, the probability of his plots, the (swift) pace of his narratives, and the raw and crude picture of life he serves up as "ordinary."

In speaking out so obtrusively, I believe that something like an edict ought to be proclaimed forbidding the spectre of the literary formalists ever to be raised again: no more Fielding *and* Smollett, only "Smollett the curious blender of literary forms," or "Smollett the experimenter with grotesque possibilities," or "Smollett the ethical and philosophical vagabond" (about which I shall have more to say), or "Smollett and cloacal stuff of social history." I have in the past tried to make out of Smollett's narratives coherent literary forms, and I could not. Nor could others. If the new prophets of literary studies, linguistic critics exploring stylistics and poetics, can forge out of Smollett's narratives a *coherent* (this is not to say Jamesian) literary form replete with organic plots, probable characters, and a credible world, they shall have accomplished what no other school could.[20] What then is left for criticism with regard to this author? If the critical act is neither "New Critical" or "Aristotelian," what is it?

There *are* other avenues of exploration, even excepting biographical and historical approaches. The historical approach studying Smollett's relation to theories of fiction in his own time is limited in value because it says nothing about achievement without regard to time (i.e. periodization). One can summon a commonsensical approach to the author, the type John Butt used very successfully. But one would have to admit—especially this critic—that Butt's strategy of quoting purple passages interlarded with elegantly poised statements about individual novels does not suffice as *analysis*. It certainly could not sustain more than the briefest type of appreciative essay.

Instead I offer this suggestion: that for the moment we dispense with formal questions about structure (organic plots, probabilities and possibilities, credible characters, grotesque elements, varieties of realism) and try to focus on "contents." This is not easily done, nor is the posture, even in limbo, fashionable: it is contrary to all our critical impulses. My generation, after all, has been warned against this very thing; and now, to have it summoned up intentionally . . . .

It *must* be at some point, for in this very critical process—involving exigencies of fashion, taste and relevance—Smollett's most rudimentary contents have somehow been lost. From *Roderick Random* to *Humphry Clinker*, and despite the tremendous disparity among the intervening books, one moral viewpoint shines through: the wickedness of this world and of the people who populate it. Although I am much less offended than our anonymous critic by Smollett's "jokes about hunchbacked people and lame matrons," there can be no debate about the prevalence of such moments in his books. Admittedly, every satirist assumes moral and physical deformity as a given. Pope would not have "writ" if there were no men to reform and no virtue to be invoked. But even in Pope's fiercest attacks in *The Dunciad* and Horatian poetry—again I find myself brought back to Smollett's debt to Pope—Pope had other things to dwell on: his love of pomp and ceremony and ritual coronation; his passion for landscape gardening and architecture; his temperamental optimism; his awesome reverence for Rome and the empire it symbolized; the delight the narrator of *The New Dunciad* takes in having found a vehicle for combining satire, vision, and apocalyptic prophecy. Nothing of this sort is true for Smollett. He practised medicine, but it meant little to him and he wrote almost nothing about it; nor does he maintain any objectivity that one would assume true of a "physician-narrator" or a "physician-satirist."[21] Avocations he had not; and he was absolutely "non-clubable." He was one of the more prolific hacks (the term is used intentionally) of his age but he wrote by the word to annihilate poverty, and only in his novels did he give way, as it were, to anything that can be called a "philosophy." For comic novelists, although they rarely have admitted it, content or substance is philosophy of a sort. Just as history is the stuff of comic drama, philosophy is essentially the novelist's province. Shakespeare knew this well:

Messenger. Your honor's players, hearing your amendment,
Are come to play a pleasant comedy;
For so your doctors hold it very meet,
Seeing too much sadness hath congeal'd your blood,
And melancholy is the nurse of frenzy:
Therefore they thought it good you hear a play
And frame your mind to mirth and merriment,
Which bars a thousand harms and lengthens life.
Sly. Marry, I will let them play. It

is not a comonty, a Christmas gambold,
or a tumbling-trick?
Page. No, my good lord, it is more pleasing stuff.
Sly. What! household stuff?
Page. It is a kind of history.[22]

What "kind of philosophy" can a voice that grasps at rawness and savagery to the near exclusion of every other quality utter? What eyes were they that continually envisioned figures hurt, humiliated, skinned, flayed, mutilated, and then revenged? These are the questions that must eventually occupy the serious reader of Smollett before such matters (merely of academic interest) as the form of his prose fictions (*à la* Sacks above) or the rhetoric of his sentences (*á la* Strauss).[23]

Those who argue that these questions must remain unanswered on grounds of unknowability must be challenged. There was a time—in the late 1940s and 1950s—when the text was everything; when external concerns were of no influence whatsoever. That day has passed. Even if it had not, the effect of its spokesmen was inconsequential for Smollett's texts. Before one dares to discuss texts, one has to decide if that text is worth discussing. All this happens before a word gets written, but occurs nevertheless. At the present rate of publication, there will not be another generation of readers of Smollett. Indeed, at a moment when the reading of Dickens is in question, can we seriously hope to find readers for Smollett?

Perhaps we can if we restore confidence in both the author and the "contents" of his novels. As I am attempting to demonstrate, both have suffered unjustly. The first has even been confused: afraid of speculation and often awed by hypotheses of any sort, distortionists have trodden the safe road and produced, biographically speaking, a Smollett who is neither human nor credible. They have consistently asked the wrong questions about his life, and treated him as something of a "man machine"—as if he had no psyche, no emotions, no subconscious. Or conversely, as Paul Boucé has pointed out, they have squandered their energies in a search for autobiographical traces in the novels.[24] Several years ago George D. Painter announced he would produce a biography of Proust composed "only from printed sources."[25] He did, and the volumes have served as a reliable reference guide to Proust's life—but they do not constitute a definitive biography on just the lines of reasoning I am arguing, because no interpretation of a man is offered. In Smollett's case, the ardor of investigating radical experimentation with prose forms has warded off certain critics, and fear of speculation in areas where extant documents are few has frightened away others. All in all, the situation has been rather grim.

IV. Speculations on a Biography of Smollett

Fantasy about a "whole personality" for Smollett, like the wish for an organic plot filled with coherent characters, must be dispelled. In Smollett's case there simply is not enough evidence: there are too few letters that reveal anything potential for the analyst; no diaries; and almost no impressions left by his contemporaries. Scholars who consider Lewis M. Knapp's reference guide "a biography" delude themselves. With all due respect to Knapp's unflagging industry in compiling the facts—and in 1949 they direly needed compiling—*Tobias Smollett: Doctor of Men and Manners*, unlike Irvin Ehrenpreis's several volumes on Swift, or Maynard Mack's *The Garden and the City*, or F. A. Pottle's *Young Man Boswell*—is an annotated telephone directory of persons, places, and titles containing no analytic content whatsoever. *Tobias Smollett* certainly does not afford a credible picture of a man, and it fails to raise psychological and social questions, let alone answer them. At best, it is a "portrait" providing outlines.

If we ought to inquire about the kind of man who would imagine a world as raw and crude as Smollett's, we should also ask about Smollett's environment—the landscapes and persons he knew, as well as the historical events and social institutions to which he was exposed. Here printed sources touching *directly* on the matter are of dubious worth. A treatise written, for instance, on just the subject one is looking for—perhaps an imagined work published in 1750 and entitled *Scottish Exiles in London in the 1740s*—would be welcome but has limited applicability. In any case, such books do not exist. The kinds of printed documents that would provide some of the clues to profound questions about Smollett's life and imagination must be reconstructed with or without the proper printed sources.

Yet in the 1940s Knapp demurred. This is all he would say, for example, about the very crucial matter of Smollett's personal religion and philosophy:

> What we know of Smollett does little to clarify his private attitude toward religion or his philosophical outlook. That he attacked Catholicism, inveighed against Protestant fanatics and hypocrites, made his Bramble rather sympathetic toward Methodists, and as a citizen of Chelsea was associated with the Church of England—these facts do not supply a satisfactory answer. Neither do they validate the view (sometimes asserted) that he entirely lacked any feeling for religion. He has, of course, been called a Pagan. He has been termed a Stoic. He has been branded a misanthropist. Such labels are not very illuminating. How his private views were influenced by Voltaire or Hume has not been discovered.[26]

It was impeccably noble of Knapp to adopt this brand of scholarly—

almost Humean—skepticism and comfort. It balances just the right amount of fact and doubt, and its insistence on the difference between fact and fiction, between hard-proved point and flaccid speculation must command respect. But Knapp wrote in accordance with notions about biography popular in the 1920s and 1930s. He could not have known in 1949 that the very basis of what constitutes "fact" could come under fire, or that even the most puritanical historians of the "kings and queens" variety would not accept this as biography in 1976. Since Knapp was educated, pathetic, intentional, affective— and many other types of—"fallacies" have influenced thinking and writing about history and literature. The desiderata expressed in Knapp's paragraph would not have satisfied many "literary critics" even if Smollett had written a manifesto of his religion (as did Milton or, in another confessional mode altogether, Beethoven); we must still inquire into his motives for writing it, the possibilities of irony and self-deception, his mood at the time, his economic circumstances, marital relations, health, and dozens of other possibly influential factors.

"Facts" do play a role in providing a sense of the naked shape of a life. In Smollett's case, that outline (although nothing more) is clear. He was born on a farm in Dumbartonshire of rather distinguished professional people: as Knapp notes, "for generations before the birth of the novelist the Smolletts representing the *noblesse de robe* of Scotland had kept alive an admirable tradition of public service in the law and military."[27] But some demon inside Smollett caused him to veer from these respectable professions; to turn from medicine (which he had probably undertaken in a temper of token respect for his family) to a writing career. At seventeen he immigrated to London, that city to which all Britons in search of a literary career eventually travelled; and he lived there until the 1760s, when departure to the Mediterranean for reasons of ill health became a matter of life or death. During these three decades he had the equivalent of a modern nervous breakdown at age thirty, lost his only daughter, Elizabeth, at the age of fifteen, and rarely made enough money to support his family and pay the rates at Chelsea. He conceived of himself—in the sense of personal identity, a subject during his lifetime very much under discussion—as an "author." Unlike Fielding but similar to Pope and in the admirable phrase of Paul Fussell, he viewed "the life of writing" as his vocation.[28] Nothing in the extant materials suggests that he was fascinated by any branch of medicine: and though he practised, he was not considered by his peers an important physician, either in his primary knowledge of that art or in the application of it. He died at Leghorn in September 1771, a few months after his fiftieth birthday.

Knapp has filled in the factual details of the outline. But he has not been able to provide anything substantial about Smollett's personal identity, religion, philosophy, politics, *Weltanschauung*—those aspects of a life that make it interesting to others. It is (of course) possible that Smollett's life, even to himself, was boring and tedious; in which event one wonders why Professor Knapp devoted his own life to such extensive documentation of a dull and almost forgotten figure. Yet other hypotheses must be entertained and explored. Until that life is shown to have been uninteresting, it must not be cast aside. In fact, the few surviving facts suggest that Smollett's life was interesting. But not according to the "old" idea of biography as "fact" substantiated by printed records.

Smollett's nervous breakdown (or in its eighteenth-century equivalent, his bout with chronic melancholy caused by psychological and physical deterioration) is the least engaging. As I attempted to demonstrate a few years ago, the coincidence of a geographical move from Westminster to Chelsea (town to country), poverty, the poor sales of *Peregrine Pickle*, the lack of family ties (his Creole wife never adjusted to London life and was in part responsible for Smollett's antisocial behaviour), the sense of isolation Smollett felt at this time, dwindling prospects, a declining medical practice—all these combined to break him.[29]

The Smolletts of Bonhill were Catholics until the last part of the seventeenth century. After the Revolution of 1688 some of the Smolletts openly asserted their Presbyterianism without embarrassment. But Tobias seems not to have converted, at least not wholly. In public, his devotion was to the Church of England, and his various historical compilations—*History of England, Universal History, Present State of All Nations*—reveal an author merely dispensing the official state religion. After the age of eighteen Smollett became a Scottish foreigner living in London and very much aware of his status as an outsider. Since he was hardly forced to emigrate, he can scarcely be called an exile. In order to understand his "religion," that of other North Britons also living as foreigners in London must be compared to his: for instance, the poets James Thomson, Mark Akenside, John Armstrong, and David Mallett; the physicians James Douglas and William Hunter; Andrew Millar (the publisher of Fielding's works), and others. None of these lives reveals unusual devotion to the Church of England. At best it was token. Foreigners in any age usually pay lip service to the religion of their new country while remaining acutely aware that another religion —a private one far more important to their welfare—takes precedence.

Politics, unlike religion in Smollett's case, is even more elusive.

His published writings reveal no consistent attitude or party affiliation, neither exclusive Whig nor Tory: he wrote for the party that paid most. When Bute came to power early in the 1760s, Smollett was hired—as everyone knows—and for a time (while he was paid!) he espoused, almost daily, Bute's party line, in the *North Briton*. But earlier in Smollett's life—in the early fifties for example—he had written at request all sorts of ephemera that suggest an allegiance to the Whigs.[30] Still later, in the mid-sixties, for a fee he wrote scientific and political pamphlets—like those for Dr. John Rutty against Dr. Charles Lucas over the controversy about the efficacy of Bath Waters.[31] From this jumble of writings over many years, no consistent political view emerges; and even if Smollett's contemporaries tended to associate him at times with particular party interests, he himself chose not to reveal his beliefs except in his novels.

Actually the six novels should have prompted this conclusion without an *excursus*. Each, from *Roderick Random* onwards, rings with political references and allusions, usually cast into an ironic or satiric mode: to some petty incident or party squabble. Experimenter with the novel as a genre, Smollett was no more consistent in his use of political materials (for example, consistently satirical or realistic), than with landscape settings (he can paint a gothic castle in sentimental as well as realistic tones). These references have been identified but it has not been possible to construct a "Smollettian politics." Even *Launcelot Greaves*, perhaps the novel containing more political references than any other, offers no unified viewpoint. Newcastle and his men are exposed, but so are others; and it would be a valiant critic who would produce a single political point of view from such varied patterns found in that novel or Smollett's fiction at large.[32] Smollett, unlike Swift, is not even known to have had personal reasons for exposing certain political figures, making it all the more difficult to specify the precise political attitude he himself may have held. The poverty-stricken Duke of Newcastle is a good case in point.[33] So far as is known Smollett knew him only as a public figure, and in 1760, when Smollett probably composed the chapter in *Sir Launcelot Greaves* in which he appears, Smollett was writing for the Tories. What Smollett personally believed about Newcastle is another matter, and it is precisely this kind of political opinion about his contemporaries that is nonexistent.

With religion, politics, and philosophy accounted for, one would think that the life of any author could be written. And yet, though other contemporary authors lend themselves more easily to such discernment, this is precisely what one cannot do to Smollett. Johnson's politics, while hardly consistent (as Donald Greene has shown),[34] have nevertheless been described at length; and his religion, while neither simple nor orthodox, can also be pieced together with reasonable assurance of its accuracy. This does not apply to Smollett, and yet it is a *sine qua non* if one is to face the largest question of all—that about his imagined rawness.

If Goldsmith has forever given us a guide to his religion in his comic portrayal of the Vicar as Job—one employing some of the best strategies of eighteenth-century typologists—Smollett has not followed suit. Fielding's deep concern for prudence, wisdom, *Fortuna*, Providence—those traditional Christian topics about which the Restoration divines and Georgian sermonists had so much to say—allows for a kind of Fieldingesque religion, derivable from the life as well as the novels. From Richardson's refusal to permit the heroically alienated but nonetheless forlorn Clarissa Harlowe to live, despite poignant imprecations, one can infer much about his relation to his own "God." Even Boswell's religion of blended hedonism and puritanism is apparent in the diaries and journals, as well as in his best-selling book about Corsica.[35] But Smollett is another matter altogether. Such deistic resolutions of novels as the *deus ex machina* at the very end of *Roderick Random* are couched in such ironic tones that one wonders how seriously Smollett or his readers took them. Moreover, Smollett composed no diaries or journals and his novels are so seemingly devoid of personal intrusion, written as they are in such a cast of objective *repos* about his third-person form, that one cannot go from the life to the novels, or vice versa, and emerge from the process with any type of dialectic about a "Smollettian politics" or "religion" or "philosophy." True, Battestin derives a fair amount of "Fieldingesque religion" from third-person narrative in *Joseph Andrews* and *Tom Jones*,[36] but then Fielding has provided all sorts of clues nowhere found in Smollett's novels: those immensely revelatory, eighteen prefatory essays of *Tom Jones*, the three volumes of miscellanies and twenty plays, to say nothing of the single monumental figure of Parson Adams.

V. The Fantasy Life of a Foreigner

The problem is that we Smollettians have been looking—if we have looked at all—in the wrong place. Smollett's "religion" is not to be discovered in extant biographical materials, or in his contemporaries' comments about him (there are few such sources anyway, and they say almost nothing of interest), or even explicitly in the novels. It is found, *au fond*, in the same psychological temperament that predisposed him to write satire at the beginning of his career, and in the fantasy life that superseded his activity as a satirist. Actually, his "religion," his most private set of beliefs about man and the universe, was submerged in the layer that was a preformation, as it were, of the world imagined in his novels. Stated otherwise, Smollett's "raw" and "crude" narratives—his episodic tales about hunchbacked septuagenarians and lame matrons—are only the visible trace of a "religion" which presupposes such figures in the first place. One can affirm this, to be sure, about almost any writer or for that matter any human being. But with a difference: for most authors, there is sufficient biographical material to corroborate the suspicion without refuge to a "reading in" of the submerged levels. George Eliot's "private religion," for example, is everywhere evident in her novels,[37] but also abounds in literary remains outside of her novels. Smollett's is not, and in my view only this type of exploration will assist us to discover his genuine *voice* and thereby allow him to stand for a position which he has never really been granted.

That position, baldly put, is that the world of man is an awful place: perilous, fraught with horror and terror, ultimately without honour or integrity of *any* sort. It is a social scene so corrupt and disreputable that the imaginative writer is left dangling: to deride it (*satire*), play games with it (*poseur*), and be inventive at its expense (*wit*). But it is not an absurd or existentialist world. There is not a trace of Beckett here, not the "Black humourists."

The view has resemblances to some of Swift's postlapsarian configurations in *Gulliver's Travels:* Reldresal, Skyresh Bolgolam, Limtoc, Lalcon, Balmuff, all particular versions of the fallen yahoos. But there is a difference with Smollett: misanthropy, that quality with which Swift's name was for so long associated, is almost wholly absent. Whether responding subjectively or objectively to experience, Smollett did not rely on misanthropic defences,[38] and he could not have written what Swift wrote to Pope: "But principally I hate and detest that animal called man, although I heartily love John, Peter, Thomas, and so forth. This is the system upon which I have governed myself many years, but do not tell, and so I shall go on till I have done with them."[39] Of course he broke his avowed promise and even "softened up" in the conclusion of this by now celebrated letter to Pope. Smollett, in contrast, had a different psyche: observation and subsequent empirical accumulation of facts had persuaded him of the validity of his point of view about the jaded people populating this cruel world. He may have recognized that he himself was jaded; if so, he accepted the evidence all the same and the consequence of this psychological process for his fiction was dire.

The reader of Smollett's fiction who sets out to compile lists of suitable Smollettian episodes will discover, not surprisingly, that malice of one form or another is found in most. Again and again the recurring, almost archetypal, image in Smollett is that of the naïf or *ingenu* being duped in some gothic or grotesque fashion. It makes little difference whether ship surgeons, wartime generals, or young rascals like Perry and his merry comrades initiate and then execute the action: the action *itself* is the important thing and it inevitably leads to a single human condition—misery. It sustains itself too and has a marvellous habit in Smollett's fictive world of paving the way to further action. This must be the solitary quality about Smollett's fiction that attracted writers like Thackeray and Dickens into unqualified admiration. Even in *Count Fathom*, Smollett's most bizarre fictive configuration, with its curious blend of romanticism, gothicism, and scenes (or *attempted* scenes) of poignant sentimentalism, "duping scenes" abound everywhere and form the single unifying pattern of otherwise disparate episodes. Someone duped, cheated, marauded, raped, or murdered, excites Smollett to infuse dramatic energy into an otherwise lethargic narrative. If such scenes are fewer and spaced further apart in *Humphry Clinker*, it must be remembered that Smollett had mellowed tremendously by 1768 and—as I have pleaded before—that any generalization whatsoever about the *totality* of his fiction has important exceptions.[40]

The question I find myself returning to over and over again is, what kind of foreigner, Scottish or other, could have developed and then sustained an imagination focusing itself on such a quasi-symbolic action? I intentionally say foreigner rather than novelist, physician, hack, Anglican, Tory, political propagandist, entrepreneur, husband, father, or any number of other roles performed or played by Smollett. For the angle of vision he eventually could call his own resulted from a constellation of emotions based on diverse forms of *exclusion:* from his family, town, country, and from those Scottish institutions with which he identified. Bitterness was merely a symptom of those emotions of deprivation (not of vocational displacement) he felt. Yet even extreme bitterness does not necessarily lead to Smollett's imagined world of raw terror and unparalleled malice—so raw that if he possessed the erotic imagination of Sade, comparison would be idiotic. Surely the known facts about Smollett's temperamental irritability—Sterne's "Smelfungus Smollett"[41] describes but only a small manifestation of that trait—do not necessitate, in the sense of cause and effect, a fiction based almost exclusively upon actions of duping or being duped. Temperamentally speaking, Smollett was irritable, even dangerously inflammable. Easily provoked, he knew his psychological tendencies all too well:

> Know then, I can despise your pride, while I honour your integrity; and applaud your taste, while I am shocked at your ostentation.—
> I have known you trifling, superficial and obstinate in dispute; meanly jealous and aukwardly reserved; rash and haughty in your

resentments; and coarse and lowly in your connexions.—I have blushed at the weakness of your conversation and trembled at the errors of your conduct.—[42]

This is Smollett in his celebrated "Dedication" to himself, Smollett secretly glimpsed in a rarely observed posture of candour. But this is not the narrative stance offering a ripple of a clue to the raw vision found in the novels. For that we must gaze elsewhere, at other traits. Smollett, a "nonclubable" and virtually antisocial man, failure in his profession of physician, seems to have had no propensity for the Augustan sorts of pastime his mentor Pope enjoyed; on the other hand he was not so solipsistically enclosed nor entrapped by his own mind that he was prevented from dwelling on outside things.[43] His was not common perception of his own personal identity. He rationalized everything on the basis of his integrity; yet the selfhood embracing that integrity he often loathed. Sometimes he failed to hear outside "voices," for example, some of the repeated advice his good friend and Scottish lanceman Alexander Carlyle offered him.[44] But solipsism did not rule him so sovereignly nor tyrannically as did his irritability, abnormal pride, and—paradoxically—belief in his own worth. Other qualities—fascination for the sensual or erotic, or, turning elsewhere, for the theological, seem not to have fazed him or roused his enthusiasm.[45]

All these are traits on the *conscious* level. The above catalogue is *faute de mieux* what Smollett might have said about himself: as he did indeed say, although in a truncated and somewhat mutilated form, in his self-dedication to *Count Fathom*, or, later on, in the self-diagnosis of his psychological disposition made to Dr. Anthony Fizès of Montpellier in the South of France.[46] On the *unconscious* level, a very different man appears. One who has developed massive guilt feelings for abandoning his Scottish family, his cultural heritage, and his native country suffering from so many problems in the 1730s and 1740s, and one who has reaped none of the guilt-mollifying reinforcements from his supposed "new life" in London. Only such a man could have created *Humphry Clinker's* almost schizophrenic hero (he is hardly a pseudohero), Matt Bramble, passionately divided as he is between encouraging misery and enacting benevolence. Most commentators of Matt Bramble notice his peculiar brand of sensibility, but in relating this curious figure to his real-life prototype (Tobias Smollett) they rarely ask what kind of man could have "imagined" such a figure.[47] Literary traditions delineating the typology of the "benevolent misanthrope" do not go far in this direction and, what is more, are incapable of producing results of a more interesting variety than the fact that Smollett's hero figures in a long line of benevolently misanthropic ancestors.[48] Much more germane to his rawness and crudity is Smollett's conception of himself and of fiction—his sense of what both ought to be.

Masochism is also evident throughout Smollett's novels and in so many forms and shapes, so often disguised in pranks and masqueraded in so many games, that it would require an entire essay to describe them. For literally dozens of pages the rascally Perry Pickle roams the world like a protean figure straight out of Ariosto, not only playing the "picaresque games" Philip Stevick has detected,[49] but mischievously indulging in infantile, hysterical actions that are ultimately more masochistic than sadistic. From the point of view of Smollett's reputation today it is Perry himself who suffers most by his exclusion from those *rites de passage* that signify manhood. True, no one in *Peregrine Pickle*, not even the memorable nun, dies or approaches death, not even in Smollett's peculiar mould of rhetorical hyperbole. But Perry, unable to wean himself from such silly behaviour, frustrates readers like the one already cited by never really growing up, never loving maturely, never showing himself capable of relationships based on compromise and giving. These are not the romantic desiderata of a post-Freudian age; they are the universal signs heralding maturity. Those who disagree with such an interpretation of *Peregrine Pickle* are forced to argue that by the end of the novel Perry has somehow outgrown his prankish imbecility. Yet the available evidence is thin and Smollett's concluding chapters do little to support such an interpretation. Not even our best reader of the *bildungsroman* in England, who might be delighted to put forward such an hypothesis, has gone so far.[50] If Smollett had possessed an unusual theory of character, he could have seen that Peregrine's development is minimal and that he never learns very much about the good and evil in this world or about his own striking limitations. Looking farther back in Smollett's oeuvre, Rory Random, despite his continual wanton attempts at charity, remains "fixated" in a stage not much beyond the oral. He warmly sympathizes; he learns from experience; he glows with fervid passion; unlike Peregrine he even feels genuine emotions of tenderness upon occasion. But he never comes to see the world as anything more than a silhouette of rogues and would-be rogues or, in other antithetical colours, divided between those who inflict pain and those who receive it. At best he would agree with John Updike (*Rabbit, Run; Rabbit, Redux*) and Ken Kesey (*One Flew over the Cuckoo's Nest*) that the whole world is basically divided between wolves and rabbits, the latter preying on the terrible fear and fright of the former. Moreover, Smollett hardly seems to possess a subconscious, nor is there any sense, as in so much other fiction of the mid eighteenth-century, of a precise physiology of that subconscious. Rory's penumbral vision is myopic and dualistic at the very best; and he has no notion of the sources—whether societal or personal—of evil or of the tremendous diversity of pain inflicted on him. Pain of this intensity treated by a George Eliot or Joseph Conrad would have provoked a veritable *metaphysics of evil* embedded within a grotesque plot bathed but not submerged in humour.[51] Smollett-the-intellectual possessed the psychological equipment for a metaphysics; but lacked a literary vehicle for expressing at the level of his protagonists this set of beliefs. Rory and Perry, frozen as it were into stances of shunning pain (usually by inflicting it on others), are the imaginative correlatives of a psyche itself predisposed to self-flagellation.

Smollett himself would not (of course) have conceded one jot of this, any more than one of us in his place would. Freud has told us why:

> Patients do not easily believe what we tell them about an unconscious sense of guilt. They know well enough by what torments (pangs of conscience) a conscious feeling of guilt, the consciousness of guilt, can express itself, and so they cannot admire that they could harbour entirely analagous feelings in themselves without observing a trace of them. I think we may meet their objection by abandoning the term "unconscious feeling of guilt," which is in any case an incorrect one psychologically, and substitute for it a "need for punishment," which describes the state of things observed just as aptly.[52]

Freud's explanation scrutinized closely also suggests the prevalence of a certain dominant action in Smollett's novels: *revenge, revenge,* and more *revenge.* This action and the formal mode it necessitates could not be more lucid. In Smollett's six imagined worlds, whether Random's treacherous London or Fathom's Central European spas, rogues and rascals of every shape and type inflict pain; as a consequence they have no difficulty in passing on revengeful acts to themselves. Indeed, they expect it. The cowards among them, usually not the major but the minor male figures, naturally flinch; but even these "minor males" dream about vindictiveness in a kind of extended moment in which each can confront his "other self" alone.[53] *Everyone* in Smollett's world, it seems, is afflicted: there is no imagined condition or sublime state as peace uninterrupted, not even in the final quarter of *Humphry Clinker,* Smollett's solitary attempt at pastoral simplicity *sans* the complications of ordinary daily life.[54]

Those afflicted to an extraordinary degree now almost "exist to revenge": that action becomes their primary *raison d'être.* For example, Jolter's mathematical explanation of the nature of motion, and Peregrine's application of this lemma to the mathematics of evil, come close to expressing in shorthand Smollett's vision of the physics of revenge.[55] The focus of a Smollett novel—as much as one can generalise about such diverse fictions as *Roderick Random* and *Sir Launcelot Greaves*, for instance—is on a counterpoint of roguish sharpers and undiscerning gulls. Dramatic tension is reached in the interludes in which recognition of hypocrites and cullies occurs. Further dramatic tension, unfortunately not always formally exploited to its fullest nor always brought to a climax by Smollett, is attained when dupe or dissembler swears revenge and then enacts it. All this can hardly be said of traditional picaresque narratives in which revenge is carried on at a much lower key and mood, generally at a more primitive level, more frugally spaced, and without the pitch of excitement or gravity of consequence one discovers in Smollett. He tried hard to unfetter himself from picaresque shackles, as is now almost universally conceded by formalist critics,[56] certainly not to innovate by retaining the basic elements of that form. But even if he had not, his struggles with a literary mode do very little to account for his peculiar actions of revenge. No modal or genetic (i.e., genre) study of Smollett's novels will ever assist us to stare plainly at his most original feature.[57] Performed in the best of possible worlds they would be but footnotes towards an understanding of the rather unique voice of this writer.

But the question stubbornly remains regarding the sources—not only formalistically speaking but the sources in the author's psyche— of this extreme grasping for revenge: in Freud's terms, the perpetual "need for punishment." Freud sketched some crude answers in an essay in 1924 entitled "The Economic Problem in Masochism."[58] Here he described the roots of masochism as a function of economic determinants, and furthermore suggested that masochism in its most rudimentary form ("erotogenic masochism") actually "lusts for pain." We ought to note the lusting. Such terminology, economic bases aside, almost tallies with the anonymous critic's estimate.[59] In Smollett's imagined world, in the notes of the voice crying out to be heard in contrast to Fielding's (with whom he was most often compared), masochism exists as a moral imperative. It is a necessity for human existence and social intercourse.[60] Even the strong shall be wounded and hurt and shall eventually avenge themselves (Perry, like Lovelace in *Clarissa Harlowe*, ultimately harms himself more than anyone else). Smollett's serious reader suspects that a constellation of money (Freud's economics), guilt, and unconscious anxiety about that felt guilt have made it—Smollett's masochism—a moral necessity for him. And yet, this is nothing that can be deduced from the facts of Smollett's life or from any known events of Scottish or

English history during that lifetime, 1721–1771.[61] It certainly cannot nor ought to be proved by demonstrating explicit cause and effect. If anything, the reader's intuition, responding to revenge and guilt thundered out at this pitch, knows all and sees everything.

By the "Economic Problem *in* Masochism" Freud did not mean (of course) to suggest that masochism is economically *determined*. Far from this, he took pains to show that (1) the guilt-causing masochism is demonstrably unconscious and (2) that its precise nature and manifestation depend upon the patient's temperamental capacity to cope with degrees of pleasure and pain.

In 1924 that was an imaginative hypothesis, but it left unresolved the relation between pain or pleasure and money—the key relation for his theory. Perhaps Freud thought the connection too obvious to be laboured but almost two centuries earlier Smollett did not, at least not in fictional form. And if Smollett could have possessed any of Freud's psychiatric knowledge he certainly would have seized on the connection in no uncertain terms.[62] Not only because Smollett had a scrupulous eye for money (as the hundreds of economic allusions in his novels suggest),[63] or because personally he felt so very much committed during the 1750s and 1760s to speak out against economic excess in the popular English and Scottish debates over luxury—or even because the ways of making and losing money were such a fashionable topic for coffeehouse and other polite conversation in mid-Georgian Britain.[64] Rather because Smollett himself was psychologically enveloped in the myth of materialism, and because he had suffered so much poverty in his most formative years. All these factors contributed something; ultimately, though, Smollett's concern for money and its unique power was prompted by his *psyche*. A child when the Age of Mercantilism was decaying, he would nevertheless have behaved as he did in any epoch, blasting luxury yet continually contemplating stratagems of revenge when deprived of it. Even when in dialogues with himself, his whole life seemed to revolve around this gravitational pole, money. At least this would have been Smollett's *conscious* explanation; the *unconscious* one depends upon his ability to cope with pain, and this one we shall never know because knowledge of the unconscious explanation requires data simply unknown in his case.

Here Smollett the-total-man must be sharply distinguished from contemporary authors like Richardson who saw himself as well as life's problems and mysteries in altogether different terms, or like Sterne who, while delighted in being wined and dined and toasted all over London, viewed himself somewhat as the ringmaster of a team of subservient *poseurs* and could have cared less about the value of a farthing.[65] But Smollett was a different type altogether.

And it may be that his economic cunning and fiscal shrewdness are too proximate to our own concerns to discover anything interesting about him in the 1970s. For instance, when printer or publisher attempted to exact a dishonest penny from the shrewd "Caledonian Smollett," a ruckus was raised as we know from his dealings with the House of Strahan and his retention of copyright for so many books.[66] Unmistakable, unclubable foreigner, tragic and lonely at home, disappointed over the shape of his whole life, especially after "Inspector Hill" ruined the sales of *Peregrine Pickle*;[67] all these were linked into a chain of emotions ultimately unleashing responses of anxiety, anger and subsequent guilt—a vicious emotional circle with no opening.

Even more consequential for the aging Smollett were familial ghosts arising from his northern past: guilt over disobedience to his parents for breaking away from the tradition of law, medicine and the military, all centuries old among the Smolletts; guilt over the precarious financial situation of the reality that he was basically a hack who lived exclusively from his earnings from book to book; and last but hardly least, guilt of which he himself was conscious over an almost hair-trigger temper.

In Smollett-the-man then there was enough of the prerequisite psychological endowment for satire (his courage, anger and wit) to recognize hypocrisy and cant when he saw it. In the *novelist* such satiric recognition took very different forms. There Smollett's invention—his "fire"—must not be minimized nor must his sense of fiction be reduced to insubstantial labels (realism, picaresque, romance, grotesque) thereby absurdly misrepresenting his most original mode. His tableaux of thieves and gulls (perhaps learned in part from observation of Pope's technique in *The Dunciad*), "fools of each fabric, sharpers of all sorts, and dunces of every degree,"[68] the interludes between chases and caricatures and the scenes of revenge occurring in a quick rhythmic tempo probably unrivalled in English fiction: all these are no mean feats even for a satirist *manqué*. Whether conscious of his final product or not, Smollett lived up to his own aesthetic that "a Novel is a large diffused picture, comprehending the characters of life, disposed in different groups, and exhibited in various attitudes, for the purposes of an uniform plan, and general occurrence, to which every individual figure is subservient."[69] In practice as opposed to mere theory the announced tapestry ("a large diffused picture") was also for Smollett a form of the baroque in prose fiction (whether consciously so or unconsciously here is irrelevant since we have his six novels in finished form). And this is why it is correct to propose that Smollett, regardless of his influence on Dickens and other nineteenth-century English humourists,[70] represents the *end* rather than the *beginning* of a set of techniques in prose loosely called "early English narrative fiction."

VI. Baroque Intentions and Further Economic Designs

We have almost come full circle. It is thus not improper to raise the spectre of Pope once again—the same imaginative Pope who perpetually hovers as a felt presence in Smollett's world, and to inquire why Smollett unlike his mentor poet did not learn, or could not learn, to see the bad *and* the good in the terrestrial universe:

> Hear then the truth: " 'Tis Heav'n each Passion sends,
> And diff'rent men directs to diff'rent ends.
> Extremes in Nature equal good produce,
> Extremes in Man concur to gen'ral use."
> Ask we what makes one keep, and one bestow?
> That POW'R who bids the Ocean ebb and flow,
> Bids seed-time, harvest, equal course maintain,
> Thro' reconcil'd extremes of drought and rain,
> Builds Life on Death, on Change Duration founds,
> And gives th' eternal wheels to know their rounds.
> Riches, like insects, when conceal'd they lie,
> Wait but for wings, and in their season, fly.
> Who sees pale Mammon pine amidst his store,
> Sees but a backward steward for the Poor;
> This year a Reservoir, to keep and spare,
> The next a Fountain, spouting thro' his Heir,
> In lavish streams to quench a Country's thirst,
> And men and dogs shall drink him 'till they burst.[71]

If Pope had gazed upon England's good men as well as her bad—her Arbuthnots and Blunts, as Howard Erskine-Hill has demonstrated in a recent essay on Pope and the "Financial Revolution"[72]—he arrived at this judicious view by considering that the spendthrift is balanced by the miser. Yet Pope was hardly blind to the English misery about him just at the time Smollett was growing up:

> "See Britain sunk in lucre's sordid charms,"
> "And France reveng'd of ANNE's and EDWARD's arms!"
> No mean Court-badge, great Scriv'ner! fir'd thy brain,
> Nor lordly Luxury, nor City Gain:
> No, 'twas thy righteous end, asham'd to see
> Senates degen'rate, Patriots disagree,
> And nobly wishing Party-rage to cease,
> To buy both sides, and give thy Country peace.
> "All this is madness," cries a sober sage:
> But who, my friend, has reason in his rage?[73]

Yet, Smollett saw only the wretch's lot. Nowhere in his fiction are there persuasive (that is the important word) portraits of such models of virtue commanding admiration as Dr. John Arbuthnot (just mentioned) and John Kyrle (Pope's Man of Ross in the *Epistle to Bathurst*). If Smollett's villains (especially Fathom and his gang of marauders) thrill the imagination and chill the blood, his "saints" (his Thomsons and Baynards) are quickly forgotten and forgiven! Since his psyche cannot conceive of genuinely amiable humourists *à la* Fielding or Dickens, his readers necessarily search elsewhere for diversion and amusement. So clear a typological figure as Baynard in *Humphry Clinker*, whose moral goodness partly derives from his rural setting (from idealised felicity rather than proved flawless character or economic sobriety), barely influences the whole canvas of Smollett's episodic series of tableaux, his "large diffused picture."[74] A few good figures scattered far and wide, as our anonymous reader has already suggested, will not change the reader's perception of the most degenerate of postlapsarian worlds.

Surely the reason is grounded in a temperamentally fixed Smollettian angle of vision —one as self-conscious of its baroque stylistic aims as of its insistence on *perpetual revenge* as an *arrière pensée*. Throughout his rather tragic life Smollett seemed unable to see goodness anywhere, certainly not in himself nor in a hope for future British progress, nor in such auspicious new institutions—to name but one—as the Society for Arts, Commerce, and Manufactures.[75] While still in his twenties (*ca.* 1741–1750), his imagination presents itself as virtually defeated and casting about for alternatives at sea and in strange territories. Broken and bitter over his theatrical failures, his true voice is not far from the poet who utters the gloomy dirge at the end of *The New Dunciad:*

> In vain, in vain,—the all-composing Hour
> Resistless falls: The Muse obeys the Pow'r.
> She comes! she comes! the sable Throne behold
> Of *Night* Primaeval, and of *Chaos* old!

Yet the failure for Smollett, unlike for Pope, lay not in the fog and mist of true wit versus false taste and black imagination, but rather in the bleak daylight of economic deviation and moral decay. Here the air was inert but still not impenetrable, and here Smollett saw eye to eye with Berkeley, not Pope:

> Though it must be owned that little can be hoped if we consider the corrupt degenerate age we live in. I know it is an old folly to make peevish complaints of the times, and charge the common failures of human nature on a particular age. One may nevertheless

venture to affirm that the present hath brought forth new and portentous villainies, *not to be paralleled in our own or any other history*. We have been long preparing for some great catastrophe . . .[76]

Apocalypse and imminent doom were closer to the pillars of Smollett's private world than all Pope's balanced estimates or (to gaze at Smollett's own plots) to the sweet optimism and pretentious felicity some rosy-eyed readers have found in the happy but improbable endings of *Roderick Random* and *Humphry Clinker*. Often Smollett pretended to be "half in love" with the warm cheer and goodness of the social world but his bloated rhetoric and defective expressions have usually given him away.[77] If Pope and Smollett were in a sense both commentators on the continuing "economic revolution" occurring in England since 1688—Pope on catastrophic developments such as the South Sea Bubble and Smollett on the fall of Walpole and the economic depressions that occurred after the War of the Austrian Succession (1740–1748) and the Seven Years' War (1756–1763)—there is nevertheless a vast difference.

For Smollett economic decay *and* baroque design—not merely one without the other, or the first as a *topoi* and the second as a principle of organization—constituted something of a literary mode.[78] Pope-the-poet would have considered the unique blend—if he could have seen it in practice in Smollett's novels (remember, even "Defoe soared no higher than a swan")—indefensible under any circumstances because fanciful and eccentric. For Smollett the mixture was original, perhaps eccentric but ancient and modern at once, his zig-zag path hewn out of an overgrown European wood of traditional picaresque and romantic narratives. By contrast, Pope's interest in economic theories and "good men" occurred on different grounds and in different ways, and is less significant for the form and shape of his poetry (partly owing to the demands of couplet rhetoric and logic) than for Smollett's fiction.[79] While these subjects may be said to form a kind of constellation of *topoi* for Pope's Horatian phase of the 1730s, they hardly shaped or camouflaged the more striking dialectic he invoked in his *Imitations of Horace* or, perhaps more evident, the sets of tableaux of contemporary London he sought to impose on "ancient paintings" in *The Dunciad*.[80] Stated differently, content and style have been blended in Smollett to a degree qualitatively insignificant in Pope. In Smollett, on the other hand, baroque ornaments (style) and economic views (content) are played against each other almost as coevals—each competing in a playful attempt to capture a long-lost world, the one Smollett thought Cervantes had lived in and which he sadly came to learn could not be revived.[81] In Pope ornament elevates all decay and can never be reduced to the level of mere *topos*, even in the wittiest satiric inversions of which Pope is capable.

Perhaps, then, the comparison for all its inherent defects has some merit. Pope's portrait of "Sir Balaam" in the *Epistle to Bathurst* can instructively be compared to Smollett's progress of "Miss Williams" in *Roderick Random* (the two works are not even chronologically separated by much more than a decade). Contrast proves illuminating in view of the extraordinary care Smollett has taken to lodge Miss Williams's history in a clear economic setting: her "father was an eminent merchant in the city who having, in the course of trade, suffered very considerable losses,"[82] and her Hogarthian "progress" from riches to rags unfolds along lines determined by economic rather than moral circumstances. So clearly described are these details that one begins to suspect the weighty validity of George Steiner's claim, his solitary one about Smollett-the-novelist quoted as an epigraph to this essay. But they are more than economic ornaments; they are elevated to baroque designs. To silence the matter about details here in no way advances understanding of Smollett but rather conceives of literary mode as mere surface while forgetting that most novelists employ techniques rather than endorse ideas. Yet the ideas are themselves not yet sharp enough. Smollett's economic lines, to continue the contrast, are not those Pope saw: the new monied interests of the 1720s, the fall of Tory empires, servants buying equipages and shopkeepers taking over the estates of gentry:

> Of all the city figures to whom Pope refers, the most conspicuous, the most fit for conservative argument, and the man whom he was in a position to know most about, was [Sir John] Blunt. His career displayed, besides a self-righteous style, that inability to conceive, or unwillingness to regard, the good of the Commonweal, which Swift, Bolingbroke and the Tories felt was the peculiar evil in the notion of creating a new monied interest, in opposition to the landed interest.[83]

This described the 1720s; but by 1740 and 1750 everything had changed again. For almost a decade (1740–1748) England was involved in Continental wars that caused her economy to boom,[84] and the familiar outcry against new monied interests (Pope in the 1720s) was by 1750 replaced by constant ridicule of the manners and mores of the hordes of middle-class people now moving to the cities. Thirty years earlier Pope lamented that the hierarchy of classes had been jumbled to a dangerous point; by 1750 Smollett recognized that the threat was no longer a matter of jumbled social hierarchies but of a patently degenerate morality, especially among the lower and merchant classes. His interest in economics was thus quasi-religious and moral, and deserves to be distinguished from Pope's. Yet even this avenue of exploration does not penetrate very far in view of the scarcity of information about Smollett's own religion. If Pope was indeed an "Erasmian Catholic"[85] (among the varieties of Catholicism he could have practiced in the early eighteenth century), this piece of knowledge allows for a reconciliation of Catholicism and his brand of deep economic dissatisfaction. Nothing like this is, or can be, known about Smollett.

Whatever Smollett's "true" religion—and all Smollettians admit that this is one of the classic mysteries about an eighteenth-century major author—his political allegiances were certainly not primarily Tory, as they had been on more than one occasion for Pope.[86] Smollett cared less about the problem of new economic interests, as his *History of England* reveals, than about the social changes they effected; but even here not without consulting his own personal, self-conscious needs first. For Smollett there would perpetually be new owners of wealth—this was but part of a grand providential scheme executed by vice and corruption. In this sense Smollett's beliefs were radical, looking backwards at Hobbes and Mandeville and forwards to post-Hegelian economic thinkers of the nineteenth century;[87] but in other areas determined by temperamental concerns, he was far more nostalgic than Pope. Considerably less politically conservative than the poet, Smollett paradoxically longed for an older world—one less Tory than Pope's, but nevertheless more "landed" even than the England Pope knew had disappeared after the "Bubble burst." Surely the paradox reveals some of the weakness in Smollett's unsystematic economic thinking. His fierce attacks on luxury[88] in *Humphry Clinker* and in the compilations derived not so much from Whiggish thinking as from the perspective of a genuine masochist feeling guiltier about himself than about the Commonweal. So too do his other random economic pronouncements, especially those centred around the possibility of restoring England's "deserted villages."

It is *in toto* a confusing picture, often paradoxical, inconsistent, rarely systematic or logical, and certainly neither genuinely Tory or Whig. If the varieties of Smollett's psychological masochism are literally placed side by side with his economic beliefs, the parallel columns reveal another way of "looking." Taken together they bear little resemblance to Swift's ingrained pessimism, the Swift for whom, incidentally, Smollett had little use and from whose prose he learned little.[89] Smollett's literary mould still reflects organisation and controlled order, even if his imagined vision cannot contain a rigorous economic programme or system. Often a vantage, different from the one most critics have discussed, guided Smollett—picaro versus realist, satirist-romanticist, Whig-Tory, Anglican-Jacobite, benevolist-misanthrope, and other traditional tensions found in his works—and it was not entirely *centred* upon economic beliefs, however economically determined it may have been.

Perhaps displacement of prose norms is the terrain that should concern students of Smollett living in a critical environment in which "misreadings" receive the highest approbation.[90] Unfortunately it almost never does. For Smollett I call this displacement "baroque"—"baroque economics" might even be more accurate—and see in its prismatic glass the traces of still another Smollett, the troubled psyche looking backwards at mythical Toryism yet also intentionally looking away from the varied patterns of traditional English narrative prose at least from the time of the Elizabethans. Still shackled, he nevertheless attempted to escape.

"Baroque" because themes developed in counterpoint appear in Smollett's novels as ornamental design not unlike the curlicues on baroque furniture. A reading of *Humphry Clinker* that proceeds from sentence to sentence reveals not only a careful continuity and discontinuity of particular words (in the sense of the weave on a tapestry) but also a sense of architecture and symmetry found especially in gardens and on monuments associated with baroque art. It cannot be accidental that the letters in that novel are so scrupulously plotted out nor that so much meaning is conveyed by the precise date, place, and the number of letters assigned to a particular character —and to the solitary undated letter.[91] Nor to another kind of "prose embroidery" manifested through the exact moment and place in which characters from previous novels (Random, Pickle, Fathom, Smollett himself) reappear in later ones. The fact that every attempt to herald these techniques extraordinary and thereby to elevate Smollett's achievement as a novelist has not completely succeeded, does not detract from his intentions to cast his novel into a baroque mould. And it certainly is not the fault of critics who have worked so hard at reconstruction of a consistent symmetrical or numerical design.[92]

Ultimately though, perhaps "unintentional baroque economics" is even the more proper label because it salvages Smollett from maniacally conservative readers of early English fiction who have not been able to conceive his works as anything more than shadows of Fielding or anticipations of Dickens.[93] "Unintentional" because there is not the slightest shred of biographical evidence that Smollett wanted to or knew how to fuse these two realms (economics and a baroque aesthetic). Moreover, since his actual execution is imperfect it may be safer to speculate that he did all this unknowingly. After all it is possible that Smollett was no more aware of his finished product than he was aware, as Freud says, of his "unconscious sense of guilt."[94]

VII. The Limits of "Beef and Bouillon"

Such a hybrid designation as baroque economics, however improbable or inchoate, must finally dislodge those modern Vladimirs and Estragons awaiting some proper god-given genre or mode for Smollett's novels. Of course he was a comic novelist who must be viewed in that tradition, and he has profound ties with artists like Hogarth, Fielding, Thackeray, Dickens and Barth. But his six novels, viewed singly or collectively, are generic misfits. As I have already suggested, they fit no genre (and it surely is not a matter of the genre not as yet having been discovered), and until now Smollett has continued to elude even a mode other than to be called a comic novelist. The Chicago neo-Aristotelian critics, especially R. S. Crane and Sheldon Sacks who have had serious interests in the eighteenth century, were prudent to avoid Smollett at every opportunity for he could only cause them bewilderment.[95] Elsewhere I have argued that all too often Smollett's narratives are explicitly judged by their proximity to or distance from Fielding's and Sterne's.[96] Here I have attempted a bolder "misreading" that prophetically discards genres and tosses away all historicism and scientific validity in the hope of restoring Smollett to a point where he is at least once again read. If not, imagine what chaos will confront the misguided critic who sets out to find a "proper genre" for Smollett's *Travels through France and Italy* within the context of all eighteenth- and nineteenth-century travel literature. Here Harold Bloom's admitted misreading of Blake is instructive and sheds indirect light on Smollett.[97] Only an interpretation permitting Smollett the maximum amount of modal expansion, and additionally one that brings no biases with regard to the role of content in modal analysis, can hope to esteem and revive his fictions—not merely to drive readers back to read them. And even this may not be enough. For these works must be deemed important enough to be read before they can have future critics. Stated in another way, if Smollett can once and for all find a genuine "misreader" then there is hope for him as a "major" novelist. All editions of the *Cambridge Bibliography of English Literature* list him as such—but they do not provide the necessary "misreading."

I have attempted to misread, to make Smollett strong, as well as to demonstrate how an author such as he was could have selected "beef and bouillon," or in my jargon "baroque economics," as the substance of his fiction. And I am persuaded that within the limits of reason Smollett knew something of what he was about. His lattices are imperfect and not commensurate with the designs perpetuated by Fielding, but to overlook them altogether is folly for the reader of good prose and tragedy for the student interested in Adam Smith's "toil and bustle of this world." Through an ornamental economics psychologically grounded he begins to emerge as the voice of the man of feeling whose sympathetic imagination demands constant *catharsis;* as the voice of down-and-out sinners and lonely sharpers of an age, as Berkeley had early envisioned,[98] steeped in sin:

> Let me not therefore be condemned for having chosen my principal character from the purlieus of treachery and fraud, when I declare my purpose is to set him up as a beacon for the benefit of the unexperienced and unwary, who from the perusal of these memoirs, may learn to avoid the manifold snares with which they are continually surrounded in the paths of life; while those who hesitate on the brink of iniquity, may be terrified from plunging into that irremediable gulph, by surveying the deplorable fate of FERDINAND Count FATHOM.[99]

NOTES

1. Actually Smollett began his career as a poet under the influence of Pope. *Advice* and *Reproof*, modelled on Pope's *Epilogue to the Satires* and published four years after *The Dunciad* in four books, shows clear influence. Unless otherwise stated the place of publication of all works cited is London. To conserve space further, these abbreviations have been used for places of publication: E for Edinburgh, P for Paris, and NYC for New York City.

2. *Humphry Clinker* (1771), letter dated 6 September.

3. *Sir Launcelot Greaves* (1760–1761), chapter xxiii.

4. *Critical Review* 1 (1756): 226–240. Smollett continued to glance at Pope's poetry throughout his own career: in some of his harsh attacks on the medical profession in *Roderick Random*, in the satiric diction in *Peregrine Pickle* (e.g. alluding to "the eel of science by the tail," *Dunciad*, B. I: 280) and the *Dunciad*-like chapters (ci–ciii) portraying "a College of Authors" in Grub Street, by adopting Pope's sense of the "Ruling Passion" in *Ferdinand Count Fathom* (1753, II, pp. 71, 154, 164) and alluding to the *Dunciad's* heroic games in the duel by *assa foetida* within the prison, by quoting in *Sir Launcelot Greaves* the *Dunciad* couplet (B, II: 105–106) about Cloacina's stinking bed and commenting extensively on the *Dunciad* in chapter 24, and less obviously but nonetheless palpably by his version of the "Augustan myth" at the end of *Humphry Clinker. The Age of Dullness; a Satire By a natural son of the late Mr. Pope. With a preface, giving an account of his mother, & how he came to the knowledge of his birth* appeared in 1757, and was just the type of work to intrigue Smollett. He may, in fact, have reviewed it; see *Critical Review* 2 (1757): 87, article 24.

5. See G. S. Rousseau, "Smollett and the Picaresque: Some Questions about a Label," *Studies in Burke and His Time* 12 (1971): 1886–1904 and P. G. Boucé, "Smollett's Pseudo-picaresque: A Response to Rousseau's Smollett and the Picaresque," ibid., 14 (1972): 73–79. I declined the invitation to reply to Boucé. Although he suggested a few revisions in my definition, his own conclusion approximated mine rather closely: "Although I agree wholeheartedly with the general thrust of Rousseau's article, I should like to offer a few brief remarks and suggestions which should prove helpful . . ." (p. 74); "The picaresque battle—or rather anti-picaresque battle—is far from over as Smollettian studies are concerned. In spite of such sensible and valuable efforts as Rousseau's important article, critics still continue to fling about carelessly

the 'picaresque' epithet with little regard for the requirements of a useful critical taxonomy" (p. 79).

6. *Roderick Random* (1754), iii. Critics discussing this passage continue to over-look Smollett's mood of despair in 1753–1754, and to notice how it then coloured his view of the world.

7. New Haven, Yale University Press, 1967, pp. 165–218.

8. I adopt and modify the phrase from W. J. Bate, "Johnson and Satire Manqué," *Eighteenth-Century Studies in Honour of Donald Hyde,* ed. W. H. Bond (NYC: The Grolier Club, 1970), pp. 145–160, and consider it admirable because it attempts to distinguish among varieties of satire while others have been satisfied to classify almost any literature as satire. But the battle is not yet won, at least not in Smollett's case. Two important correctives attempting to discriminate are D. L. Evans, "Pere-grine Pickle: The Complete Satirist," *Studies in the Novel* 3 (1971): 258–274 and Michael Rosenblum, "Smollett as Conservative Satirist," *English Literary History* 42 (1976): 556–579. The difficulty with Rosenblum's perceptive essay is that he wants to find a "typical hero" for all Smollett's novels: "Smollett's typical hero is a figure who demonstrates a belief . . . in the orderly society" (p. 560). Few readers will be persuaded that this is true of, or even important to, *Roderick Random* and *Peregrine Pickle.*

9. *Humphry Clinker* (1771), letter dated 8 October.

10. Two authors have strained more than others: Donald Bruce, *Radical Doctor Smollett* (1964) and M. A. Goldberg, *Smollett and the Scottish School* (Albuquerque, 1959).

11. The best of these is P. G. Boucé, *Les Romans de Smollett: Étude critique* (P, 1971), recently translated into English and published in 1976 by Longmans. See also R. D. Spector, *Tobias Smollett* (NYC, Twayne Publishers, 1968), who provides individual readings but who has nevertheless hoped to find a common thread as his subtitles for the five novels indicate: "Roderick Random: The Rogue Sets Forth," "Peregrine Pickle: The Rogue in High Society," "Ferdinand Count Fathom: Smol-lett's Iago," "Launcelot Greaves: Quixotic Picaresque," "Humphry Clinker: The Picaresque Ménage." Spector's interpretations must be considered tentative; if the Bramble family is anything collectively speaking, it is certainly not a "picaresque ménage."

12. See John Butt, "Smollett's Achievement as a Novelist," *Tobias Smollett: Bicentennial Essays Presented to Lewis M. Knapp,* ed. G. S. Rousseau and P. G. Boucé (NYC, Oxford University Press, 1971), pp. 9–23.

13. This may be an illusion, of course, and some of Fielding's ablest students, Martin Battestin, Henry Knight Miller, Claude Rawson and others connected with the Wesleyan Fielding Edition, may not concur with the judgement. I mean that Smollett's works, much less so than Fielding's, lend themselves to the kind of overview found in Andrew Wright's *Henry Fielding: Mask and Feast* (University of California Press, 1966) or G. W. Hatfield's *Henry Fielding and the Language of Irony* (University of Chicago Press, 1968). The notion that Smollett has not yet found an able enough critic is possible but improbable. Still it might be worthwhile for a very able critic to give meaning to experience by writing a book entitled *A Critic's Criticism of the Book about Smollett's Novels That Would Not Be.*

14. See Sheldon Sacks, *Fiction and the Shape of Belief* (University of California Press, 1967), pp. 270–271. Presumably Sacks tried to discover a "principle of co-herence" in *Humphry Clinker* and could not.

15. Such is the main point of Edmund Wilson's by-now classic essay "The His-torical Interpretation of Literature," *The Intent of the Critic,* ed. Donald A. Stauffer (Princeton, 1941), pp. 91–124. My friend Anais Nin informs me that Wilson, in the last year of his life, repeatedly asserted that he had now arrived at a point in which he could read nothing but eighteenth-century novels for pleasure, and that *Roderick Random* and *Peregrine Pickle* were among his favourites. I have been unable to con-firm the validity of this report with Mrs. Edmund Wilson of Wellfleet, Massachusetts.

16. See G. S. Rousseau, "Smollett and Sterne: A Revaluation," *Archiv für das Studium der Neueren Sprachen und Literaturen* 208 (1972): 286–297.

17. See M. E. Novak's treatment of the love scenes between Roderick and Narcissa in "Freedom, Libertinism, and the Picaresque," *Racism in the Eighteenth Century,* ed. H. E. Pagliaro (Cleveland, Case Western Reserve University Press, 1973), pp. 41–42.

18. Alexander Pope, *An Essay on Man*, Epistle IV, pp. 205–216.

19. Robert Paltock's novel *The Life and Adventures of Peter Wilkins* (1751) and Edward Kimber's *The Life and Adventures of Joe Thomson* (1750), both of which appeared within six months of the publication of *Peregrine Pickle*. The entire paragraph should be closely scrutinized and compared with the very different conclusions reached by Michael Rosenblum and referred to in n. 8.

20. I.e., school of criticism: formalist, new critical, historical, Aristotelian, Humean, Chicagoan, Marxist, structuralist. There is no such thing as a "Smollett school," only individual students (Boucé, Spector, Preston, Paulson *et al.*) who interpret his works. For reasons unknown to me *The Critical Heritage Series* has omitted only Smollett among the major eighteenth-century novelists; students therefore must make do with F. W. Boege's *Smollett's Reputation as a Novelist* (Princeton, 1947) which is often incomplete. A thorough survey of Smollett's critical heritage would probably reveal that he, somewhat like Goldsmith, his contemporary, has been a plaything for the tides of taste, reverenced by Scott, imitated by Dickens, neglected by the Edwardians, and discovered a bore to Henry James and his circle. To my mind John M. Warner's attempt to confront Smollett's literary career succeeds more than most others, but it, too, fails in the attempt to find meaningful coherence in a radical novelist who continued to experiment with form. See John M. Warner, "Smollett's Development as a Novelist," *Novelist 5* (1972): 148–161. Warner views Smollett's literary career as culminating in *Humphry Clinker*, a coherent masterpiece; yet he cannot demonstrate wherein lies the *coherence*.

21. The type of a "physician satirist," a satiric narrator who describes his experience by the use of medical analogues, reached its peak in the Renaissance, and declined afterwards; see Mary Claire Randolph, "The Medical Concept in English Renaissance Satiric Theory: Its Possible Relations and Implications," *Studies in Philology* 38 (1941): 125–157. Although vestiges of the tradition are apparent in the period 1700–1760 (Swift in *A Tale of a Tub*), it seems to have died out by then. To believe that Smollett consciously wrote in this tradition—i.e., Matt Bramble as a "physician-satirist" type—is critically as woolly headed as loosely styling him a picaresque novelist or calling the Bramble family (see note 5) a "picaresque ménage." True, all Smollett's novels, as I know very well, refer to medicine in an essential way (see G. S. Rousseau, "Doctors and Medicine in the Novels of Tobias Smollett," Ph.D. dissertation, Princeton University, 1966), but this is a very different matter, critically speaking, from calling Bramble a "physician satirist." Even then the tradition was fast decaying as a result of the new literary image of the medical man (Pope's Cheselden, Mead, and Arbuthnot). Sir John Colbatch, the Worcester physician whom George I knighted and at whose expense Garth found such cause for ridicule and mirth in canto 5 of *The Dispensary*, distinguished sharply between "the functions" of a satirist and physician. See *A Dialogue between Alkali and Acid* (1698; BM 1034, a. 12. 1). U. C. Knoepflmacher's title is misleading: "The Poet as Physician: Pope's Epistle to Dr. Arbuthnot," *Modern Language Quarterly* 31 (1970): 440–449. Nowhere does he suggest that the satirist (Pope) and physician (Arbuthnot) are the same, neither fictionally nor in real life. Much more curious than Smollett's relation to the tradition of the "physician satirist" is his ambivalent attitude in the novels to physicians: his heroes both adore them (the knight's long paean at the opening of chapter xxiv of *Launcelot Greaves*) and deplore them (Roderick's ordeals with Lavement in chapters xix–xx of *Roderick Random*).

22. Shakespeare, *The Taming of the Shrew*, Ind. Scene ii, pp. 131–144.

23. See Albrecht B. Strauss, "On Smollett's Language: A Paragraph in *Ferdinand Count Fathom*," *English Institute Essays* (1959), pp. 25–54.

24. See P. G. Boucé, "Eighteenth- and Nineteenth-Century Biographies of Smollett," *Tobias Smollett*, ed. G. S. Rousseau and P. G. Boucé (NYC, Oxford University Press, 1971), pp. 201–230. Boucé's essay chides biographers who have "read into" his fictional characters. This is a very different matter from the asking of Jacques Derrida's main question in his essay "Freud and the Life of Writing," namely, "what is a text, and what must the psyche be if it can be represented by a text?" We *must* continue to ask the question, and Boucé must also if he wishes to further his understanding of Smollett, "what are these novels, and what must Smollett's psyche have been if it will continue in literary criticism to be represented by these texts?" The answer of course depends upon the definition of "represented."

25. See G. D. Painter, *Marcel Proust: A Biography* (1959–1965).

26. Lewis M. Knapp, *Tobias Smollett* (Princeton, 1949), pp. 307–308.

27. Ibid., p. 4.

28. Adopted from Paul Fussell's title, *Samuel Johnson and the Life of Writing* (NYC, 1971).

29. See G. S. Rousseau, "Tobias Smollett," *Journal of the American Medical Association* 216 (1971): 85–89. Two other authors have sensed an unusually distraught psyche, the first in the representation of fathers and sons in Smollett's novels, the second in Smollett's fascinated attitude to crime and punishment. See William Park, "Fathers and Sons—*Humphry Clinker,*" *Literature and Psychology* 16 (1966): 166–174 and Angus Ross, "The Show of Violence' in Smollett's Novels," *Yearbook of English Studies* 2 (1972): 118–129. Ross's reading of Smollett is rather close to our anonymous critic's on pp. 14–15.

30. The point has been repeatedly made, the ephemera meticulously documented in Knapp's biography, and Smollett's Whig and Tory loyalty periodically questioned. For the most recent attempt, see Robin Fabel, "The Patriotic Briton: Tobias Smollett and English Politics, 1756–1771," *Eighteenth-Century Studies* 7 (1974): 100–114. Fabel is surely right to argue that in this period the labels Whig and Tory did not divide men according to any political ideology. Smollett's constant concerns were with issues (e.g., the national debt, subsidy of the House of Hanover, peace with France), not parties.

31. Smollett probably edited or wrote *A Free and candid Examination of a Pamphlet . . . of Mineral Waters* (1758) and *The Analyser analysed . . .* (1758). Smollett's role in the Rutty-Lucas controversy has been extensively surveyed by G. S. Rousseau in "Matt Bramble and the Sulphur Controversy in the Eighteenth Century: Some Medical Background of *Humphry Clinker,*" *Journal of the History of Ideas* 27 (1967): 577–589.

32. Smollett's targets in *Sir Launcelot Greaves* have recently been identified by G. S. Rousseau and Roger Hambridge in "Smollett and Politics: Originals for the Election Scenes in *Sir Launcelot Greaves,*" *English Language Notes* 14 (1976): 32–37. But this essay merely names figures and produces suggestions about Smollett's reasons for viewing the whole enterprise of electioneering with less than a sincere smile. Essays and books (e.g., Arnold Whitridge, *Tobias Smollett: A History of His Miscellaneous Works,* privately printed [1925]) that attempt to discover a consistent political point of view in Smollett's novels always disappoint.

33. See *Sir Launcelot Greaves,* chapter ix and the elaborate portrait of the Duke of Newcastle in *Humphry Clinker,* letters of 2 and 5 June. Ray Kelch, who had admirably surveyed the duke's career in *Newcastle, A Duke without Money: Thomas Pelham-Holles, 1693–1768* (University of California Press, 1974), has very little to say about the representation of Newcastle in Smollett's writings.

34. See *The Politics of Samuel Johnson* (Yale University Press, 1960).

35. James Boswell, *An Account of Corsica; The Journal of a tour to that island and memoirs of Pascal Paoli* (1768).

36. See Martin C. Battestin, *The Moral Basis of Fielding's Art* (Middletown, Conn., 1959) and, more recently, his learned edition of *Tom Jones* in the Wesleyan Fielding Edition (1975). Any book aimed at "the moral basis of Smollett's art" would have to look elsewhere than to sermons—to social conditions in town and country, to economic aspects of Georgian England; these, not religious ideas, fired up Smollett's satiric imagination.

37. Especially the private religion of Dorothea Brooke in *Middlemarch* (1871–1872) and Maggie Tulliver in *The Mill on the Floss* (1860), both third-person narratives unlike *Roderick Random, Peregrine* and *Humphry Clinker.*

38. As Thomas R. Preston has suggested in "Smollett and the Benevolent Misanthrope Type," *Publications of the Modern Language Association* 79 (1964): 51–57 and *Not in Timon's Manner: Feeling, Misanthropy, and Satire in Eighteenth-Century England* (University of Alabama Press, 1976), pp. 69–120. Of the latter Claude Rawson has written (*Times Literary Supplement,* 21 November 1975, 1381): "Since Smollett is one of Mr. Preston's main authors, and Matthew Bramble the culminating manifestation of the tradition he is describing, Mr. Preston devotes his longest chapter to a stultifying novel-by-novel run-through of Smollett's fiction, designed to chart the progress of the type until it 'reaches perfection' in Smollett's last novel. But in fact the

account reads like a set of bread-and-butter lecture notes, taking in all the usual points (relations with picaresque, travel-themes, country versus city) in a manner which seems more concerned with filling pages than advancing the argument." This plodding may be true; more consequential though to my argument is Preston's cubby-holing of Bramble into a neat label with accompanying tradition. Of course Bramble is a type of "benevolent misanthrope"; but he also belongs to many other types (the man of feeling, the hypochondriacal traveller, the splenetic humourist, the English squire undergoing change in his views of society as a result of changing social conditions, etc.), not least of these the new "nervous creature" of mid-Georgian England, somewhat anxious, highly irascible, perversely irritable, visibly eccentric, and always possessed of a most exquisitely "nervous constitution" (see *Humphry Clinker*, letter of 18 April).

39. Swift to Pope, 29 September 1725. See *The Correspondence of Jonathan Swift*, ed. H. Williams (Oxford, 1963–1965), III, 103.

40. See G. S. Rousseau, "Smollett and the Picaresque: Some Questions about a Label," *Studies in Burke and His Time* 12 (1971): 1886–1904.

41. In *A Sentimental Journey through France and Italy*, ed. Gardner D. Stout, Jr. (University of California Press, 1967), p. 116. See also Stout's very useful discussion of "Smelfungus Smollett" on pp. 32–35. Everyone mentions Sterne's allusion but usually without recognizing the reader its tone and details imply: a reader who has of course read Smollett's novels and who knows his reputation in general, but who is not so familiar with Smollett's splenetic side. How otherwise explain Sterne's celebrated caricature of Smollett? If Smollett's nervous sensibility and extraordinary irritability were common knowledge in 1768, why did English readers need to be told so again and why did Sterne need to say it once more so *straightforwardly?* This is hardly Sterne in one of his posing moods. The whole passage deserves restudy.

42. *Ferdinand Count Fathom* (1753), I, pp. iii–iv.

43. This raises again the question of Smollett's psyche and its representation in the selfhood and sensibility of his main characters. During this century, the pervasive line has been that Smollett-the-man was a Hobbesian or at least a Hobbesian-*manqué*, and that his characters reflect this in their antipathy to the role of feelings in shaping their moral integrity and selfhood. And yet this seems, at least to me, a partly distorted reading of the novels. If sensibility is construed in a broad sense, as capable of embracing ethical, moral, and even philosophical dimensions, then Smollett's main characters are certainly not hostile to the life of feelings and the capability of emotion to shape good, moral beings. As for Smollett-the-man, alive in the 1740s and 1750s, it is impossible to imagine, under any biographical circumstances, that he had not heard talk or read books about the various powers of sympathy. More interesting to me is the nature of "self" and "personal identity" in his imagined worlds. His main characters are defined almost exclusively in relation to their society—at what distance they are from an implied norm. Other than this they seem to have no self or other identity. To this degree, at least, Smollett was "Humean": Hume had been denying the existence of a "self" as anything other than the sum of individual actions. It doesn't matter whether Smollett actually *read* Hume's *Treatise of Human Nature* (1739–1740)—at the least, there is no way of proving or disproving it. More important is Smollett's sense of the self or identity of fictive characters. Although A. D. Nuttall does not mention Smollett in *A Common Sky: Philosophy and the Literary Imagination* (University of California Press, 1974), his sound treatment of solipsism in the eighteenth century should set all readers of Smollett's fiction thinking.

44. Carlyle's (1722–1805) role in Smollett's life remains somewhat murky. While Smollett confided some things to him (the events of the day, his yearning to return to Scotland), he apparently omitted others. Although Carlyle's *Autobiography*, first published in 1860, says much about Smollett, it reveals surprisingly little about the Smollett-Carlyle friendship and leaves readers wondering who were Smollett's best friends.

45. What were Smollett's interests *other* than literature? Knapp's biography (see above note 26) offers no clue, nor tells us what it *felt like* to be Smollett.

46. The whole episode is discussed by Edouard Rist in "Une consultation médicale au xviiie siècle," *Revue de Paris* 63 (1956): 112–125. Roger Fielding also deals with Smollett's psychosomatic illnesses in "Unlucky Doctor Smollett," *History of Medicine* 3 (1971): 11–12.

47. Ultimately P. G. Boucé's appealing phrase, "inverted autobiography," the process by which one reads in Smollett's life to his main characters (i.e., Bramble as Smollett), is a red herring. While it needed clear assertion in the 1960s when the state of Smollett scholarship was more primitive than it is today, it still leaves the big question, Derrida's question referred to above in note 24, unanswered. It would be nice if higher criticism were merely a matter of accumulating facts; see, for example, Olive Hamilton, "In Search of Smollett at Livorno," in *Paradise of Exiles: Tuscany and the British* (1974), pp. 49–61. Such efforts, while pleasant enough as recreations, have no interpretative value.

48. See T. R. Preston, "Disenchanting the Man of Feeling: Smollett's *Ferdinand Count Fathom*," in *Quick Springs of Sense*, ed. L. S. Champion (University of Georgia Press, 1974), pp. 223–239. While Preston repeats T. O. Treadwell's lucid insight about the dual struggle of forms in this novel, he seems unaware of, or if aware forgets to acknowledge, Treadwell's earlier essay; see T. O. Treadwell, "The Two Worlds of *Ferdinand Count Fathom*," in *Tobias Smollett*, ed. G. S. Rousseau and P. G. Boucé (Oxford University Press, 1971), pp. 131–153.

49. Philip Stevick, "Smollett's Picaresque Games," ibid., pp. 111–130.

50. See J. H. Buckley, *Seasons of Youth: The Bildungsroman from Dickens to Golding* (Harvard University Press, 1974), pp. 18–31, in which eighteenth-century novels are discussed.

51. Curiously, little has been written about this aspect of Smollett's fiction. The clearest (if brief) statement is by Robert Hopkins, "The Function of Grotesque in *Humphry Clinker*," *Huntington Quarterly* 32 (1969): 163–177. Actually the first of the four 1751 volumes of *Peregrine Pickle* contains the largest amount of concentrated "grotesque" material in any of Smollett's novels and deserves closer scrutiny in this regard than it has received.

52. See Sigmund Freud, "The Economic Problem of Masochism" (1924), in *The Standard Edition of the Complete Psychological Works of Sigmund Freud*, ed. and trans. James Strachey *et al.*, 23 vols. (London: The Hogarth Press, 1953–), xix, pp. 157–170.

53. The coy and wily Roderick Random is an exception, especially in chapter 19, the scene with Miss Snapper.

54. These sections of *Humphry Clinker* have been repeatedly discussed: see A. Shoumatoff, "Matthew Bramble's Rural Ideal," unpublished B.A. Honors Thesis, Harvard University, 1967; David L. Evans, "*Humphry Clinker*: Smollett's Tempered Augustanism," *Criticism* 3 (1967): 257–274; W. A. West, "Matt Bramble's Journey to Health," *Texas Studies in Language and Literature* 11 (1969): 1197–1208; and in a half dozen essays dealing with Smollett's attitude to Scotland. Here again is still another connection with Pope, for the reader who looks closely will see that Smollett's conception of an "Augustan myth" is close to Pope's (rather than Thomson's, Smollett's acquaintance), and that he has preserved many of Pope's notions about the enchanted grove and sacred wood of the country.

55. See *Peregrine Pickle* (1751), I, chapter xxvii.

56. Especially P. G. Boucé, G. S. Rousseau, M. E. Novak, and T. O. Treadwell. See also, for still another reservation about Smollett's use of picaresque techniques, Alice G. Fredman, "The Picaresque in Decline: Smollett's First Novel," in *English Writers of the Eighteenth Century*, ed. J. H. Middendorf (Columbia University Press, 1971), pp. 189–207.

57. I tried in 1970–1971 to formulate a scheme or "threshold of genres" for all Smollett's novels and could discover no principles of consistency. Some of the results of my toil were presented in the essay listed above in note 5.

58. See note 52.

59. Quoted on pp. 14–15.

60. And so is sadism, which deserves as much attention as masochism. From the very start Smollett had isolated these two aspects of behaviour—sadism and masochism—and endowed them with more energy than any of his contemporaries. The reader of *Ferdinand Count Fathom*, for example, is perpetually placed in the position of peeper: wondering if he has seen all, or if still more violence is to come. Only in *Humphry Clinker*, Smollett's last novel, is the sado-masochistic violence displaced and transferred to a dynamic process in which figures are hurt by grotesque aspects of the city, London, Bristol, Bath, Edinburgh, etc. Some perceptive comments on sado-

masochism in English fiction of this period are found in R. F. Brissenden, *Virtue in Distress* (1974), although without specific reference to Smollett.

61. Cause and effect, though, are in this case more complicated. Smollett's psyche notwithstanding, his fiction would doubtlessly have been different if he had lived a generation earlier (as a contemporary of Pope's), or later (as a contemporary of Chatterton, Godwin, and Blake); but this is true of all novelists. The point is not this at all but rather that Smollett's fictions are sensitive to, or alive to, certain economic and social changes very much evident in his time, and that extensive knowledge of these changes—never demonstrated by any of his students—would certainly illuminate his novels. Among these conditions 1740–1760 are: (a) shifts in the practice of Scottish presbyterianism; (b) the dispersion of wealth among a new class; (c) the effects of luxury on various social classes; (d) population changes in villages, towns, and cities; (e) urban planning, especially in the largest cities; (f) Wesleyanism and the evangelical revival of the 1740s and 1750s; (g) political corruption in the period of Newcastle's reign; (h) the stability of the self in a period of such local turmoil. There are different approaches to these problems: the works of Gordon Mingay shed much light, especially his book on *English Landed Society in the Eighteenth Century* (1963), or one can trace the history of a quasi-economic simile, as Louis A. Landa has done in "London Observed: The Progress of a Simile," *Philological Quarterly* 54 (1975): 275–288, which addresses itself to (d) above. But in either approach (there are others too) the question about illuminating a specific set of texts nevertheless arises: how to chart out the social and economic background in such manner that enhances a reading of Smollett's fiction?

62. His attempts to find technical language to describe this idea are abundantly evidenced by his cribbing of whole pages verbatim from Dr. William Battie's *Treatise on Madness* (1758) in *Launcelot Greaves* (1760–1761). The point has been made by every recent student of this novel, as well as in every book on madness in the eighteenth century. See, for example, Max Byrd, *Visits to Bedlam* (University of South Carolina Press, 1974), pp. 43–44, and W. Parry-Jones, *The Trade in Lunacy* (1972), chapter i *passim*. Less obvious, though, was Smollett's perpetual interest in the medical aspects of madness. As early as 1756 he had written in the first volume of the *Critical Review*— and as a digression within the context of the passage—"Dr. Mead observes that opium never assuages madness" (1, 1756: 385). Smollett was doubtlessly reading in the 1750s all types of books about madness, the same Smollett who would read in the next decade as preparation for his *Travels* such works as Bianchi's *Ragguaglio Delle Antichità e Rarità* (1759) and Travessac's *Abrégé de l'Histoire de la Ville de Nismes* (1760). He read to understand better his own nervous exhaustion in the early 1750s, later on for reviews he was writing, and at the end of the decade as necessary background for the mad characters and madhouses in *Launcelot Greaves*. One wonders in this last instance, and in view of Smollett's insistence that *Launcelot Greaves* was a "modern English *Don Quixote*," if Smollett had read books about the nature of madness in Cervantes' time. For example, did he know about the learned treatises after 1616 dealing with Quixote's brand of delusion? Had he read or heard of Vasari's disquisition on Leonardo's "romantic madness?"

63. They have never been gathered and discussed, and more than mere accumulation is needed. For example, Smollett's attack on the whole class of medical men is relentless and ultimately made on economic, not medical grounds. But no clarification about this vigorous attack will be forthcoming until historians document the precise lot of medical men, their numbers in Georgian England, their income in relation to its purchasing power, their social standing and religious attitudes, and, as far as can be generalized, their collective role as a professional class. Some preliminary steps have been taken by members of the Faculty of Sociology at the University of Leicester. See especially N. D. Jewson, "Eighteenth-Century Medical Theories: A Sociological Analysis," *Working Papers in Historical Sociology* No. 1 (1974). Smollett's attacks on certain social groups (physicians, lawyers) offer a sounder basis for understanding his economics than does a comparison of his general economic attitudes with those of the age. For example, Hume's essay *Of Luxury* (1752) will offer only limited help; ideas about luxury were being discussed in every quarter, and it is difficult to pinpoint a single source, or even series of sources, as Smollett's origin.

64. As diaries and letters of the period reveal. Smollett, unlike Sterne, seized upon money and harsh economic reality from the very start of his literary career: one of the

aspects of *Roderick Random* that distinguishes it from traditional picaresque fiction is its incessant concern for the making and losing of money.

65. As George Steiner sensed; see the epigraph above.

66. This matter will be fully treated with precise figures given in my introduction to *Peregrine Pickle* in the *Bicentennial Edition of the Works of Tobias Smollett*.

67. See William Scott, "Smollett, Dr. John Hill, and the *Failure of Peregrine Pickle*," *Notes & Queries* n.s. 2 (1955): 389–392.

68. *Ferdinand Count Fathom* (1753), I. pp. 138–139.

69. Ibid., I, v. Although several critics have suggested that such aesthetics of the novel permitted Smollett to give free reign to his satirical tendencies, ultimately his pronouncement here derives from theories about history painting current or popular *ca.* 1750.

70. This approach almost always leads to poor results. The argument usually proceeds as follows: (a) Smollett was not a great novelist himself; but (b) his influence on nineteenth-century comic novelists was so considerable that (c) this influence alone entitles him to a privileged position; therefore (d) his influences, not his novels, are at the centre of his achievement. This is to take us farther and farther from Smollett's own texts.

71. Pope, *Epistle to Bathurst*, 1.161–176.

72. H. Erskine-Hill, *The Social Milieu of Alexander Pope* (Yale University Press, 1975), especially chapter vii, "The Betrayal of Society."

73. Pope, *Epistle to Bathurst*, 1.145–152. This passage, probably composed in 1732, was written while Smollett was a young man and applies to the economic world he was entering.

74. Smollett's most common figures are "humourous" or Jonsonian, and in more cases than not they are evil, as their names suggest: in *Roderick Random* (Smollett's first novel) there are (among others) Weazel, Potion, Crab, Crampley, Cringer, Gawky, Gripewell, Lavement, Medlar, Narcissa, Quiverwit, Simper, Snapper, Straddle, Wagtail, Whiffle; in *Humphry Clinker* (Smollett's last novel) Blackerby, Bullock, Gill, Drab, Friponean, Hopeful, Prig, Tabby, Eastgate, Blackberry, Crumb, Ivy, Potatoe, Guy, Buzzard, Skinner, Macaroni *et al*.

75. Smollett, alone among his literary contemporaries, was uninterested in the new society. For his probable reasons, see G. S. Rousseau, "No Boasted Academy of Christendom': Smollett and the Society of Arts," *Journal of the Royal Society of Arts* 121 (1973): 468–475, 532–535, 623–628.

76. See Berkeley, "An Essay toward preventing the Ruin of Great Britain," in *The Works of George Berkeley Bishop of Cloyne*, ed. A. A. Luce and T. E. Jessop (1953), VI, p. 84.

77. This point raises the perpetual question of Smollett's use of rhetoric, and much more importantly, his relation to a tradition that may be loosely called "the rhetorical ideal of life." Smollett certainly does not belong to this tradition, as do Rabelais, Swift, Sterne, and perhaps Lewis Carroll, but he has enough commitments to the "ideal" to make the question worth asking. Furthermore, Smollett's style and rhetoric have never received anything approaching the close scrutiny Swift's has, especially in recent times by computer analysts (Milic *et al.*). I am most grateful to Ruth Mitchell (UCLA) who has performed the essential legwork on the computer from which to generalize cautiously about Smollett's style; the results of her work will be presented as an appendix to my annotated edition of *Peregrine Pickle*. Several critics have objected to Smollett's intensity of rhetorical figures; others find this a virtue. Two articles discuss the matter but should be read with extreme care: Gary N. Underwood, "Linguistic Realism in *Roderick Random*," *Journal of English and Germanic Philology* 69 (1970): 32–40, professes to have discovered "linguistic realism" in Smollett's style but never defines his key term, and T. Pratt, "Linguistics, Criticism, and Smollett's *Roderick Random*," *University of Toronto Quarterly* 42 (Fall 1972): 26–39, whose attempt to discover a "transformational grammar" for Smollett must be viewed by those with genuine background in linguistics. See also P. Stevick, "Stylistic Energy in the Early Smollett," *Studies in Philology* 64 (1967): 712–719 for some discussion of Smollett's rhetoric, and O. M. Brack and J. B. Davis, "Smollett's Revisions of *Roderick Random*." *Publications of the Bibliographical Society of America* 64 (1970): 295–311 for a sound treatment of Smollett-the-writer actually at work.

78. Mode, not genre; the first is much broader and less restrictive. The difficulty

with many studies of the so-called "genre" of Smollett's works is that neat categories are established which reduce his fiction embarrassingly. See, for example, S. Auty, *The Comic Spirit of Eighteenth-Century Novels* (Kennikat Press, 1975), chapter iv and Scott B. Rice, "Smollett's *Travels* and the Genre of Grand Tour Literature," *Costerus* 1 (1971): 207–220.

79. H. Erskine-Hill's essay, cited in note 72 above, tells us why; there is no similar essay of Smollett's social milieu.

80. See T. Gneiting, "Pictorial Imagery and Satiric Inversion in Pope's *Dunciad*," *Eighteenth-Century Studies* 8 (1975): 420–430, who studies Pope's use of Raphael, Titian and Veronese. Pope did more than "impose": he consciously attempted in the *Dunciad* to discover a new poetic form by a radically new conception of space, only partly Newtonian in origin and influenced by the ideas present in such then popular books as Edmund Law's *Enquiry into the Ideas of Space, Time, Immensity and Eternity* (Cambridge, 1734). Smollett's debt to the world of art glances elsewhere, notably to the traditions of caricature; see George Kahrl, "Smollett as a Caricaturist," in *Tobias Smollett*, ed. Rousseau and Boucé (Oxford University Press, 1971), pp. 169–200. But Smollett knew much more than this about European art, and during the time of composition of his *Travels* became something of a connoisseur on the art works in such cities as Paris, Nice, Rome.

81. As was especially evident in *Launcelot Greaves*. It is most curious that it took critics so long to see what Smollett was up to in that novel. In 1764, just three years after its publication, James Beattie, the Scottish philosopher-poet, compared *Launcelot Greaves* to *Don Quixote* in *Essay on Laughter and Ludicrous Composition*. But the comparison seems to have died afterwards and was not revived until 1797 when John Moore, Smollett's editor and biographer, took it up. After this it was repeated by every critic to the present time and almost universally to Smollett's disadvantage.

82. *Roderick Random* (1747), chapter xxii, the prominent opening sentence.

83. See H. Erskine-Hill, "Pope and the Financial Revolution," in *Alexander Pope*, ed. P. Dixon (Ohio University Press, 1975, 2nd ed.), p. 228.

84. First the war with Spain, and then the much longer War of the Austrian Succession. Smollett comments extensively on the economic aspects at home caused by the wars in his *History of England*.

85. See Chester Chapin, "Alexander Pope: Erasmian Catholic," *Eighteenth-Century Studies* 6 (1973): 411–430, and Erskine-Hill's discussion of the idea in *The Social Milieu of Alexander Pope* (1975), pp. 66–67.

86. Pope's politics are not in question here, Smollett's are. In his own time Thomas Birch thought that Smollett was a Tory and wrote about his belief to his "Saturday correspondent" Philip Yorke. Since then, the legend has persisted but without much evidence. Recently D. J. Greene has closely examined Smollett's *History* and concluded that he was a "skeptic" rather than a "Tory": "Smollett's skepticism as an historian, it can be confidently maintained, on the basis of a comparative sampling of the two works [Smollett's and Hume's *History*], is certainly no less than Hume's. Mossner's argument, however, has not prevented authors of manuals of literary history from continuing to parrot the old phrase, Hume's 'Tory history.' Smollett has suffered even more, since even fewer modern commentators on his work have bothered to read it before settling this judgment on it" ("Smollett the Historian," in *Tobias Smollett*, ed. Rousseau and Boucé, 1971, p. 46). Still more recently, Robin Fabel has ably argued that Smollett's politics were based upon "issues rather than party labels" in "The Patriotic Briton: Tobias Smollett and English Politics, 1756–1771," *Eighteenth-Century Studies* 7 (1974): 100–114. Both arguments caution future students not to repeat the glib old saw about Smollett's Tory allegiance, but neither can explain how Smollett came to work for Bute in 1761, or how he could conceivably have written in the *Continuation of the Complete History of England* (1760–65), V, p. 211: ". . . a periodical publication of a paper called the *North Briton*, which was insolent and attrocious beyond the example of all former oppositions, in the most distempered periods of government." Concerning the first problem, the best guess has been that George Bubb Dodington, the patron of James Ralph, recruited Smollett, but it is equally possible that Smollett was hired by Henry Fox through his chaplain and political scribe Dr. Philip Francis (translator of Horace and father of Philip Francis of Junius fame). The latter is especially likely in view of Smollett's relations with the elder Pitt.

87. To the Ricardians, not to Bentham and J. S. Mill or Adam Smith's mercan-

tilism. Jacob Viner has put forward some of the profound questions in "Man's Economic Status," in *Man Versus Society in Eighteenth-Century Britain* (Cambridge University Press, 1968), pp. 22–54 but Smollett is not mentioned.

88. *All* Smollett's references to luxury deserve to be brought together so that his attitude to this popular topic of discussion can be settled once and for all. Anti-luxury passages, like the one in which Tom Clarke describes the hero of *Launcelot Greaves*, should also be considered:

> . . . he always had plenty of cash for the asking as my father was ordered to supply him liberally, the knight thinking that a command of money might help to raise his thoughts to a proper consideration of his own importance. He never could endure a common beggar, that was either in a state of infancy or of old age; but, in other respects, he made the guineas fly in such a manner, as looked more like madness than generosity. He had no communication with your rich yeomen; but rather treated them and their families with studied contempt, because forsooth they pretended to assume the dress and manners of the gentry: they kept their footmen, their saddle-horses, and chaises: their sattins, their negligees and trollopees; their clumsey shanks, like so many shins of beef, were cased in silk-hose and embroidered slippers: their red raw fingers, gross as the pipes of a chamber-organ, which had been employed in milching the cows, in twirling the mop or churnstaff, being adorned with diamonds, were taught to thrum the pandola, and even to touch the keys of the harpsichord . . . I have heard Mr. Greaves ridicule them for their vanity . . . (*Launcelot Greaves*, 1760–1761, I, 126).

See also Smollett, *Complete History of England* (1762–1765), IV, p. 93 and *Continuation* (1765, I, pp. 56, 128). Berkeley's concluding paragraphs in *An Essay toward preventing the Ruin of Great Britain* (1721), especially their imagery of jumbling, should be compared with Bramble's letter to Dr. Lewis dated 29 May in *Humphry Clinker:* ". . . every trader in any degree of credit . . . in short, there is no distinction or subordination left—The different departments of life are jumbled together." Some of Smollett's anti-luxury ideas were stimulated by the medical effects of luxury on health; see, for example, Dr. George Cheyne's *The English Malady* (1733)—a book Smollett knew well—pp. ii, 28–29, 49–52, 59, 158–159, 174.

89. By "learned" I mean primarily in the literary sense, i.e., in the way Jane Austen "learned" about plot and character from Samuel Richardson. Cervantes, Pope, and Fielding were Smollett's "teachers," not Rabelais or Swift. And yet it is surprising that Smollett was not more impressed by Swift's *persona*, irony, and the possibility his texts offered for instant paradox. Daniel Turner, M.D., a colleague of Smollett's, although a much weaker stylist, quickly discovered in Swift a master of prose to be imitated. See D. Turner, *A Remarkable Case in Surgery* (1709), p. viii: "But leaving these Romantick Boasters, amongst Knaves and Fools, the bare mentioning of whom I fear is a Trespass upon your Patience: I hope 'tis now no novel Assertion, if I do affirm, that the wounded Brain is conditionately [sic] curable . . ." and the rest of this passage parodying Swift's "Digression on Madness" (IX) in *A Tale of a Tub*. Smollett apparently did not see the possibilities of such parody in *Launcelot Greaves* in which madness is such an important concern.

90. I am of course thinking of Harold Bloom's challenge to the modern literate world in defence of "misreading": "Poetic history, in this book's argument, is held to be indistinguishable from poetic influence, since strong poets make that history by misreading one another, so as to clear imaginative space for themselves" (introduction to *The Anxiety of Influence: A Theory of Poetry*, Oxford University Press, 1973, p. 5).

91. The seventy first, J. Melford to Sir Watkins Phillips, in which Matt Bramble comes close to death "by water" and is symbolically regenerated at "Mr. Dennison's estate." The eighty-two letters in *Humphry Clinker* would seem to lend themselves to all sorts of external analyses yet most neat arrangements ultimately prove Procrustean. See Scott Garrow, "A Study of the Organization of Smollett's . . . *Humphry Clinker*," *The Southern Quarterly* 1 (1966): 349–364; 22–46. Smollett scrupulously plots out certain details—the only undated letter, the fact that each major figure's surname contains exactly seven letters (BRAMBLE, MELFORD, JENKINS, CLINKER), the strange appearance of figures (Random, Grieves from *Count Fathom*, Dr. ---------- from *Peregrine Pickle*, etc.) from all five previous novels, and the further—astonishing —fact that if *Humphry Clinker* is divided into its seven natural geographical sections,

each section is discovered to comment *chronologically* on each of Smollett's six previous works, section seven, the reconciliation section, corresponding to *Humphry Clinker* itself—but not enough details to add up to complete coherence or to permit a brilliant "new-critical reading" *à la Tom Jones, The Rime of the Ancient Mariner*, or *Ulysses*. This is what is so tantalizing about *Humphry Clinker*.

92. See, for example, the long chapter on Smollett in Douglas Brooks, *Number and Pattern in the Eighteenth-Century Novel* (1973), pp. 123–159. I realize perfectly well that "baroque economics" has not been defined here—this is not the proper place, nor is there space. Actually "ornamental economic design" approximates Smollett's intentions better since "baroque" suggests period associations not helpful here. When I originally settled on the term "baroque" I allowed it because it embodied those characteristics of energy, elaborate ornamentation, and contrasting effect so very evident in Smollett's later works as well as in his particular brand of Methodism.

93. Most histories of English fiction are culpable here, even as penetrating a student of the novel as Ian Watt in *The Rise of the Novel* (University of California Press, 1962).

94. See above, note 52.

95. Not only the Chicagoans but all major "schools." Overlooking for the moment the fact that novelists write to be appreciated by individual readers, not studied by "schools of criticism," it is still probably true to say that Smollett's fiction lends itself best to Marxist or quasi-socialist criticism. I have no doubt that a critic like the Hungarian Georg Lukács would know very well what to say about Smollett and his "alienated figures." Perhaps it is true: formalism has no means by which to cope with Smollett's degree of alienation, his person and his figures.

96. See above, note 16.

97. See Bloom's prophetic allegorical essay, *Kabbalah and Criticism* (NYC, The Seabury Press, 1975).

98. In still another prophetic essay referred to in note 76 above.

99. *Ferdinand Count Fathom* (1753), I, pp. vi–vii.

VIII

Quackery and Charlatanry
in Some Eighteenth-Century Novels,
Especially in Smollett

I

The history of quackery in Britain, especially in the eighteenth century remains to be written. Two books purport to treat the subject, perhaps even to exhaust it: Eric Jameson's *The Natural History of Quackery* (1961) and Grete de Francesco's *The Power of the Charlatan* (1939). Yet the eighteenth century, an era in which quackery flourished to an unprecedented degree, for some reasons suggested later, is shabbily treated in these books; and one author, Tobias Smollett, the brilliant prose stylist with an historical and sociological flair, is never mentioned at all. This omission is startling considering that Smollett, of all the writers of the mid-Georgian period, is the first author to whom anyone knowledgeable would turn if he wished to find an anatomy of charlatanry at that time. We cannot survey all Smollett's charlatans; instead we discuss his two most interesting ones, in part because each is representative of a typology of charlatans evident in Smollett's writings, and in part because we may have identified hitherto unknown originals for each.

II

Of all the characters who comprise the main cast of Smollett's *Sir Launcelot Greaves* (1760–1761), the most engaging is the cynical, protean misanthrope Ferret. His Hobbesian philosophy of life and his ability to disguise himself—hence the protean description—call to mind his literary ancestors in Smollett's previous novels, especially Cadwallader Crabtree in *Peregrine Pickle* and, on a grander scale, Ferdinand Count Fathom.[1] In addition to his representation as the "Timoanin misanthrope" of *Sir Launcelot Greaves*,[2] Ferret is interesting because he is thought to have been drawn from a real-life original, Smollett's inveterate enemy Doctor John Shebbeare (1709–1788).

Smollett and Shebbeare need to be related meaningfully. Although the conduct of domestic and foreign policy during the Seven Years' War was exposed and defended by a multitude of partisan hacks, those who have compared the form and content of Shebbeare's political writings, particularly his series of *Letters to the People of England* issued at intervals during 1755–1758, with Ferret's compulsive political harangues, have noted their essential similarity.[3] If an awareness of Smollett's suspicions expressed in his reviews of Shebbeare's *Letters* . . . is added to a familiarity of the exchanges between the two men, it is easy to see why Smollett wanted to satirize Shebbeare. And not only satirize him, but in such an extended manner. Having established this much, a number of questions about Ferret's character remain unanswered. If he had appeared only in the first several chapters of the novel set at the Black Lion Inn, critics could point to Shebbeare's political writings, his feud with Smollett, and explain Ferret as a satire on a persistent enemy. In fact this case has been made; yet an unanswered question remains: why does Ferret reappear as an itinerant mountebank in chapter ten and how did Smollett go about creating Ferret's very complex character?

Sir Launcelot Greaves finished its serialised run in the *British Magazine* in 1761. James R. Foster has presented the best account of Smollett's relationship with Shebbeare from the early 1750s until *ca.* 1770, that is including the years when Smollett was editing the *British Magazine*.[4] In his account of the continuing battle between the two men, Foster makes use of the *Critical Review* mainly as a chronicle of the feud's progress. His primary concern is to present the available information about Shebbeare's life, works and opinions. References to the *Critical Review* serve primarily to elucidate Shebbeare's political views while tracing the attacks and counter-attacks that marked each stage of the logomachy. Direct quotation of the *ad hominem* attacks in Smollett's reviews are confined to comparisons of Shebbeare to lunatics and even fishmongers. While such characterizations possess relevance to one of *Sir Launcelot Greaves's* major motifs, madness, they reveal nothing about Ferret-the-quack and probably have more connection with the conventional rhetoric of eighteenth-century pamphlet warfare than with the composition of *Launcelot Greaves*. Concerning Ferret-the-quack: Foster suggests, somewhat optimistically, that Smollett may have been aware of, and credited, the uncorroborated report that Shebbeare dabbled in alchemy during 1736 to 1748 while in Bristol.[5] A close inspection of Smollett's reviews of Shebbeare's works and of his sarcastic references to Shebbeare in reviews of works by others provides materials that shed light on the origins of Ferret/Shebbeare-the-quack and also on Smollett's method of composition.[6] Such a survey indicates that when Smollett chose to present Ferret as an itinerant mountebank and fortune-teller, he was reifying a metaphorical similitude: one that he had begun to sketch in the *Critical Review* in 1756. This partook of a comparison that had become commonplace among eighteenth-century satirists and social commentators.

When Smollett reviewed Shebbeare's *Third Letter to the People of England* . . . in the initial number of the *Critical Review*[7] he allowed that "perhaps there may be some truth in what this monitor advances," but he questioned Shebbeare's honesty and motivation:

> His production is not the language of sincerity and true patriotism, but the raving of spleen and disappointment. He is not the real person he represents, but *a poor player, who struts and frets his hour upon the stage, and then is heard no more.* He either does not understand his subject, or he purposely makes absurd inferences and false calculations . . . (p. 89).

In the months between this review and that of the *Fourth Letter* . . . in the August 1756 number (*Critical Review*, II, pp. 35–44), Smollett persuaded himself of Shebbeare's self-serving intentions. He also reconsidered his comparison of Shebbeare: he remained a person performing a role but the deceitful motive behind the deception was clarified. In this review Shebbeare is labelled "an empiric in language as well as in politics" (p. 35); in the final chapter of *Sir Launcelot Greaves*, Smollett calls Ferret "the empirical politician."[8] Smollett, by positing a similarity between rhetorical strategies of political oratory and the equally shameless ploys practised by quacks, mountebanks and empirics, was endorsing a view that had become commonplace by mid-century.[9] After listening to Ferret's harangue, Sir Launcelot observes that Ferret "mixed some melancholy truths with his scurrility,"[10] and there is little doubt that one of those truths is his insistence that "the kingdom is full of mountebanks, empirics, and quacks . . . quacks in religion, quacks in physic, quacks in law, [and] quacks in politics . . ."[11]

Smollett's sensitivity to this apparent plague of quacks is also evidenced in reviews of works by authors other than Shebbeare: most importantly in reviews of balneological treatises. There is good reason to think that Smollett connected Shebbeare's career with that of the equally controversial Dr. Charles Lucas (1713–1771). Like Shebbeare, he had transformed himself from apothecary to doctor, a significant progression in mid-Georgian England; he was also a chemist who shared Shebbeare's almost compulsive interest in political rhetoric. The review in the March 1756 number of the

Critical Review (I, pp. 169–70) roundly condemns Lucas's *Appeal to the Commons and Citizens of London*. Its strategy is to provide a clear historical background of the nefarious circumstances of Lucas's arrival in England eight years previously. Just as Ferret's presence in the north of England is explained by his having "received intimation of a warrant from the secretary of state, who wanted to be better acquainted with his person,"[12] Lucas's flight from Ireland, we are told, was to avoid arrest and confinement:

> This gentleman, heretofore an apothecary in *Dublin*, and now a doctor and chemist, in consequence of a transformation very common in these days, was by the parliament of *Ireland* unanimously voted an enemy to his country, for having, in certain printed papers, scandalously and maliciously misrepresented the proceedings of the house of commons, and highly reflected on the honour and dignity thereof. If was at the same time resolved, that he should, upon Mr. Speaker's warrant, be committed close prisoner to the common Jail. But this warrant he very wisely eluded by a well conducted and immediate retreat.[13]

Similarly, just as Ferret is accused of having joined the "desperate emissaries of a party endeavor[ing] to poison the minds of his Majesty's subjects . . . who act as emissaries of France both in word and writing . . . and scatter the seeds of dissatisfaction through the land,"[14] Lucas is labelled "a turbulent partisan, who wanted to fish in troubled waters; who having miscarried in his own country, endeavours to foment factions and disturbance in the city of *London*."[15]

Although Shebbeare is neither explicitly mentioned nor cunningly alluded to in this review, Smollett's review of Lucas's *Essay on Waters* published two months later (*Critical Review*, I, May 1756, pp. 321–45) is an entirely different matter. It makes quite clear that he viewed the two men—Shebbeare and Lucas—as separate manifestations of the same phenomenon, and it does so by lacing itself with irony. Perhaps its opening passage lends some idea of the whole thing:

> Nature still continues to produce great and stupendous geniuses, howsoever they may be overlooked or opposed by the ignorance of envy of mankind. Two such have lately appeared like comets in our hemisphere; in the contemplation of whose labours, we know not whether most to admire, the acuteness of perception, the extent of learning, the strength and solidity of argument, the candour, modesty, patriotism, or singularity in station, study and circumstance, that denote them so consummate and congenial. Both have shone like *Phosphorus* amidst the mists of ignorance and prejudice: both have corroded like the *lapis infernalis*, an imposthumated administration big with foulness and corruption; and

both have been overwhelmed and well-nigh dissolved in the discharge that ensued. Many moons have not revolved since one of these illustrious adepts obliged the world with a performance, in which he plainly demonstrated the absurdity of the practice adopted by all his contemporaries, and blew up their whole medical system by means of a mine kindled with electrical fire.[16] Thus illuminated, the subject has been considered in a new light, the whole faculty begin to study the doctrines of the ancient magi; and doctor *Sh*[ebbeare] (as he himself prophesied) shines forth the second founder of the healing art.

That judicious reformer's worthy compere [sic] is the learned author of the treatise which now falls under our examination.

During this lengthy review of almost 15,000 words Smollett excoriates Lucas's immodesty. He charges him with plagiarism from predecessors such as Aristotle, Dioscorides, Celsus, Van Helmont, Boerhaave, and Paracelsus Bombast. Lucas, according to Smollett, has not even had the decency to acknowledge his debt to forbears. By this means the whole review takes a side in the "Ancients–Modern" medical controversy set off thirty years earlier by Dr. John Freind's *History of Physick; from the time of Galen to the beginning of the sixteenth century* (1725–26). Smollett does not go so far as Louis Dutens a few years later in a 459–page *Enquiry into the Origin of the Discoveries Attributed to the Moderns. Wherein it is Demonstrated, that our most celebrated Philosophers have, for the most Part, taken what they advance from the Works of the Ancients* (1769)—attempting to prove that Newton's law of universal gravity was known to Plutarch and Lucretius, and his theory of colours to Pythagoras and Plato. But Smollett still makes his case against Lucas. The list of ancient and modern balneological authorities in this long review extends to more than two dozen names and includes most of those Ferret attacks in his harangue to the mob.[17] Moreover Smollett devotes over a page to what he calls "the great pains the author [Lucas] has taken to reform the orthography of the English tongue; and a few other singularities which may conduce, if not to the instruction, at least to the entertainment of the reader."[18]

Smollett's sardonic reference to Shebbeare's radical theory about "electrical fire" indicates familiarity of some type with Shebbeare's *Practice of Physic*, 2 Vols. (1755). In view of Smollett's interest in balneology it is likely, not merely possible, that he also knew Shebbeare's *New Analysis of the Bristol Waters* which had been published in 1740.[19] Because Shebbeare's chemical analysis of those waters produced no evidence of sulphur, he had allied himself with balneologists (including Lucas) who advanced theories denying the presence of sulphur in Bath and Bristol waters. Consequently

Shebbeare opposed the medical theories of such adversaries as Diederich Wessel Linden, Alexander Sutherland, Dr. John Rutty and Tobias Smollett himself. The last mentioned had followed this controversy for more than two decades, had indeed taken a part in the mid-fifties.[20] The publication of Lucas's *Essay on Waters* led to yet another flare-up of the "sulphur controversy," and Smollett is now known to have had a hand in the pamphlet war that raged during 1757–58 occasioned by Dr. John Rutty's publication of a *Methodical Synopsis of Mineral Waters* in late summer 1757.[21] Years later Smollett remembered with passion the opposing sides and delineated them satirically in the opening pages of *Humphry Clinker*. For him the matter was scientific and political in the same degree: over three decades he had seen positions taken—as in the case of Shebbeare—for political reasons and not only for reasons related to objective veracity.

Smollett's review of Shebbeare's *Fifth Letter* . . . appeared in the same number of the *Critical Review* that praised Rutty's work and savagely ridiculed Lucas's attack on it.[22] Here Shebbeare is once again labelled a quack. This time Smollett amplifies the similitude, expanding on his previous sketches in a savage attack that demonstrates his sense of the *modus operandi* of quackish medical men. One passage in particular offers a sense of Smollett's harsh tone:

Again our political quack appears in public, and with effrontery exhorts the good people of *England*, who are in hazard of perishing, to follow his prescriptions, if they have any regard for their own welfare. *Itaque ite mecum, qui & vosmetipsos, (salvos) & rempublicam salvam vultus. (vid.* title page). Like all other quacks, he loves to be mysterious, and therefore addresses us in *Greek*, which he has even adulterated in transcribing, so great is his love for misrepresentation, or ignorance in that language. That he may fill the poor gaping crowd with ideas of his own importance, he begins with a furious and a railing harangue full of high sounding metaphors, in which, without any decency, he abuses his superiors, dictates to them in a swaggering magisterial manner, and at length concludes with assuring us, "that the nation is now agonizing at the last gasp, drained to the last drop by the miserable transfusion of the vital power of *England* into *Germany*." Miserable state! nevertheless he says, take but his two shilling remedy, he offers to the public from mere disinterested motives, and all will be well. How greatly is the nation obliged to this worthy doctor, who with great modesty declares himself the saviour of a lost people? However, as his remedy is much more nauseous than salutary, we counsel our readers not to throw away their money upon such trash, which is more apt to create a distemper than to procure health.[23]

Commentary such as this is unusual even for the irritable and splenetic Dr. Smollett. At the very least it reveals how profoundly Shebbeare and all he represented had jolted Smollett. At about the same time Smollett was embroiled in the Rutty–Lucus controversy (1757–58), an amusing notice appeared in the *Critical Review*. Though brief it conjoins Shebbeare the politician, Shebbeare the balneologist, and Shebbeare the potion peddler. The review, written in an ironic style not unlike Smollett's, deflates claims made by the anonymous author of *An Exposition of the virtues of the all-healing mixture, which powerfully removes, and certainly prevents, in every stage of life, the disorders incident to both sexes. . . .* The reviewer begins without reference to Shebbeare:

> If we may believe the assertions contained in this performance, the temple of immortality is opened by Thomas Norris, at the Golden Head, the south-side of St. Paul's Church-yard, and no where else: and he who chooses to die the death of nature, rather than walk in and drink of *the all-healing mixture*, must be accessary to his own destruction.[24]

But soon the reviewer's intentions are made known:

> This admirable medicine will soon repair that waste of men, by which Dr. Brakenridge has proved the number of our people diminished. Nay, we shall be in danger of becoming too populous, if Mr. Thomas Norris, at the end of some centuries, should not think it proper to break the charm. As this sovereign mixture equals in virtue the famous balsam of Tuerabas, the soldiers that march to battle, may be supplied with small canteens filled with it; and if a man swallow a gulp, after he is shot through the head with a musket-ball, his life may be saved. The nation will never want a Sh[ebbear]e to reform a weak or wicked ministry; and the same cobbler will sing in the same stall to the day of resurrection.[25]

It is clear that Smollett continued to think of Shebbeare within a context of quackery even after the publication of *Sir Launcelot Greaves*. This is evident in his characterization of Shebbeare in the *Adventures of an Atom* (1769) as "an empiric who had out-lived his practice." In brief, Smollett's decision to satirize Shebbeare by presenting Ferret as an itinerant mountebank hawking an "Elixir of Long Life" reflects Smollett's earlier assessment of Shebbeare's public career. Shebbeare the private man held no interest for Smollett; it was Shebbeare's tactics on the platform and on the printed page that vexed and angered Smollett. That Shebbeare may have dabbled in alchemy in the 1740s could add further colour to a character already sullied in Smollett's eyes. We cannot be positively assured that Smollett possessed knowledge of these dubious alchemical activities; but so far as Smollett was concerned, Shebbeare's medical and political activities had placed him in the ever-increasing ranks of charlatans whose practises were destroying England's basic fabric at a time when she seemed to have reached the zenith of civilization. Smollett could not have agreed with Dryden in *Mac Flecknoe* that a single playwright, Thomas Shadwell, had caused any palpable decline in the national vitality; nor could he fully agree with Pope's *Dunciad*, which he greatly admired, that the heart of English decadence was geographically, symbolically, and literally centred in Grub Street. Smollett saw something more ominous on the English horizon: a debasing turn for the worse in politics, a recent decay threatening the continuance of English civilization. If he could have debated with Dryden or Pope, he might have contended that this was now another England requiring another rhetoric altogether.

III

Smollett's second representative charlatan is altogether different and appears in an earlier novel, *The Adventures of Ferdinand Count Fathom*. The notion of an original for the anti-hero of *Ferdinand Count Fathom* (1753) may seem odd in light of Smollett's contention in the Dedication that Count Fathom is a typological villain, the epitome of evil.[26] This notwithstanding, a large amount of circumstantial evidence suggests that when Smollett was creating his "hero" his attention was drawn especially to one man and to the many conflicting and contradictory accounts that circulated concerning him since his arrival in England in about 1743. The Count Saint-Germain (?-1784) was one of the most spectacularly successful charlatans of the eighteenth century, far more notorious than Shebbeare or any one else associated with the villainous Count Fathom. Though not, perhaps, as well known as Mesmer or Cagliostro, Saint-Germain frequented and captivated the courts of Europe for a generation. Nowhere, though, was his career followed with more avid interest than in England.

Concerning his life little is known with certainty, particularly of his early years.[27] He is known to have been at The Hague in 1735; but neither the nature of his business there nor the length of his stay is known.[28] According to Horace Walpole, who met him on at least one occasion, he arrived in England sometime late in 1743. The length of his stay is shrouded in mystery: sudden departures are an occupational hazard of a career in charlatanry; and he was still very popular in 1748 when an English song he had composed was thought sufficiently fashionable to warrant its being printed in the *Gentleman's*

Magazine.[29] Whether he exploited his popularity to enhance the fortunes of his favourite confidence scheme, the industrial hoax usually involving the production of luxury goods from *ersatz* materials, appears not to have been recorded; at least it has eluded an extensive search in American and European libraries. It is also possible that Saint-Germain may have been operating as a French informant: such a suspicion had surfaced during the Jacobite rising of 1745 and the fact that he next appears in 1759, as a favourite of the Pompadour, and in the following year playing a brief and puzzling role as a French diplomat in the negotiations for peace between France and England at The Hague, seems to lend plausibility to the conjecture. After dismissal from the French Court in 1761 or thereabout he disappears yet again, but in 1763 he surfaces in Brussels. There he succeeded in extracting almost two hundred thousand gulden from Count Carl Cobenzl, Minister Plenipotentiary in the Austrian Netherlands, in exchange for "industrial secrets," apparently with the approval of the Statthalter of the Netherlands, Prince Charles of Lorraine. Still later Saint-Germain turns up in Russia and Italy, and during 1774–1776 he is known to be residing at the court of the Margrave of Ansbach, Karl Alexander (1736–1806), in Germany. He is said to have died at Eckernförde,[30] near Kiel in Holstein, in 1784, though at what age no one knows.

Resemblances between Count Saint-Germain and Count Fathom are not, to be sure, exact: considered individually some similarities may be dismissed as part and parcel of the charlatan type so familiar in Europe from the Renaissance onward. And even if the similarities were exact, the resemblance could not extend beyond Fathom's entrapment by the rapacious Trapwells in Chapter XXXVI, the halfway point in the novel. What seems most significant, however, are the number of idiosyncratic resemblances: can it be, we ask, that all these are mere chance, merely the result of a common typology of the charlatan? It is after all possible, and perhaps even probable, that Smollett, having decided to depict Fathom practising successfully amongst the English aristocracy and upper classes, may have seen the value of giving his anti-hero some unmistakable resemblances to a real figure who had proved that such success was possible. A dimension of realism would be added; besides, Smollett had done exactly that in his two previous novels, *Roderick Random* and *Peregrine Pickle*, where the technique was applauded.

Some of the compelling similarities are worth considering. Fathom's origins remain a puzzle to the English: upon arrival he assumes the title of "Count Fathom from Germany" and proceeds to act out his appointed role. Efforts made by his jealous "brother sharpers" to uncover his background prove fruitless:

In vain they strove to discover his pedigree, and detect the particular circumstances of his life and conversation; all their inquiries were baffled by the obscurity of his origin, and that solitary scheme which he had adopted in the beginning of his career. The whole fruit of their investigation, amounted to no more than a certainty that there was no family of any consideration in Europe, known by the denomination of Fathom; and this discovery they did not fail to divulge for the benefit of our adventurer, who had by this time, taken such firm root in the favour of the great, as to set all those little arts at defiance; and when the report reached his ear, actually made his friends merry with the conjectures which had been circulated at his expence.[31]

When two English sharpers return from the Continent and circulate reports about his previous identity as "Count Fadome from Poland," Fathom maintains the appearance of being untroubled. The Count Saint-Germain's origins also mystified the English public: in fact from all reports the number of different stories that circulated concerning his past seemed to gratify him and heighten his sense of self-importance. Horace Walpole describes his arrival:

In the year 1743 or thereabouts there came into England a person who called himself Count St. Germain, which he owned was not his name, but would never own what was, nor give any account of himself, nor could it be discovered who he was. He had little or no colour, his hair and beard were extremely black. He dressed magnificently, had several jewels, large remittances but made no other figure.[32]

Walpole, writing to Mann in December 1745, catalogues some of the various conjectures then being made about the Count's past: "he is called an Italian, a Spaniard, a Pole; a somebody that married a great fortune in Mexico, and ran away with her jewels to Constantinople; a priest, fiddler, a vast nobleman."[33] At various times the Count assumed other names including the Marquis de la Croix Noire, Comte Surmont, and Count Welldone.[34] So, too, did Count Fathom, as Smollett makes abundantly plain.

Both figures possess a number of common talents. In addition to their cultivation of a sense of mystery about their past, both possess a flair for grasping the dramatic moment; and both cultivate a poised and dramatically assertive personality that is the *sine qua non* of the high-class imposter; especially in England. On a number of occasions Smollett points out Fathom's ability to simulate expertise in political, mathematical, military or artistic matters.[35] Walpole finally concluded that Saint-Germain must be "a man of quality who had been in or designed for the Church." He also found the Count to be a brilliant raconteur whose table talk was memorable: "he had parts, was said to understand the mathematics, had apparently much scholastic knowledge, and was a vehement disputant." Walpole goes on to note that Saint-Germain "had been a great traveller, spoke Italian and French with the greatest facility, though it was evident that neither was his language; he understood Polish, and soon learnt to understand English and talk it a little. . . . But Spanish or Portuguese seemed his natural language . . ."[36] Fathom too is a master of several languages: in chapter XVIII Smollett reports that Fathom became a "master of the French tongue, and learned to speak Italian with great facility."[37] In addition to English and Polish—the languages, respectively, of his parents and foster parents—he also demonstrates competence in "high-Dutch, Italian, Hungarian, and Latin."

Even more compelling are their particular musical accomplishments. Walpole records that Saint-Germain's chief talent lay in music: "he sung in a most agreeable taste, but with little or no voice, composed genteely, particularly several songs for the operas here, *musique raisonnée*, and played exquisitely on the violin. . . . He was too great a musician not to have been famous if he had not been a gentleman."[38] While Walpole was not a skilled musician himself, he was nevertheless a connoisseur as his letters reveal on many occasions. Nor was he the kind of dupe to be taken in by a performer, especially by someone with as bizarre a past as Saint-Germain, unless his musical technique were truly extraordinary. Fathom's musical abilities are also well developed in Smollett's novel. Early in life he became "proficient in playing the violin"[39] and he sharpened these talents and greatly refined them before coming to England by posing as a fiddler. Soon after his arrival in London, the aristocracy is agreed that Count Fathom "sung with great melody and taste, and played upon the violin with surprizing execution."[40]

Several other similarities also deserve attention. Although Saint-Germain generally avoided medicines, he did have strong medical opinions which he dispensed in much the same manner Fathom employs when practising for his own amusement at Bristol Hot Well prior to becoming ensnared by the Trapwells. Moreover, Saint-Germain continually advocated, according to several biographers, that "health depended on the delicate balance of the 'life machine.' " Walpole reports that the Count distributed medicines, in particular a costly "rejuvenation water," gratis to women.[41]

In conclusion we can only speculate about Smollett's source or sources for his knowledge of Saint-Germain. The Count appears to have remained in England until 1750, and the many myths and stories about him surely circulated widely. Walpole records that the Count was on intimate terms with Lord and Lady Chesterfield, and this is just the kind of fact that Walpole usually gets positively right. Therefore, it is possible, although this cannot be proved, that Smollett met the Count in 1746 or 1747 when he was seeking Chesterfield's assistance in getting *The Regicide* produced.[42] A further possibility—although it remains just this until proved—is that Smollett, who had few aristocratic connections, may have derived his information from his circle of well-connected Scottish friends who remained loyal to him. Many of them, especially the prominent medical men in the circle, were on intimate terms with the aristocracy. But this question about Smollett's sources is ultimately less important than the parallels already discussed: indeed the similarities between Saint-Germain and Fathom seem to argue that Smollett did know about the Count, and that his knowledge occupied some region of Smollett's imagination, however small a territory, while composing *Ferdinand Count Fathom* in 1752. Now that criticism of this novel increasingly focuses on Count Fathom in terms of his relationship to the stock villains of Renaissance drama or as an animated symbol of evil locked in combat with similarly animated symbols of good,[43] it is important to keep in mind the fact that living, breathing scoundrels of this type flourished to an extraordinary degree in Smollett's London.

NOTES

1. In chapter LXXVII of *Peregrine Pickle* (1751), Crabtree reports: "I have travelled over the greatest part of Europe, as a beggar, pilgrim, priest, soldier, gamester, and quack. . . . After having suffered innumerable hardships, dangers, and disgraces, I returned to London, where I lived some years in a garret, and picked up a subsistence, such as it was, by vending purges in the streets, from the back of a pied horse; in which situation I used to harangue the mob, in broken English, under pretence of being a High German doctor." Crabtree adheres to Hobbesian principles, renouncing his religious "beliefs" to escape the Inquisition, taking advantage of chance occurrences and of people who trust him, all the while interested only in his own preservation and advancement. Like Ferret, he holds mankind in general in high contempt and is adept at playing roles: from priest to spy to pilgrim to quack. Ferret's assumption of the role of fortune teller in chapter XXII mirrors Crabtree's in chapters XC–XCI of *Peregrine Pickle*. Fathom's similar versatility and his Hobbesian world view are well documented. Unless stated otherwise the place of publication of works cited is London.

2. The phrase is Thomas R. Preston's; see his *Not in Timon's Manner: Feeling, Misanthropy, and Satire in the Eighteenth Century* (University, Alabama: The University of Alabama Press, 1975). The best single interpretation of the novel remains P.-G. Boucé's *The Novels of Tobias Smollett*, trans. Antonia White (1976), pp. 174–190.

3. Despite Smollett's satirical treatment of Shebbeare's rhetoric, there is good reason to believe that Smollett agreed with the essence of much that Ferret advances. Ferret repeats imitative distillations of Shebbeare's sentiments rather than direct quotations; and Smollett carefully selected the substance of Ferret's criticisms from among Shebbeare's far more wide-ranging list of political complaints. This enabled Ferret to voice objections ("melancholy truths," I, p. 515) relating to the war in Germany with which Smollett agreed. Smollett's opposition to a continuation of the war in Germany has been documented by Robert D. Spector in *English Literary Periodicals and the Climate of Opinion During the Seven Years' War* (The Hague, 1966), who notes that "on the question of Germany, of all the periodical writers, the *Critical* reviewers were the most outspoken in opposition to the alliance. . . . Smollett himself rejected all arguments based on the mercantile advantages to be gained by

continental measures, and, commenting on the treaties protecting Hanover, he insisted that they were designed without regard for British interests and that a European defence alliance would ultimately bankrupt the nation" (pp. 47–48). See the *Critical Review*, XI (January 1761) pp. 78–79; XII (October 1761), p. 292, (December 1761), pp. 473–474, and Smollett's similar comments in his *History of England*, 6 vols. (Philadelphia, 1796), III, 375–377.

4. "Smollett's Pamphleteering Foe Shebbeare," *PMLA*, LXVII, pp. 1053–1100. It should be noted that Foster's lengthy article is valuable for the context it provides for Shebbeare's relationship with Smollett, but the amount of new biographical information presented by Foster is small and mainly confined to information about his publications after 1753. While the article provides valuable summaries of obscure works, Shebbeare's life prior to the publication of *The Marriage Act* in 1754 remains shrouded in mystery and speculation.

5. Foster, "Smollett's Pamphleteering Foe Shebbeare," p. 1056.

6. The material presented here parallels and enlarges upon the thesis advanced by Louis L. Martz in his *Later Career of Tobias Smollett* (New Haven, 1942). Martz excluded Smollett's work as a reviewer in the *Critical Review*, focusing instead on the creative and stylistic influence of his labours during 1753–1765 as a compiler of histories; he comments on *Sir Launcelot Greaves* only in passing (pp. 13–16, 188). Richard L. Lettis, in his "Study of Smollett's *Sir Launcelot Greaves*" (Yale Ph.D. dissertation, 1957), pp. 138–151, has pointed out a number of borrowings from the *Critical Review* but relies on Foster's speculations (see above, n. 5) to explain Ferret's appearance as a quack.

7. I (January and February 1756), pp. 88–90.

8. *The Life and Adventures of Sir Launcelot Greaves* first published in *The British Magazine*, II (1761), p. 204.

9. The entire matter will be considered by Roger A. Hambridge in an extensive study of Charlatanry in the eighteenth-century English novel.

10. *Sir Launcelot Greaves*, p. 81. R. L. Lettis, in his "Study of Smollett's *Sir Launcelot Greaves*," pp. 140–141, has noted the resemblance between Ferret's catalogue and that in a passage from the anonymous *Yorick's Meditations upon Various Interesting and Important Subjects* . . . (1760) which is quoted at length in the July 1760 number of the *Critical Review* (X, p. 71).

11. *Sir Launcelot Greaves*, p. 74.

12. *Sir Launcelot Greaves*, p. 79.

13. When Dr. Johnson came to review Lucas's *Essay on Waters*, 2 vols. (London, 1756), in the *Literary Magazine* (I, 15 July to 15 October 1756, pp. 167–168, 225–229, 288–293), he treated Lucas's flight with more sympathy, charging Dublin officials with driving Lucas out of "his native country by a proclamation, in which they charged him with crimes of which they never intended to be called to the proof, and oppressed him by methods equally irresistable by guilt and innocence" (p. 167).

14. *Sir Launcelot Greaves*, p. 16.

15. Both accusations also echo Smollett's charge against Shebbeare in the review of the *Fourth Letter* . . . (*Critical Review*, II, August 1756, p. 44): ". . . we shall not scruple to pronounce him a desperate incendiary, who avails himself on the present fears, jealousies, and disgusts of the nation, to create a spirit of discontent and disaffection, which may destroy the union so necessary for opposing the designs of a powerful enemy, and involve the kingdom in civil broils and confusion."

16. The allusion is to Shebbeare's *Practice of Physic*, 2 vols. (London, 1755). Shebbeare devotes an entire chapter (II, "Of the reality of fire," I, 27–51) to prove the existence and physiological functions of "electrical fire."

17. *Sir Launcelot Greaves*, pp. 79–80.

18. *Critical Review*, I (1756), pp. 322–324. At one point Smollett speculates that "the doctor would have *geberous* for *gibberish*, which is derived from *Geber* the *Arabian* alchymist, of whom our author might, from his writings, be supposed a worthy disciple" (p. 323). Interestingly, Ferret labels Tom Clarke "a true disciple of Geber" (1.4.12–13B) as a result of Clarke's eccentric idiolect.

19. Its publication was noticed in *Gentleman's Magazine*, X (June 1740), p. 320. A second edition appeared during 1760.

20. This controversy has been studied and reviewed with respect to Smollett's *Humphry Clinker* by G. S. Rousseau in "Matt Bramble and the Sulphur Controversy

in the XVIIIth Century," *Journal of the History of Ideas*, XXVIII (1967), pp. 577–589.

21. In brief, the controversy developed when Lucas issued his scathing *Analysis of Dr. Rutty's Methodical Synopsis* not long after Rutty's work had appeared. Predictably Rutty's work had been favourably received in the *Critical Review* (IV, August 1757, pp. 121–130; September 1757, pp. 242–256), and Lucas's attack was savagely ridiculed in a review that L. M. Knapp has said "only Smollett would have written" (*Tobias Smollett: Doctor of Men and Manners*, Princeton, 1949, p. 207). Knapp also notes (p. 207) that Smollett had a hand in preparing either or both of the replies of Lucas's attack published under Rutty's name early in 1758.

22. Lucas's *Analysis* . . . was reviewed in the *Critical Review*, IV (August 1757), pp. 160–162.

23. *Critical Review*, IV (August 1757), pp. 274–275.

24. Ibid., IV (October 1757), p. 370.

25. Ibid., p. 371. It is also possible that Smollett's later review of Mrs. Elizabeth Nihell's *Treatise on the art of Midwifery* (*Critical Review*, IX, March 1760, pp. 187–197) assisted him in constructing Ferret's harangue to the mob in chapter X.

26. *The Adventures of Ferdinand Count Fathom*, ed. Damian Grant (London: Oxford University Press, 1971), p. 3. All references are to this edition.

27. Sources of biographical information about him tend to provide little, if any, information about his actual activities in England. Horace Walpole's correspondence provides some important information, particularly his letter to Mann dated 9 December 1745 OS (*Horace Walpole's Correspondence*, ed. W. S. Lewis *et al.*, New Haven, 1937–   , XIX, 181–82; cited hereafter as *HW*) and his prose portrait of Saint-Germain in his MS *Commonplace Book of Verses* (*HW*, XXVI, 20–21). Isabel Cooper-Oakley's *The Comte de St. Germain* (London, 1927) is not a reliable or balanced account of the Count's life. As the *HW* editors correctly note, it was written "from the point of view of the Theosophical Society, which, on the strength of some dubious French memoirs, decided that St. Germain was still living in the 19th century, being supposedly immortal." Perhaps the best account of Saint-Germain is found in Grete de Francesco's *The Power of the Charlatan*, trans. M. Beard (New Haven, 1939), pp. 174–187. It uses materials in Charles-Henri, Baron De Gleichen's *Souvenirs* (Paris, 1868), pp. 120–134, and in the *Memoires of the Pompadour's lady-in-waiting*, Mme. *du Hausset* (Paris, 1824; trans. S. F. Flint, New York, 1928). De Francesco also relies upon a biography, *Der Graf von Saint Germain* (Dresden, 1932), written by the celebrated historian Frederick the Great, Gustav B. Volz.

28. De Francesco, *The Power of the Charlatan*, p. 175.

29. XVIII (August 1748), p. 372.

30. Eckernförde Castle MSS, uncatalogued. By kind permission of the Castle Curator.

31. *Ferdinand Count Fathom*, p. 152.

32. *HW*, XXVI, 20.

33. *HW*, XIX, 181–182. The Baron de Gleichen accepts the account that Saint-Germain was the illegitimate son of the wife of Charles II of Spain. Isabel Cooper-Oakley's contention that he was the son of Prince Rágóczy (or Rákóczy) of Transylvania deserves some consideration (*The Comte de St. Germain*, pp. 9–24).

34. De Francesco, *The Power of the Charlatan*, p. 174.

35. See *Ferdinand Count Fathom*, especially pp. 148–149.

36. *HW*, XXVI, 20.

37. *Ferdinand Count Fathom*, p. 136. Count Fathom's mastery of French is discussed by Smollett on p. 73.

38. *HW*, XXVl, 20.

39. *Ferdinand Count Fathom*, p. 24.

40. Ibid., p. 149.

41. De Francesco, *The Power of the Charlatan*, pp. 192–193. The Count's "rejuvenation water" still survives today as Saint-Germain Tea.

42. Curiously Saint-Germain is not referred to in Chesterfield's correspondence, nor is the Count mentioned in any biographies of Chesterfield.

43. See, for example, T. O. Treadwell's "Two Worlds of *Ferdinand Count Fathom*" in *Tobias Smollett*, ed. G. S. Rousseau and P. G. Boucé (New York, 1971), pp. 131–153, and Thomas Preston's recent *Not in Timon's Manner: Feeling, Misanthropy, and Satire in Eighteenth-Century England* (University, Alabama, 1975), pp. 85–100.

IX
Smollett and Politics

Sir Launcelot Greaves, published serially during 1760–1761 in the first two volumes of Smollett's *British Magazine*, has always been one of his least read novels.[1] Most critics have given it short shrift, dismissing it with a minimum of commentary on its hasty composition, its self-plagiarization, and the seeming ineptness of its quixotic frame.[2] Critics anxious to find some good in the novel usually register appreciation for a few selected episodes on grounds of their effectiveness as satiric vignettes. The portrait of the country election in Chapter ix is one such episode.

A satire on "typical" borough politics (and a microcosm of "typical" national politics), this episode has gained additional notoriety because critics see it as the original of the strikingly similar episode in Chapter xiii of Dickens' *Pickwick Papers*.[3] Beyond this, Smollett's chapter has not seemed to require further comment; he seems clearly to be concerned with presenting a general portrait of a typical borough election and not an exposé of politics in a particular locale. It takes place in an unspecified market town; the Jewish-stockbroker-Whig, Mr. Isaac Vanderpelft, and the foxhunter-Tory, Sir Valentine Quickset, are both caricatures espousing the most extreme positions of their respective parties; and, within the novel's quixotic framework, all this seems orchestrated to allow Sir Launcelot (speaking for Smollett) to damn the extremists of both sides while excoriating their violent, mindless supporters.

Because Smollett's fiction frequently has some relation to particular historical events and figures, the serious student of his work never discounts the possibility that any given episode might have some historical correlative in Smollett's life or in events with which he was familiar. Without attempting to make Chapter ix any less a general satire on partisan politics, it should not surprise us that several elements in this vignette have counterparts in eighteenth-century political history. First, by tracing Sir Launcelot's movements during the first eight chapters, we can identify the market town where the election takes place.

The novel opens, as George Kahrl has pointed out, at the famous

Black Lion Inn located on the Great North Road near Weston, Nottinghamshire.[4] Sir Launcelot arrives there late in the day in the midst of a fierce storm. The events of the evening, during which we meet most of the main characters, learn the knight's history, and witness several midnight pranks, and through all of which Sir Launcelot vainly attempts to rest, are described in Chapters i–vii. At the end of Chapter vii, finding rest impossible, Greaves arms himself and announces his immediate departure to his squire, Timothy Crabshaw.

Chapter viii begins by noting that from the Black Lion the knight "proceeded in a southerly direction, insensible of the storm that blew, as well as of the darkness, which was quite horrible" (I, 393). The two adventurers ride on in the stormy darkness discussing madness and cowardice, and at the conclusion of their dialogue (about midway through the chapter) we are informed that "by this time a very disagreeable night was succeeded by a fair, bright morning, and a market-town appeared at the distance of three or four miles . . ." (I, 395–396). Following the Great North Road south from Weston, the knight and his squire would have passed through Sutton-on-Trent, Carlton-on-Trent, and Cromwell (respectively $1\frac{3}{4}$, $3\frac{1}{4}$, and $4\frac{3}{4}$ miles from Weston).[5] By the time they reached North Muskham ($6\frac{3}{4}$ miles from Weston), they would have been $3\frac{1}{2}$ miles from the nearest market town to the south of Weston, Newark-on-Trent.[6] The next market town on their route, Witham (in Essex), is $34\frac{1}{4}$ miles from Weston—too far, one would think, for an early morning's ride. Additionally, Witham was not a parliamentary borough.

It is to Newark, then, that Sir Launcelot finally comes, but not before he and his companion confront two would-be highwaymen who have stopped a coach in the vicinity of North Muskham. Shortly after his arrival in Newark, Greaves, "Being very much fatigued, [and] resolved to indemnify himself for the loss of last night's repose" (I, 398) retires to an inn where, after two hours' rest, he is awakened by the uproar of the election.

A brief survey of the history of Newark, which regularly sent two members to Parliament, indicates that during 1715–1740 its politics were controlled by three powerful families. The Whig interest was totally controlled by Thomas Pelham-Holles (1693–1768), the powerful Duke of Newcastle, lord of the manor of Newark. The Tory interest, on the other hand, was divided between Sir Thomas Willoughby (ca. 1670–1729), 1st Lord Middleton (and after his death by his son Francis [1692–1758], 2nd Lord Middleton), and Robert Sutton (1662–1723), the last Lord Lexington, who owned the nearby estate of Kelham (upon whose death his interest passed to his son-in-law, John Manners [1696–1779], 3rd Duke of Rutland). By means of an accommodation reached between these contending interests "Newcastle shared the representation of Newark with the Manners-Sutton family, each returning one Member, usually after a contest with a Tory."[7] In 1741 Newcastle absorbed the Middleton interest by nominating a common (Whig) friend, and during 1741–1760 the Newcastle (Middleton)/Manners-Sutton accommodation regularly returned their respective candidates—not, however, without some opposition.[8]

With this broad overview of Newark politics in mind, let us examine the biographies of the Whig and Tory members returned during 1741–1760.[9] The Whig member during this period was Mr. Job Staunton Charlton (1700–1778) of Staunton Hall, a Whig in principle but closely connected with Middleton (the leader of the Nottinghamshire Tories) and descended on both sides from Royalists and Tories. His selection in 1741 (as we noted) served to consolidate the Newcastle and Middleton interests. Romney Sedgwick (*Sedgwick*, I, 543) notes that

> besides acting as an intermediary between Newcastle and Middleton, Charlton was Newcastle's manager at Newark, a position combining the duties of an estate agent with those of an election agent.[10] . . . For these services he was rewarded by Newcastle in 1751 with a place in the Ordnance [as Clerk of Deliveries] at a salary of £400 a year. In the same year[11] he became chairman of the [House of Commons] committees of supply and ways and means for which he received £500 a year from secret service funds.[12]

The Tory representative for Newark during 1739–1754 was Lord William Manners (1697–1772) of Croxton Park, Lincolnshire. The younger brother of the 3rd Duke of Rutland, Manners, a bachelor all of his life, fathered seven illegitimate children upon the daughter of a Shrewsbury apothecary. Upon his death he left this family over £100,000 in cash as well as other property. A considerable part of this fortune derived from his highly successful career as a gamester.[13] He was also an ardent foxhunter, and Sedgwick observes that Lord William "spent much of his time looking after the Belvoir foxhounds and his extensive racing studs" (*Sedgwick*, II, 241). He retired from Parliament in 1754 and his eldest son, John (1730–1792), took over his seat, representing the Tory interest until 1774.

Since, admittedly, Smollett's overriding artistic aim in Chapter ix is to present general, not specific, satire, we need not expect that his descriptions there will necessarily correspond point for point with any specific events or figures outlined above. But while most of the events in the chapter have been fashioned to depict the most vivid extremes against which to promote his own moderate views, many circumstantial details from Newark's political history are reflected in his descriptions of the two candidates provided to the knight by a London tradesman, "well acquainted with all the particulars which our adventurer wanted to know"[14]:

> . . . the competitors were sir Valentine Quickset and Mr. Isaac Vanderpelft; the first a meer fox-hunter, who depended for success in this election upon his interest among the high-flying gentry; the other a stock-jobber and contractor, of foreign extract, not without a mixture of Hebrew blood, immensely rich, who was countenanced by his grace of —————, and supposed to have distributed large sums in securing a majority of votes among the yeomanry of the county, possessed of small freeholds, and copyholders, a great number of which last resided in this burrough. He said these were generally weavers; and that the mayor, who was himself a manufacturer, had received a very considerable order for exportation, in consequence of which, it was believed, he would support Mr. Vanderpelft with all his influence and credit.
>
> (I, 451)

Sir Valentine Quickset surely mirrors Lord William Manners. Mr. Isaac Vanderpelft, on the other hand, presents some problems.

The largest part of Vanderpelft's portrait describes his use of wealth and commercial influence to secure support, and these actions compare favourably with those of Job Staunton Charlton. Charlton, as we have noted, was "countenanced by his grace of [Newcastle]" and it is known that during the election of 1754 he "distributed large sums in securing a majority of votes."[15] Additionally, as Clerk of Deliveries in the Ordnance and with his places at the head of two powerful committees in the Commons, he was certainly in a position to offer mercantile concessions in return for political support. Notwithstanding this, however, Charlton wielded no immense personal fortune, had no known "mixture of Hebrew blood," nor was he a "stock-jobber and contractor, of foreign extract." In fact, no figure in Newark politics during 1715–1760 possessed these attributes.

We may speculate about Smollett's decision to draw his typical Whig candidate as a Jew. He may have decided to capitalise on the satiric possibilities afforded by Charlton's Biblical (and Hebrew) first name. His decision may also have been influenced by the uproar during the most recent general election (in 1754) occasioned by the debates on the ill-fated Jewish Naturalization Bill of 1753.[16] Whatever Smollett's reasons were, the history of the period provides a prominent figure whose attributes match those we are unable to connect with Charlton. The most famous "stock-jobber and contractor" of the period was the immensely wealthy Sampson Gideon (1699–1762), a Jewish financier of Portuguese extraction.[17] He had begun business in 1719 with £1500, and at his death his estate was valued at £580,000. Frequently consulted on financial matters by the Walpole, Pelham, and Newcastle administrations, he raised £1,700,000 for the government in 1745, and four years later advised upon and executed the consolidation of the national debt. During the Seven Years' War he paid bounties from his estates for the recruiting of the army, and during 1758–1759 the government relied almost exclusively upon him for loans. His Jewish heritage denied him the opportunity to stand for Parliament, but there seems little doubt that Smollett had Gideon in mind when he drew parts of the portrait of Vanderpelft. His staunch financial support of the Whigs may also have contributed to the rhetoric of Vanderpelft's speech.

NOTES

1. All quotations from the novel are from this version, cited by volume and page numbers. A book version in two volumes appeared in March 1762.

2. See, for example, John Butt, "Smollett's Achievement as a Novelist," in *Tobias Smollett: Bicentennial Essays Presented to Lewis M. Knapp*, ed. G. S. Rousseau and P.-G. Boucé (New York, 1971), pp. 18–19; Louis L. Martz, *The Later Career of Tobias Smollett* (New Haven, 1942), pp. 13–14; George M. Kahrl, *Tobias Smollett, Traveller-Novelist* (Chicago, 1945), pp. 56–60; and Lewis M. Knapp, *Tobias Smollett: Doctor of Men and Manners* (Princeton, 1949), pp. 320–321.

3. For example, Frans Wierstra, *Smollett and Dickens* (Den Helder, 1928), p. 60, and Martz, *Later Career*, p. 14.

4. *Tobias Smollett*, p. 57. Kahrl's statements here and on p. 58 must be viewed with caution since a certain amount of the information he supplies is simply incorrect (e.g., his Ashenton "in the hundred of Stafford [sic], West Riding, Yorkshire" is actually Aston, in the hundred of Strafforth), Nevertheless, Smollett, by locating his Black Lion Inn on the Great North Road, provides the information necessary to validate Kahrl's identification. While there may have been a number of Black Lion Inns in the North (and we should note that this sign was not nearly so ubiquitous as the White Hart, the George, or the Red Lion), *the* Black Lion on the Great North Road was that located at Weston. We are grateful to Mr. S. J. Best and Mrs. Sheila M. Cooke of the Nottingham Central Library for enabling us further to verify Kahrl's identification.

5. The route and distances are provided in Charles G. Harper's *The Great North Road: The Old Mail Road to Scotland*, 2nd ed., rev., 2 vols. (London, 1922), I (*London to York*), [front matter].

6. We have used the designations in Stephen Whatley's *England's Gazetteer*, 3 vols. (London, 1751), to determine market towns.

7. Romney Sedgwick, *The History of Parliament: The House of Commons, 1715–1754*, 2 vols. (London, 1970), I, 300; hereafter cited as *Sedgwick*.

8. The various attempts of Newark's vicar, Dr. Bernard Wilson, D.D. (1689–1772), to establish a fourth interest during 1739–1754 never met with success, although at a by-election in 1751 his candidate came within five votes of unseating Newcastle's man. In 1754, when it appeared that Wilson might finally succeed, his efforts were quashed when the two ducal candidates closed ranks against him and Newcastle poured £1000 of government secret service funds into the purchase of votes (see Sir Lewis Namier, *The Structure of Politics at the Accession of George III*, 2nd ed. [London, 1957], pp. 200, 202).

9. The standard authorities are *Sedgwick* and Sir Lewis Namier and John Brooke's

The History of Parliament: The House of Commons, 1754–1790, 3 vols. (New York, 1964); the latter cited hereafter as *Namier and Brooke.*

10. Charlton's activities as Newcastle's estate agent are detailed by Ray A. Kelch in *Newcastle, A Duke Without Money: Thomas Pelham-Holles, 1693–1768* (Berkeley and Los Angeles, 1974), pp. 157, 162–165, 175.

11. *Namier and Brooke,* II, 209, give the year as 1752.

12. Namier, *Structure,* p. 229 [*Sedgwick's* note].

13. Hogarth portrayed him in the gambling scene (Plate 6) of "The Rake's Progress" (see Ronald Paulson, *Hogarth's Graphic Works,* rev. ed., 2 vols. [New Haven and London, 1970], I, 167–168), and Horace Walpole described him to Mann as "better known in the groom-porter's annals than in those of Europe" (to Mann, 28 March 1754; *Horace Walpole's Correspondence with Sir Horace Mann,* ed. W. S. Lewis and George L. Lam, 11 vols. [New Haven, 1954–71], IV, 418).

14. Smollett's information about Newark's politics may have come from just such a source.

15 See note 8 above. As Namier notes, total expenses for the election eventually neared £1700.

16. See, for example, the comments of "The Connoisseur," a periodical essayist whose observations on the effect of the "Jew Bill" on the 1754 election were reprinted in the *London Magazine* for May 1754 (pp. 212–213).

17. For the most complete account of Gideon's life see Lucy Stuart Sutherland, "Sampson Gideon: Eighteenth-Century Jewish Financier," *Transactions of the Jewish Historical Society of England,* 17 (1951–1952), 79–90; see also James Picciotto, *Sketches of Anglo-Jewish History,* rev. and ed. Israel Finestein (London, 1956), pp. 55–59.

X

Smollett and the Eighteenth-Century Sulphur Controversy

"I have had an hospital these fourteen years within myself, and studied my own case with the most painful attention; consequently may be supposed to know something of the matter, although I have not taken regular courses of physiology."[1] Thus Matt Bramble writes to Dr. Lewis from the Hot Wells in Bristol. Actually, Tobias Smollett, the author of *Humphry Clinker*, had "taken regular courses of physiology" at Glasgow University, and had become a physician. Bramble proceeds to note in his letter to Dr. Lewis that he has "for some time been of opinion (no offence, dear Doctor) that the sum of all your [Dr. Lewis'] medical discoveries amounts to this, that the more you study the less you know." Views expressed by the character Matt Bramble in *Humphry Clinker* reflect in brief three basic attitudes concerning medicine which Smollett entertained throughout his medical career: (1) the value of careful observation, (2) the necessity of full knowledge, and (3) a persisting skepticism. As an invalid, Smollett, like Bramble, had observed his own ailments and nursed himself for twenty years; in so doing, he kept abreast of contemporary medicine, particularly in the field of balneology; and, although a doctor himself, he was strongly skeptical of doctors who were quick to prescribe panaceas.

This combination of almost clinical self-observation, learning, and skepticism is blended in Matt Bramble in such a way as to produce medical satire of the finest sort. Smollett's satire is always built upon a foundation of extensive learning, and if Matt Bramble pokes fun at notable contemporary physicians, it is because his creator previously had spent much time weighing the pros and cons of the medical theory of each doctor. And if Matt appears to be unusually aware of the names and remedies of countless maladies of the time, we may be certain that this author is using him as a mouthpiece to display his own extensive medical learning. Inasmuch as the medical background of *Humphry Clinker* has never been explored, I will examine this aspect of Smollett's masterpiece, treating the opening scenes in the pump room at the Hot Wells, Bristol, in some detail, because much of the *materia medica* is concentrated here.

It is not accidental that the Bramble family begins its tour in search of health at the famous Bristol Hot Wells. In the letter already cited, Bramble writes to Dr. Lewis, "I have read all that has been written on the Hot Wells."[2] Bramble's remark is suspect: after Bath, the Hot Wells was the second most popular watering place in XVIIIth-century England, and no one person is likely to have read all that had been written about it. Yet we can be fairly certain that Smollett himself had read extensively about this much frequented spa, in addition to having visited it, at which time he met several of its better known inhabitants.[3]

One of these inhabitants was Diederich Wessel Linden, or as Matt Bramble's nephew, Jery, refers to him, "the famous Dr. L——n, who is come to ply at the Well for patients."[4] Readers of the novel will recall the brilliant satire of Dr. Linden: in this hilarious scene, Linden diagnoses Bramble as a possible victim of a conglomeration of diseases, ranging from the common gout and dropsy to the more serious "*lues venerea*," or venereal disease. He lectures on the splendid virtues of stink and stercoraceous matter, and finally, offers to remove from his own nose "a little suspicious wart," which Bramble has spied. After the operation, Linden returns to the pump room, his face marred by "a considerable inflammation, attended with an enormous swelling," disgraced in the eyes of all, and ludicrous to behold.[5]

Whether Smollett ever met Linden cannot be determined with any degree of certainty. He is, nevertheless, so familiar with Linden's medical theories that he either read or, at least, was aware of some of Linden's writings. It was customary for Linden to accompany his patients to the Hot Wells every summer from 1754 to 1762,[6] passing his time in the company of the well-known Drs. Lucas and Sutherland.[7] There is a likelihood that Smollett, who visited the Hot Wells in the early 1760s, made his acquaintance. It is also possible that Smollett knew about a complaint Linden issued to the *Gentleman's Magazine in* 1761,[8] concerning the pollution of the atmosphere of the Hot Wells by a lead-smelting works on the opposite bank of the Avon. In either case, Smollett was so very much influenced by Linden's medical theories and personality that the author made the doctor the focal figure of this satirical scene.

In his study of English balneology, Professor Mullett writes, "I regret very much my inability to find anything about Linden; so prolific an author deserves something better than silence."[9] Linden was indeed prolific in several languages. A full bibliography of his published works does not exist.[10] As Professor Mullett notes, "Dr.

Linden was especially prolific during three decades, with his accounts both general and specific, descriptive as well as controversial." One of the few things we know about Linden's extant works is their alchemical bent: in a review which Smollett probably wrote, we learn that Linden "possesses the quality of a true alchymist, namely, that of being sometimes so dark and mysterious, that none but adepts can understand his meaning."[11]

If all his works are not known, even less are the facts of his life. Linden, a German by birth, came to England in the early 1740s. He writes in his *Treatise on . . . Chalybeat Waters* that in six years of residence in London he had heard little about the waters of the spring at Islington and had never seen them; he was "happy therefore to visit them on the 27th of June 1748," and thus one may presume he was in England by 1742.[12] In the Preface to his *Treatise*, Linden asks forgiveness for any errors of language, pleading that he is "a foreigner of no long sojournment in this country." From his dedication of the book to Frederick II of Prussia, and from his enthusiastic and detailed description of Cleves, it is tempting to think that he may have lived there before coming to England.[13] After his residence in London, Dr. Linden visited some Welsh spas for reasons of personal health. In 1754 he went to Llandrindod Wells, and in the following year to Llanrwst. He spent a considerable part of the next eleven years at the Bristol Hot Wells. Returning to Llanrwst in 1765, he wrote a *Reply to Dr. Lucas's Cursory Remarks*[14] cast in the form of an "Open letter to the Mayor, Aldermen, and Common Council of Bath."

This *Reply* summarises the issues in the sulphur controversy,[15] and offers a key to an understanding of Smollett's medical satire in *Humphry Clinker*. In his *Reply to Dr. Lucas*, Linden claims friendship with Sutherland and states that he is replying to Lucas in Sutherland's defence because the latter is away. The liaison between Sutherland and Linden may have been personal as well as medical, but for our purposes only the medical aspect of their relationship is important. That their views on the important issues of the day were similar is clear: both doctors were more inclined to the theories of the chemists than to those of the Galenists,[16] both had accompanied their patients to Bath and the Hot Wells, and as a result of their strong recommendation of these waters, both had gathered about them a host of patients, from whose subscription they lived rather comfortably. Each had the warm baths of the Hot Wells and Bath at heart, inasmuch as it was these spas which enabled the doctors to flourish as well as they did. But if the medical sympathies of Linden and Sutherland are compatible, what roles do Lucas and, finally, Smollett play in popular medicine of the day?

Dr. Charles Lucas had written about every aspect of balneology,[17] analysed particular waters, and was well known to have engaged in controversies with his contemporaries, notably with Dr. John Rutty. When Rutty in 1757 published a quarto of over seven hundred pages on the nature of sulphur in specific mineral waters, Lucas wasted no time in attacking Rutty's thesis. His rebuttal appeared before the year was out. Put simply, Rutty maintained that most of the English baths, particularly Bath and the Hot Wells, were rich in sulphureous content. Lucas, who believed that the value of bathing arose from the ability of the water to induce evacuation in the body, and thereby restoration of proper balance of the "humours," denied the presence of sulphur.

A Fellow of the Royal Society, Rutty decided to bring the issue before the men of Gresham College, and therefore prepared a paper which he read to them on November 15, 1759.[18] Rutty's purpose in debating the issue was not only "to sum up the evidences of sulphur in waters, in order to show, that antiquity hath not altogether rashly attributed sulphur to water," but also to prove the existence of sulphur at Bath from an argument of smell. He writes: "The effects of these waters, and their vapours, in discolouring metals, and their peculiar smell and flavour, like that of boiled eggs, and in the stronger like that of rotten eggs, are perfectly similar to those of the artificial solution of sulphur."[19] Everyone who had ever been in the pump room at Bath, including Matt Bramble, knew how putridly the waters smelled—from what we would call a hydrogen-sulphur compound— but few doctors were in agreement about the source of the smell. Was the stink derivative from an element of sulphur or some *other* chemical present in the water? The answer to this question was complicated by those who denied the presence of sulphur in waters; they named a variety of other chemicals.

Exactly two years earlier, when Rutty brought the issue before the learned men of Gresham, Lucas appealed his point to the Royal College of Physicians, of which he was a member, in a paper read in December, 1757.[20] The immediate issue was the presence or absence of "sulphureous contents" in the Harrigate waters, but the larger, and more important concern was the search for a precise definition of sulphur: is sulphur a principle of combustion, as Paracelsus had asserted, or the yellow flakes of brimstone which yield a noisome odour? Eighty years earlier, Boyle and other doctors of the Royal Society,[21] had used the term sulphur in many ways, although there was no controversy over a precise definition.

Smollett himself formally entered the controversy between Lucas and Rutty in the summer of 1757. As Professor Knapp has stated, Smollett spent the summer months of 1757 in Bath where, we are told, he had an opportunity to observe Lucas.[22] It is also likely that Rutty was in Bath at this time, battling with Lucas over this sulphur question, thus making it possible for Smollett to meet Rutty. Smollett had depleted his funds while at Bath, and it may be that he turned to a journalistic endeavour to sustain himself. It is possible that Rutty approached Smollett while both were still at Bath, seeking his assistance in preparing his rebuttal to Lucas. Smollett's unfavourable review of Lucas's *Analysis of Dr. Rutty's Methodical Synopsis of Mineral Waters* in the *Critical Review* of August 1757 was probably influenced both by his direct observations of Lucas and by his financial association with Rutty. It is not surprising to find Smollett requesting from his printer, William Strahan, in October 1757, a copy of Lucas's treatise: "I have perused the m.s. from Dr R—y, which is very sensible and correct; but, I cannot well prepare it for the Press, without having the Synopsis and L——s's Pamphlet, which I desire, may be sent out, and I shall take care to return them in good Condition."[23]

In view of the fact that Smollett's thinking paralleled Lucas's, the savage tone of his August 1757 review can be explained, as I have said, only by Smollett's need for funds and his personal contact with Lucas at Bath. Smollett asserts ironically that he has observed "the personal virtues of the cool, the candid, the patriotical Dr. Lucas."[24] In typically Smollettian fashion, he says: "He [Dr. Lucas] challenges Dr. Rutty to shew where Boerhaave says there are but two vitriols. It is pretty strange that a professed chemist should not know where to find this position. We will refer him to a book entitled *Boerhaave Chem. pars prim. de arte theoria, de semimetallis.*"[25] Boerhaave, an iatrochemist had modified Paracelsus' "three vitriols" (sulphur, mercury, and salt) to "two vitriols," or principles of heat, which he called "*feu et chaleur,*" and by so doing, had avoided the problem of precisely defining sulphur, and was able to explain expansion and contraction.[26] Smollett attacked Lucas for being a pretender rather than a true chemist, since he did not keep abreast of recent theories of sulphur, not even one so important as that of Boerhaave. Smollett, as we have observed, involved himself in this clash between Lucas and Rutty; later we will see him re-enter this controversy by means of personal satire.

Lucas's dispute about sulphur with Sutherland several years later was to be of the same nature as his dispute with Rutty. Sutherland had engaged in a study of the chemical contents of the waters of the Bristol Hot Wells and Bath, and concluded that "sulphur was very prevalent." Lucas, who believed that sulphur not only was absent from the waters, but that the sulphur in this controversy was, in reality, scum and excrement, quickly rose to the challenge and published a scathing refutation of Sutherland's theory, which he called *Cursory Remarks on the Method of Investigating the Principles and Properties of Bath and Bristol Waters* (1763).[27]

In the *Cursory Remarks*, Lucas indicates that he has made extensive investigations of the Bath waters and has proved conclusively that they contain neither sulphur nor brimstone. He offers an analysis of the so-called Bath sands, and the "scum" contained in these sands, which, he maintains, have passed for "sulphureous elements." Finally, he refutes the very common notion of the water's being impregnated with sulphur and joyfully repeats his previous discovery of "having detected the fraud of the guides, who tinge the shillings of a yellow hue, and pretend the colour is owing to the sulphur in the waters." In addition to his exposure of what we may call "tingeing the shillings," Lucas insists that he has had "ocular demonstration" of such occurrences, and, moreover, that "by the help of a sagacious nose, he discovered an old woman in the very act of attempting to impose upon him with putrid wine."[28] His conclusion is that the medicated waters at Bath contain "iron, absorbent earth, sea-salt, a portion of oily matter, and the universal acid"—anything but sulphur.

Actually Lucas had advanced these theories of the absence of sulphur in the Bath and Bristol waters in the 1750s. He had reached his conclusions nine years earlier in the *Essay on Waters*, to which he added an appendix "on the improvement of Bath Waters." Like the *Cursory Remarks* (1764), the *Essay on Waters* (1756) had been poorly received, especially in a review probably written by Smollett that appeared in the first volume of the *Critical Review*.[29] Despite the similarity of their views on the chemical content of water, there is reason to believe that Smollett's early attack on Lucas in the *Critical Review* was attributable to plagiarism: "The candour of this curious chymist would have appeared more conspicuous, had he taken some notice of those gentlemen and others from whom he seems to have almost literally borrowed many of his most valuable hints of reformation." Smollett knew only too well the host of doctors who had constantly badgered the officials of Bath with petitions suggesting ways to improve the medicated waters. He himself had attacked the Bath Corporation, together with the managers and directors of the Bath Hospital, in his own *Essay on Waters*.[30] The tenor of his review becomes increasingly indignant and culminates in this sarcastic remark: "After having read this learned treatise of Dr. *Lucas*, we cannot help wondering how the hot-springs at *Bath*, acquired their reputation, considering how injudiciously they have been administered—is it possible that any person could ever return alive from the use of the waters at *Bath?*"

The controversy ramified, and just as Lucas had attacked Sutherland so did Linden attack Lucas. The principal participants now in
the Lucas–Sutherland fracas were Dr. Linden, Dr. Philip Thicknesse,
and Dr. Rice Charleton, all of whom appear in the early sections of
Humphry Clinker, explicitly by name.[31] In the Foreword to his *Bath
Guide*, Thicknesse had said, "a chemist ought to settle the matter
once and for all." He himself agreed with Lucas, and he went on to
remark that competent men had generally supported Lucas, even
though Lucas had suffered from persecution. In particular, Thicknesse defended Lucas's analysis of the waters against Charleton's.
Opposing Lucas was Charleton, who vigorously maintained, on the
evidence of "nearly a thousand cases," that the Bath waters were
impregnated with sulphur, and thereby especially effective in treating
a large number of diseases.

Lucas's most eloquent adversary, by far, was D. W. Linden. His
Reply to Dr. Lucas's Cursory Remarks, appearing at the height of the
controversy (1765), five years before Thicknesse and Charleton
published their views, was written from Llanwrst, Wales. In his
prefatory epistle, Linden stressed the fact that Lucas's denial of
sulphur created a serious crisis in chemical science. Linden had
grown interested in the precise mineral content of sulphur more than
a decade earlier, when, in a work on practical mineralogy,[32] he had
devoted long sections to the definition of sulphur. His conclusions in
the *Lettres sur la minéralogie* were anything but definitive, and he
admitted that he had not progressed very far in view of iatrochemical
theories. It is likely that he maintained interest in the sulphur question
throughout the fifties. In 1765, he announced the importance of his
own recent medical investigations, at a time "when one of the agi-
tating ingredients [sulphur] of this natural Medicine, is positively
and obstinately denied by one of the greatest ornaments of the
Faculty [Lucas] the Kingdom of Ireland has ever produced."[33]
Affirming that his only reason for entering into the controversy was
"the establishment of truth" rather than malice, Linden answered
Lucas point by point, drawing a conclusion in the form of nine key
points.

It is significant that Linden never uses the word "sulphur" in his
conclusion (he does occasionally in the treatise), but instead speaks
of brimstone. Although the two words are considered to be defini-
tively different by most doctors in the mid-XVIIIth century,[34]
confusion about the precise chemical meaning of each is at the heart
of the Lucas controversy in Bath. To the followers of Paracelsus and
the iatrochemists, that is, the New Chemists, sulphur was still, as Dr.
Robert James says in his *Medicinal Dictionary* (1743–1745), "that
Vapour which Physicians recommend," namely, what we would

simply call "heat." The physicians of the XVIIth and XVIIIth centuries had prescribed baths primarily on the grounds that the "heat" (sulphur) of these waters would re-establish a balance of the "humours," which would restore health to the patient. But to those doctors still sympathetic with the notions of the Galenists, who continued to oppose the new-fangled theories of the chemists, "sulphur" primarily meant "brimstone," whether in a solid or liquid state.

We now can see how the two factions—Lucas and Thicknesse versus Sutherland, Linden, and Charleton—were continuing the old quarrel of the preceding century, that of the Galenists ("humourists") versus the Paracelsians ("chemists"). Lucas, a staunch believer in the humours as a basis for physiological explanation, was forced to deny the presence of sulphur in waters, since he never could comprehend how a solution of brimstone could mix with water, nor why this Paracelsian "principle of sulphur," in the first place, was necessary for hot baths. On the other hand, Linden, together with other followers of the chemists, had to postulate the existence of sulphur in hot baths in order to explain the beneficial effects of the heat in the baths. Moreover, according to their explanation of physiological changes, it was this combining of the water's sulphur with the sulphur of the body that restored health to the body. In other words, like combined with like, and by a process of evacuation, detrimental elements were discharged. Linden's agreement with the chemists may be observed in his conclusion, in which he charges Lucas with "no more learning than what properly appertains to an apprentice of a sensible Apothecary." Such denigration of the Galenists on grounds of little or no understanding of the "elements of chemistry" was typical of the times.

The sulphur controversy had a profound effect upon Smollett. We have already seen that he participated in this controversy in 1757 by defending Rutty. But even before this, in 1752, thirteen years prior to the Lucas–Linden flare-up, he wrote an *Essay on Waters*, with the primary intention of clarifying his position on the matter. In the Introduction to the *Essay*, he remarks, in reference to Sutherland, what must have been at this time (1752) the central issue of the controversy at Bath:

> One writer denies that the Water in the generality of Hot Wells, is impregnated with *Sulphur*; while another affirms, that, without *Sulphur*, no such natural Hot Waters can exist. Yet, both these authors quote experiments to vouch for the truth of their different asseverations.[35]

This is, in simple terms, precisely the crux of the controversy.

Next, Smollett proceeds to give an objective statement of the claims of both:

> One asserting, that although he had immersed silver in many of the most noted *Thermae* on the continent of *Europe*, he could not perceive the colour of the metal changed; neither could he procure any real brimstone by evaporating the water; nor would the residue, when mixed with Salt of *Tartar*, produce the *Hepar Sulphuris*. But, in opposition to this Doctrine, there are so many concurring observations, that it is amazing to see it maintained by an author of *Hoffman's* reputation; for, besides the Hot Baths of *Austria* and *Hungary*, described in the Philosophical Transactions, and the Spaw at *Harrigate*, in which Dr. *Shaw* found actual brimstone floating in flakes; *Hoffman* himself owns that the Waters at *Aix la Chapelle*, which are better known than any other in *Europe*, abound with this Mineral in such quantities, that whole pounds of the flowers of *Sulphur* are found sticking to the stones that line the fountain-head of the Springs.

It is clear from these two passages that by sulphur Smollett means the mineral brimstone, and not the principle of heat, which it connoted to the chemists. The entire *Essay* is, in fact, a justification of his own Galenist or "humourist" preferences with regard to the sulphur controversy, for Smollett concludes his *Essay* with the statement that "in the use of bathing and pumping, that Efficacy is often ascribed to the mineral particles [sulphur particles], which properly belongs to the Element [water] itself."[36] That is, the water itself and not the brimstone cures the valetudinarian. He apparently would have cast his lot with Lucas rather than with the chemists, questioning, as he does, the statements of medical authorities who have found sulphur (the mineral) in bath waters. This in no way contradicts my previous remarks about Smollett's attacks on Lucas (which were prompted by monetary and personal reasons). Basically, Smollett's view paralleled that of Lucas in that they both agreed that water rather than sulphur was the healing ingredient.

Smollett's concern with the sulphur controversy did not wane in the next twenty years (1752–1771), respecting either that aspect of the controversy concerned with smell, or the argument about its presence in waters. He especially remembered the countless doctors, such as Rutty, who had referred to the "stink of sulphur" as similar to that of "rotten eggs." Indeed, he put these very words into the mouth of his hero: "Some people say it smells of rotten eggs, and others compare it to the scourgings of a foul gun."[37] But Smollett, the novelist and satirist, was not satisfied to have Matt simply echo the medical issue; he wished to use the ludicrous aspect of the dispute over the source of the stench emanating from the baths. Therefore, in the very first scene at the Bristol Hot Wells, Dr. Linden, the great exponent of sulphur in waters, is found indulging in a "learned investigation of the nature of stink":[38]

> He [Dr. Linden] observed, that stink, or stench, meant no more than a strong impression on the olfactory nerves; and might be applied to substances of the most opposite qualities; that in the Dutch language, *stinken* signified the most agreeable perfume, as well as the most fetid odour, as appears in Van Vloudel's translation of Horace, in that beautiful ode, *Quis multa gracilis*, etc.—The words *liquidis perfusus odoribus*, he translates *van civet & moschata gestinken*: that individuals differed toto caelo in their opinion of smells, which, indeed, was altogether as arbitrary as the opinion of beauty; that the French were pleased with the putrid effluvia of animal food; and so were the Hottentots in Africa, and the Savages in Greenland; and that the Negroes on the coast of Senegal would not touch fish till it was rotten; strong presumptions in favour of what is generally called *stink*, as those nations are in a state of nature, undebauched by luxury, unseduced by whim and caprice: that he had reason to believe the stercoraceous flavour, condemned by prejudice as a stink, was, in fact, most agreeable to the organs of smelling; for, that every person who pretended to nauseate the smell of another's excretions, snuffed up his own with particular complacency; for the truth of which he appealed to all the ladies and gentlemen then present.

This passage further justifies Sterne's impression of Smollett's nasal sensibility, in referring to his fellow novelist as the "learned Smelfungus" in *A Sentimental Journey* (1768). In the next sentence of Smollett's passage, he includes Dr. Barry in the general satire of those learned chemists who find sulphur wherever they look: Barry had explained human digestion in terms of "sulphuric effervescence," whereby the stages of digestion are compared to fire burning in a flask.[39]

Nor did Smollett forget the ridiculous assertion of Dr. Shaw,[40] who, as he says in the *Essay on Waters*, "found actual brimstone floating in flakes" at the Harrigate Spa. In *Humphry Clinker*, we find Matt Bramble commenting on Shaw's discovery of sulphur flakes at the very same spa, Harrigate Waters: "It [Harrigate] is generally supposed to be strongly impregnated with sulphur; and Dr. Shaw, in his book upon mineral water, says, he has seen flakes of sulphur floating in the well."[41]

But, as Bramble continues, we discover remarks which probably reveal Smollett's ultimate position, an unchanging one, about the matter:

> *Pace tanti viri;* I, for my part, have never observed anything like

sulphur, either in or about the well, neither do I find that any brimstone has ever been extracted from the water.

In the sarcastic tone of *"Pace tanti viri,"* peace to all those men, one finds a clue to Smollett's real attitude toward the famous sulphur controversy. A long-time resident of Bath and other spa waters both in Great Britain and on the Continent, Smollett, one suspects, considered ludicrous the hair-splitting feud about the definition of sulphur. Although he himself was interested sufficiently to express his position, nevertheless the situation must have seemed to him a "much ado about nothing," especially the sophistic positions to which some doctors were driven. The issue was now over a hundred years old and nothing new had been said about sulphur and the sulphureous principle since Paracelsus; moreover, the renewed arguments over the element were a mere rehashing of the former quarrels of quacks. Any serious experimentation with sulphur in the 1760s would have been performed by the Royal Society, the College of Physicians, or in either of the universities, but not in the pump room at Bath.[42] As he observed the squabbles of these doctors— Shaw, Sutherland, Rutty, Lucas, Linden, Charleton—each confident that he had reached the ultimate truth, Smollett's skepticism, I venture to say, grew and became more manifest. In any case, he seems to have preserved all this *materia sulphurica* for the culminating work of his life.

Although Smollett may have been sympathetic toward Lucas's views, his sympathy probably would do little to vindicate the folly of these doctors—"chemists" and "humourists" alike. However, in the belief that Linden was farther from the "truth" than Lucas, Smollett parodied the former all the more savagely in the opening scenes of *Humphry Clinker*. This attack on Linden does not indicate a deeper hostility toward Linden than to the other doctors in the sulphur feud. It is simply that Linden, with his pro-sulphur attitude, his Germanic background, and his flaunting pedantry possessed the qualities which Smollett seized upon for his satiric purposes.

NOTES

1. *Humphry Clinker* (London, 1771, 3 vols.), I, 40.
2. *Humphry Clinker*, I, 41.
3. The Bristol Hot Wells is located in Clifton, a section of Bristol on the Avon River. For an XVIIIth-century account of the Hot Wells, see E. Shiercliff, *The Bristol and Hotwell Guide* (Bristol, 1779).
4. *Humphry Clinker*, I, 26.
5. *Humphry Clinker*, I, 32.
6. John Latimer, *Annals of Bristol in the Eighteenth Century* (Bristol, 1893), 321. No record exists of Linden in Bristol during these years, except his own testimony in the Preface to *A Reply to Dr. Lucas's Cursory Remarks . . .* (Llanrwst, 1765) ii. Miss Mary E. Williams, Chief-Archivist of Bristol, informs me that no record of Linden is

contained in the City Archives. I have discussed Smollett's satire of Dr. Linden in *Sir Launcelot Greaves* (1762) in "Smollett and the *acidum vagum*," *Isis*, LVIII (1967).

7. Charles Lucas (1713–71) was a lively controversialist in medicine, attacking among other things, abuses in drugs. He wrote extensively. Alexander Sutherland practised at Bath and Bristol. His concern with balneology was interwoven with a campaign to revive ancient medical doctrines, as a consequence of which his ideas received attention in the periodicals.

8. 341–42. This was the first of a series of letters which Linden wrote to leading periodicals. See *Scots Magazine*, XXIV (1762), 235–36, 630, 631–32 (four letters); *Gentleman's Magazine*, XXXVI (1766), 328.

9. Charles F. Mullett, "Public Baths and Health in England, 16th–18th Century," *Supplements to the Bulletin of the History of Medicine*, No. 5 (Baltimore, 1946).

10. The extant works in English and French are: *A Letter to Dr. Peter Shaw concerning the Black Epileptical Powder* (London, 1746); *A Treatise on the Origin, Nature and Virtues of Chalybeat Waters, and Natural Hot Baths* (London, 1748); *Three Letters on mining and smelting* (London, 1750); *Directions for the Use of that . . . Mineral Water, commonly called Berry's Shadwell-Spaw, in Sun Tavern Fields, Shadwell* (London, 1749); *An Experimental Dissertation on the . . . Hyde Saline Purging Waters, commonly called the Hyde Spaw near Cheltenham in Gloucestershire* (London, 1751); *Lettres sur la minéralogie et métallurgie pratiques* (Paris, 1752); *A Treatise on the Three Medicinal Waters at Llandrindod, in Radnorshire, South Wales* (London, 1756); *A Medicinal and Experimental History and Analysis of the Halys-Spa Saline, Purging and Chalybeate Waters, near Shrewsbury* (London, 1768); Linden also wrote a work of balneistic nature in Welsh which is not preserved in the United States, although there is a copy at the British Museum. This list does not include articles in periodicals. No German or Dutch works by Linden are in the British Museum or in the major German libraries to which I have sent inquiries. Contained in the library of the Archives of Cleves, Germany, is a work by him entitled *Chemische Anmerkungen über Herrn D. Schüttens Physicalische Nachricht vom Ursprung der mineralischen Wasser und den Bestand-Theilen in dem Clevischen Sauer-Brunnen-Wasser . . .* (Amsterdam and Leipzig, 1746). The work was published by Peter Mortier, a Dutch printer of small repute. There are also Dutch works by Linden in the Archives Library at Cleves that I have not had an opportunity to examine.

11. *Critical Review*, II (1756), 97–98.

12. *A Treatise on the Origin and Virtues of Chalybeat Waters, and Natural Baths* (London, 1748), iii.

13. It is curious that, although his German works are found in the Archives Library of Cleves, no record of Linden survives in the Archives themselves. His name is not mentioned in the works of famous men of Cleves, nor is he included in the most complete dictionary of XVIIIth-century German doctors, *Biographisches Lexicon der hervorragenden Ärtze* (Berlin, 1925–35, 3 vols.).

14. London, 1765.

15. It is important to note that by "sulphur," scientists of all ages up to the XVIIIth century did not mean that which we mean today. The Ancients, particularly Aristotle and Hippocrates, made a distinction between sulphur and brimstone. In classical times, the difference between sulphur and brimstone was elaborated into four basic distinctions. "Pliny and Isidorus describe four kinds of sulphur. The *apuron* of Dioscorides, or the *Sulphur vivum* of the Latins, is native sulphur. The *Sulphur ignem expertum* (*to pepuromenon*) is sulphur which has been subjected to the action of fire. Sulphur (*theion*) was applied by the Ancients to various uses in medicine and other arts. For the use of the physician was required translucent native sulphur, which the Greeks called *apuron*. That which had been freed from impurities by an artificial process, which had passed the fire, was called *pepuromenon*, and distinguished into various kinds, appropriated to various uses, according probably, to their several degrees of purity. Thus, one kind was used for fumigating woolens, to render them whiter and softer; another for making matches. The employment of sulphur in expiration and lustration, which was very common, we find referred to by many ancient authors" (*Collection of Scientific Terms* [Edinburg, 1826] under "Sulphur," by Francis Adams, the Scottish surgeon). By the XVIth century, sulphur and brimstone had acquired so many different meanings, especially in scientific circles, that it is not always possible to differentiate them accurately. To Paracelsus and his descendants,

the iatrochemists, sulphur, together with air, water, earth, salt, and mercury, comprised the six basic elements. When he used the term sulphur he implied "principle of sulphur" or "sulphureous principle," that is, the combustible quality in matter which renders heat, and not the yellow deposits with which we identify solid-state sulphur. The word for these yellow deposits in the XVIIth and XVIIIth centuries was "brimstone." Certain scientists during these two centuries used the terms interchangeably. For further distinctions between sulphur and brimstone, see Hélène Metzger, *La Génèse de la science des cristaux* (Alcan, Paris, 1918); *Les Doctrines chimiques en France du début du XVII à la fin du XVIII siècle* (Paris, 1923); *La Chimie* (Paris, 1930). The distinction between sulphur and brimstone is also treated in Andrew Kent, "Phlogiston, Caloric and Heat," in *An Eighteenth-Century Lectureship in Chemistry* (Glasgow, 1947), 66–77.

16. For the best and most complete study of this controversy in the XVIIth and XVIIIth centuries, see R. F. Jones, *Ancients and Moderns: A Study of the Rise of the Scientific Movement in Seventeenth-Century England* (St. Louis, 1961), revised edition with index.

17. Some of his works are: *An Essay on Waters* (London, 1756, 3 vols.); *The City and Thermal Waters of Bath addressed to the Right Honourable The Earl of Chesterfield* (1756); *An Analysis of Dr. Rutty's Synopsis of Mineral Waters* (1757); *The Tonnelett [Spa Water] Vindicated* (London, 1766).

18. *Philosophical Transactions*, LI (1759), 275–282.

19. *Phil. Trans.*, LI (1759), 276.

20. *An Analysis of Dr. Rutty's Methodical Synopsis of Mineral Waters. Addressed by Way of Appeal to the Royal College of Physicians of London* (London, 1757).

21. See Marie Boas, *Boyle and Seventeenth-Century Chemistry* (Cambridge, 1958), 83–85, and *Phil. Trans.* for 1674. An anonymous Fellow of the Royal Society read two papers on sulphur in 1674, in which he considered sulphur to be neither principle of heat, nor mineral, but "a Vitriol Salt, the very same with that, which is separable from Common Vitriol" (*Phil. Trans.*, IX, 47).

22. Lewis M. Knapp, *Tobias Smollett: Doctor of Men and Manners* (Princeton, 1949), 207, n. 49.

23. This letter addressed to "Mr. W. Strahan Printer in New Street" is now in the Pierpont Morgan Library, New York. It is reprinted in Knapp, 206–207.

24. *Critical Review*, IV (1757), 160.

25. *Critical Review*, IV (1757), 161.

26. See Walter Pagel, *Paracelsus* (Basel, 1958), 82–105, and Hélène Metzger, *Newton, Stahl, Boerhaave et la Doctrine Chimique* (Paris, 1930), Chapter iii. The term "vitriol" meant sulphuric compound or acid until the XIXth century.

27. Actually Sutherland had put forth his view, that sulphur was present at these spas, in preceding works. See *The Nature and Qualities of Bristol Water* (Bristol, 1758). This work went through a second edition in 1764, bearing the title, *An Attempt to Ascertain and Extend the Virtues of Bath and Bristol Waters by Experiments*, and appeared before Lucas's *Cursory Remarks*.

28. *Cursory Remarks*, 19 and *Essay on Waters*, § 380.

29. 1 (1756), 321–345.

30. See the two Appendices to Smollett's *An Essay on the External Use of Water* (Baltimore, 1935, ed. Claude E. Jones), 77–81.

31. Linden is satirized throughout the opening scenes at the Hot Wells. Philip Thicknesse, the eccentric son of a more eccentric and very contentious father, appears in Henry Davis' letter to the Reverend Jonathan Dustwich, in the prologue to *Humphry Clinker* (I, p. xv). The work by Thicknesse referred to is *Useful Hints to those who make the Tour of France* (London, 1768). Rice Charleton (1710–89), an M.D. from Oxford and physician to the Bath General Hospital, appears in *Humphry Clinker* (I, p. 90) at Bath. The works in which Thicknesse and Charleton refer to the Lucas controversy are, respectively, *The Valetudinarian's Bath Guide* (London and Bath, 1770), and *An Enquiry into the Efficacy of Warm Bathing in Palsies* (Oxford, 1770). Charleton's analysis of Bath Waters was previously expounded in *A Treatise on the Bath Waters* (Bath, 1754).

32. *Lettres sur la minéralogie et métallurgie pratiques* (Paris, 1752).

33. *Reply*, i.

34. See note 15. There was also confusion in the preceding century. For example,

Michael Sandivogius, a French doctor, writing *A Treatise on the Nature of Sulphur* (London, 1650), classifies both heat and the yellow particles of "brimstone flower" under the heading sulphur. Twenty years later, however, Thomas Vincent, who had written about the Plague of London, differentiates sulphur and brimstone very carefully, as may be quickly gathered from the title of his work, *Fire and Brimstone* (London, 1670). In 1693, Christopher Packe published a work entitled *A Short Discourse on the Nature of the Sulphurs of Minerals and Metals, in Curing the most Chronical and Pertinacious Diseases* (London, 1693), in which he is clearly discussing that "principle of heat, called sulphur" which is said to cure diseases; at no point, however, does he question whether the cure arises from the chemical quality of brimstone or from the heat. The same confusion is displayed in the following fifty years in England and on the continent. Writing in 1757, at the time that Lucas and Smollett were questioning the meaning of sulphur, Gustavus Harmens considers sulphur to be the "mineral brimstone," as opposed, apparently, to its more common concept as heat; cf. *Dissertatio de Sulphure Minerali, ejusque usu praecipue Medico* (London, 1757). See also, for a contemporary definition of sulphur, Robert James, *A Medicinal Dictionary* (London, 1743–1745, 3 vols.), article on "Sulphur": "There are two different sulphurs . . . the Sulphur of the Shops, called θεῖον . . . and the Vapour of Sulphur which Physicians recommend." James remarks that "Sulphur is commonly called Brimstone."

35. *An Essay on the External Use of Water*, ed. Claude Jones, 52.

36. *An Essay on the External Use of Water*, 53.

37. *Humphry Clinker*, II, 100.

38. *Humphry Clinker*, I, 26. See my forthcoming article on Sterne's use of "Smelfungus" for Smollett, which takes on fuller significance in light of this controversy.

39. Sir Edward Barry (1696–1776), F. R. S., *A Treatise on the Three Different Digestions, and Discharges of the Human Body. And the diseases of their principal organs* (London, 1759). Smollett incorrectly quotes Barry's work in *Humphry Clinker* when he refers to the "learned Dr. B——, in his treatise on the Four Digestions." See T. P. C. Kirkpatrick, "Sir Edward Barry," *The Dublin Journal of Medical Science*, CXXVIII (1909), 442–461.

40. Peter Shaw (1694–1763), one of the great doctors of the XVIIIth century and a radical "new chemist," wrote extensively on chemical subjects. He had taken a leading part in the sulphur controversy, but died before Lucas and Linden entered it. Shaw wrote *An Enquiry into the Contents, Virtues, and Uses, of the Scarborough and Harrigate Spaw-Waters* (London, 1734) and was responsible for translating the chemical works of the distinguished German physician, Friedrich Hoffman, *New Experiments and Observations upon Mineral Waters* (London, 1740). For Dr. Shaw and *Peregrine Pickle*, see Judd Kline, "Three Doctors and Smollett's Lady of Quality," *Phil. Quart.*, xxvii (1948), 219–228.

41. *Humphry Clinker*, 195. Most scholars agree on 1765–68 as the time of composition of *Humphry Clinker* just after the controversy had reached its most feverish point at Bath. See Knapp, *Tobias Smollett*, 289.

42. The allusions to the sulphur controversy in literature dealing with Bath and the Bristol Hot Wells were many. For example, it is mentioned several times in Charles Anstey's *The New Bath Guide* (London, 1766):

> Take a smack of the brimstone contained in the water.
> But, what is surprising, no mortal e'er viewed
> Anyone of the physical gentlemen stewed.
> Then, all on a sudden, two persons of worth,
> My Lady Pandora Mac'scurvy came forth,
> With General Sulphur arrived from the North.
> So Tabby, you see, had the honour of washing
> With folks of distinction and very high fashion. (Epistle VI)

Anstey's *New Bath Guide* is one of the most important sources of the novel.

XI
Smollett and Paracelsian Medicine

Several years ago in attempting to annotate a passage dealing with the *"acidum vagum"* in Tobias Smollett's novel *The Adventures of Sir Launcelot Greaves*, I came to the conclusion, with the assistance of several historians of chemistry, that no such acid existed and that Smollett had fabricated the term.[1] I now wish to correct myself in view of the fact that the "vague acid" appears at least twice in eighteenth-century chemical texts, once in Boerhaave's *Elementa chemiae* (1732)[2] and several times in a manuscript copy of William Cullen's *Chemical Lectures at Edinburgh University*, now in the possession of W. A. Smeaton of University College London.[3] It is plausible that Smollett, a medical student at Glasgow University in 1736–1739, first learned about the acid in Boerhaave's *Elementa chemiae*. In 1735 Timothy Dallowe's English translation had appeared and by 1736–1739 some students at Glasgow were studying Boerhaave's chemistry in their courses on the materia medica.[4] It is also possible that Smollett never read Boerhaave but instead heard about the *acidum vagum* from his Glasgow medical teachers, Drs. John Gordon and William Stirling. Both had studied in Leiden and both had been exposed to Boerhaave's theory of chemistry. *Acidum vagum* as found in Boerhaave and Cullen is "vague" for two reasons, first because it is contained in a hidden part of the earth, and second because it is one of the numerous names given to sulphuric acid. Nomenclature in chemistry posed a considerable problem for scientists in 1761, and Dr. Smollett, like his Scottish friend Dr. Cullen, may well have satirized the term for its chemical vagueness. The acid is accordingly referred to in Smollett's novel by a quack physician, Dr. Ferret, who is unable to appreciate recent innovations in chemical terminology:

> Nor shall I expatiate on the alkahest of that mad scoundrel Paracelsus, with which he pretended to reduce flints into salt; nor the *archaeus*, or *spiritus rector*, of that visionary *Van Helmont*, his simple, elementary water, his *gas*, ferments, and transmutations; nor shall I enlarge upon the salt, sulphur, and oil, the *acidum vagum*, the mercury of metals, and the volatilized vitriol

of other modern chymists, a pack of ignorant, conceited, knavish rascals, that puzzle your weak heads with such jargon.[5]

NOTES

1. *Doctors and Medicine in the Novels of Tobias Smollett* (Ph.D. thesis, Princeton University, 1966), pp. 77–78. Outstanding alchemical and chemical lexicons of the 17th and 18th centuries were then consulted as well as J. R. Partington's massive *History of Chemistry* (3 vols., London: Macmillan; New York: St. Martins, 1961–).

2. "The fifth of the simple fossil Salts, is an acid, vague, volatile, liquid one, dispersed perhaps every where throughout the Mines: This being united with a fossil Oil, as the *Petroleum*, *Oleum terrae*, and the like, may possibly produce the different sorts of native fossil pellucid Sulphurs, called quick Sulphurs" (*Elements of Chemistry*, trans. Timothy Dallowe, 2 vols., London, 1735, Vol. I, p. 28). In Peter Shaw's translation of 1741 the acid is called the "Vague universal acid" and is said "to be diffused in all parts of the earth" (Vol. I, p. 112). By the time of the 1753 Shaw translation the *acidum vagum* must have attracted a great deal of attention among chemists for in that edition Shaw has a long footnote (Vol. I, pp. 112–113) discussing recent theories of the "vague acid."

3. Mentioned in Vol. I, pp. 180, 192, in lecture notes entitled "Vitriolic Acid." "It is supposed to be in all Cavities of the Earth, whence it is sometimes called *Acidum Vagum*." Dr. Smeaton dates the lectures 1756–1758. Cullen drew of course a good deal from Boerhaave's *Elementa chemiae*. I am greatly indebted to Dr. Smeaton for drawing this passage to my attention.

4. The unauthorized Latin edition appeared in 1724, the authorized in 1731, and the first full English translation by an unknown author in 1732; but Boerhaave had been lecturing on chemistry to English-speaking students at Leiden since 1702. For the difficult chronology of these editions and translations see F. W. Gibbs, "Boerhaave's Chemical Writings," *Ambix*, 1958, 6:117–135, and William P. D. Wightman, "William Cullen and the Teaching of Chemistry," *Annals of Science*, 1955, 11:154–165; 1956, 12:192–205. See also "Hermann Boerhaave and Scottish Chemistry" in *An Eighteenth-Century Lectureship in Chemistry. Essays and bicentenary addresses relating to the Chemistry Department of Glasgow University*, ed. Andrew Kent (Glasgow: Jackson, 1950), pp. 41–48.

5. *Sir Launcelot Greaves* (Oxford: Shakespeare Head Press, 1925), p. 108.

XII
Smollett's Wit and the
Traditions of Learning in Medicine

"This young lady, who wanted neither slyness nor penetration
. . . replied with seeming unconcern, that for her own part she should
never repine, if there was not a pineapple in the universe, provided
she could indulge herself with the fruits of her own country."[1] Mrs.
Pickle's remark is calculated and represents the basis of a plan to rid
herself of the "teizing and disagreeable Mrs. Grizzle." In fact,
Smollett tells us that if a certain "gentleman happening to dine with
Mr. Pickle" had not mentioned pineapples, Peregrine might not
have seen the light of day: the ridiculous Mrs. Grizzle would have
remained at the side of her sister-in-law throughout gestation, teasing
and torturing her with obsequiousness, dementing her imagination,
which at this period seemed to be strangely diseased, and "marking"
her still unborn child.[2] A "diseased imagination" in the mother, Mrs.
Grizzle would have argued, produced inferior progeny (Peregrine
born with the image of a pineapple clearly defined on his body!), but
a "dish of pineapples" could produce no progeny at all. Mrs.
Grizzle's search for pineapples for "three whole days and nights" is
thus futile: Peregrine, our hero, must be born. But then, a pregnant
woman's desires must not be balked—Mrs. Grizzle would have
continued—and Mrs. Pickle had told her that "she had eaten a most
delicious pineapple in her sleep." Unaware of the consequences of
these alternatives, Mrs. Grizzle makes the wrong choice, furnishing
her sister-in-law with two ripe pineapples, "as fine as ever were seen
in England." Propitiously, however, Mrs. Pickle did not partake of
the fruit—at least, Smollett never tells us that she did. Her swooning
at the dinner table, the ensuing hysteria, the nocturnal dream—all
are devices to encourage Mrs. Grizzle to leave the Pickle household.

It is curious that these chapters (v–vi) describing the incubation
and birth of Peregrine have never received any attention. This fact is
further puzzling when one recalls that they are among the most
amusing in the novel. Smollett's eighteenth-century readers would
have been amused by Mrs. Grizzle's obstetric handbooks and pious
medical beliefs, and perhaps entertained by Mrs. Pickle's intense

dislike of her "sister". But they must have been doubly amused by the elder's "researches within the country" (Smollett's hyperbole) for pineapples: such peregrinations for fruits "which were altogether unnatural productions, extorted by the force of artificial fire, out of filthy manure!"[3] For her distaste for pineapples and her pretentious medical learning—Aristotle and Nicholas Culpepper[4]—eighteenth-century audiences could have forgiven Mrs. Grizzle; they could not forgive her for an inability to put learning into practice. Her immense concern for pineapples, however, must have struck them as particularly topical, for readers of *Peregrine Pickle* would have understood Mrs. Grizzle's new-fangled theories of the effects of this fruit on pregnant women in the context of eighteenth-century medicine. We, as modern readers, view her actions and statements as part of Smollett's use of learning for the purposes of wit. A clue to the extensiveness of Smollett's knowledge of the subject can be observed in the first full-length book on pineapples in English, John Giles's *Ananas, a Treatise on the Pine Apple* (London, 1767), a book which Smollett may or may not have read. This technical handbook for scientists and expert gardeners confirmed Mrs. Grizzle's belief that pineapples were an unlucky sign for pregnant mothers. Much of Smollett's comic irony in these chapters derives from the audience's familiarity with contemporary ideas about pineapples. It is not surprising, however, to discover medical learning used for comic purposes in the novels of an author who was a physician by profession and whose works abound with a variety of scientific references.

For our purposes chapters v and vi of *Peregrine Pickle* contain the key passages in which Mrs. Pickle describes her unexplainable desires: for a fricassee of frogs, for a porcelain chamber-pot, for three black hairs from Mr. Trunnion's beard—and for pineapples. Then we are told that only in the case of exotic foods did Mrs. Grizzle interfere:

She restricted her [Mrs. Pickle] from eating roots, pot-herbs, fruit, and all sort of vegetables; and one day when Mrs. Pickle had plucked a peach with her own hand, and was in the very act of putting it between her teeth, Mrs, Grizzle perceived the rash attempt, and running up to her, fell upon her knees in the garden, intreating her, with tears in her eyes, to resist such a pernicious appetite. Her request was no sooner complied with, than recollecting that if her sister's longing was baulked, the child might be affected with some disagreeable mark, or deplorable disease, she begged as earnestly that she would swallow the fruit, and in the mean time ran for some cordial water of her own composing, which she forced upon her sister, as an antidote to the poison she had received.[5]

The witty context of this description and the ridiculous actions of the women it involves should not lead us to conclude that Smollett was distorting or ridiculing contemporary theories of embryology. Actually Smollett's accounts of the treatment of pregnant women (such as Mrs. Pickle) were based upon experiments with foetuses performed in the third and fourth decades of the eighteenth-century and speculations of respected scientists of the Royal College of Physicians such as James Augustus Blondel, Daniel Turner, and William Smellie, a leading obstetrician to whom Smollett was apprenticed and in whose medical library he educated himself. It is essential to note biographically that at the very same time—1750— Smollett was composing *Peregrine Pickle*, he was also editing, annotating, and preparing for the press Smellie's *Treatise on the Theory and Practice of Midwifery*, which was published the same year as Smollett's novel. In 1750, then, Smollett was deep in the study of obstetric medicine and, particularly, in abnormal pregnancy, for that subject occupies the largest portion of Smellie's book. Smollett's novel was the first in English (a decade before *Tristram Shandy*)[6] to refer to heated controversies about the role of imagination in abnormal pregnancy, a subject Smellie treated at length and which abundantly stimulated Smollett's own imagination. The humorous episode built upon Mrs. Grizzle's extreme distrust and dislike of pineapples also reflects the popularity of this exotic fruit in England and in Scotland in the 1740s and 1750s, its alleged medicinal qualities, and its being a forbidden fruit to pregnant women. Although Smollett did not live long enough to see the appearance of Edward Topham's widely read *Letters from Edinburgh written in the years 1774, and 1775*, he would have taken Scottish pride in Topham's observation that in the 1740s and 1750s Scotland, no less than England, was the garden of Europe—at least as far as exotic *ananas* were concerned:

> . . . if the Scotch are deprived, by the nature of their situation, of enjoyment of natural fruit, they have the opportunity of furnishing themselves with hot-houses . . . and, in this respect, have the advantage of the rest of Great Britain. There are few gentlemen of any consequence that are not supplied with fruit by this means; and indeed, melons, pineapples, grapes . . . are produced here with great success.[7]

I

"Mrs. Pickle's longings," Smollett tells us, "were not restricted to the demands of the palate and stomach, but also affected all the other organs of sense, and even invaded her imagination, which at this period seemed to be strangely diseased." The notion that a mother's "imagination" influenced her foetus and subsequently, her child, was as old as Aristotle. In his treatise *De Generatione et Corruptione*, the Greek philosopher had discussed the matter at length in "Rules for the First Two Months of Pregnancy." "Let none present any strange, or unwholesome thing to her, not so much as name it, lest she should desire it, and not be able to get it, and so either cause her to miscarry, or the child have some deformity on that account."[8] The sections in Aristotle's book dealing with gestation and pregnancy were extracted in the seventeenth century and bound together, under the title *The Experienced Midwife*. Galenic medicine of the seventeenth century had little to add to Aristotle's precepts. Occasionally an author such as Shakespeare capitalised upon Aristotle's admonishment: thus Pompey, the jester in *Measure for Measure*, comes on stage bellowing that his Mistress Elbow "came in, great with child, and longing for stewed prunes; Sir, we had but two in the house, which at that very distant time stood in a fruit dish, a dish of some three-pence." Distinguished physicians like Thomas Sydenham and Thomas Willis adhered to the ideas stated in *The Experienced Midwife*, and less illustrious doctors were equally obeisant.

Throughout the seventeenth and early eighteenth centuries this work was a standard textbook for physicians and midwives, and was the major source for Nicholas Culpepper's *Directory for Midwives* (first published in 1651), a book which Smollett must have read at least by the time he prepared Smellie's *Treatise on Midwifery* for the press. Culpepper's *Directory* had become so popular by the 1730s—years during which Smollett was in medical school—that it evoked in 1735 enthusiastic rhapsody from an anonymous commentator:

> And if he [any young doctor] applies himself to the Obstetrical Art, let him turn over Culpepper's *Midwife enlarg'd* night and day. That little Book is worth a whole Library. All that is possible to be known in the Art is there treasur'd up in a small *Duodecimo*. Blessed, yea for ever blessed, be the memory of the inimitable Author, who, and who alone, had the *curious happiness* to mix the profound learning of Aristotle with the facetious Humour of Plautus.[9]

A physician himself, Culpepper repeated Aristotle's advice to pregnant women who, like Mrs. Trunnion, wished to give birth to unscarred infants. "Sometimes there is an extraordinary cause, as imagination, when the Mother is frighted, or imagineth strange things, or longeth vehemently for some meat which if she have not, the child hath a mark of the colour or shape of what she desired, of which there are many examples."[10]

It was not the pregnant mother's "strange longings"—a condition known as "pica"[11]—that disconcerted physicians and midwives so much as the ill effects of these yearnings on the foetus. According to Culpepper even a single instance of bizarre desire would produce "Hermaphrodites, Dwarfs or Gyants," and this idea was repeated again and again in medical works of the period. John Maubray discussed it at length in *The Female Physician, Containing all the Diseases Incident to that Sex, in Virgins, Wives and Widows* (1724). In a chapter entitled "Of Monsters" he complained that too few authors were "ready to discuss the proper Causes of *Monstrous* BIRTHS," and continued to give his explanation for the occurrences:[12]

> First then, I take the Imagination to have the most prevalent *Power* in Conception; which I hope may be readily granted, considering how common a Thing it is, for the *Mother* to mark her child with *Pears, Plums, Milk, Wine*, or any *thing else*, upon the least trifling *Accident* happening to her from thence; and *that* even in the latter ripening *Months*, after the Infant is entirely formed, by the *Strength of her Imagination* only, as has been already manifestly set forth at large.

Maubray extended his case to the male as well, noting that "a Foetus with a *Calf's, Lamb's, Dog's, Cat's-Head*, or the Effigy of any other thing whatsoever," might be the result of "a *copulating* Man, if he should imprudently set his Mind on such Objects, or employ his perverted *Imagination* that way." The powerful and lasting effects of the imagination, Maubray contended, were not limited to human-kind, but extended also to lower species. "This absurd *Imagination* takes place even among the very *Brutes*, as Lemnius relates of a Sheep with a Seal's, or *Sea* Calf's-Head, having no doubt seen that Animal in the critical Time of *Conjunction* or *Conception*." Like many doctors in the previous century, Maubray enjoined would-be mothers to suppress their "absurd Imaginations," lest they bring into the world no children but "Monsters formed in the Womb."

An incident late in 1726 which Smollett probably had heard about, contributed much to the popular fear that women with "absurd Imaginations" during pregnancy would bring forth monsters: this was the extraordinary case of the pregnant Mary Tofts of Godalming who insisted that she had eventually given birth to at least seventeen rabbits and other curious progeny. Unable to afford rabbits, she nevertheless craved them throughout her pregnancy, and one day, while working in the fields, she actually saw one who may or may not have frightened her. The case itself has recently been discussed in such detail that I do not pretend to add new discoveries or theories,[13] but will suggest that its widespread fame and the satires it provoked —for example, Hogarth's "Credulity, Superstition, and Fanaticism" —added further fuel to existing fears. On 5 December 1726, Pope wrote to John Caryll who lived not far from Godalming and might be expected to have heard more details than Londoners: "I want to know what faith you have in the miracle at Guildford; not doubting but as you past thro' that town, you went as a philosopher to investigate, if not as a curious anatomist to inspect, that wonderful phenomenon. All London is now upon this occasion, as it generally is upon all others divided into factions about it."[14] If Caryll replied to Pope's inquiry, as he may well have, the letter is not extant, but numerous Scriblerian satires are. One of these was a series of verses by Pope, "The Discovery: Or, *The* Squire turn'd Ferret. An Excellent New Ballad. To the Tune of *High Boys! up go we; Chevy Chase;* Or what you please," published in December 1726, again in January, and several times thereafter. Here Pope turned his light artillery particularly upon two scientists, Nathaniel St André, a Swiss anatomist and medical attendant on the King, and Samuel Molyneux. Mary Tofts had first been attended by John Howard, a Guildford surgeon and male midwife who had not known her until he was called in on her case. After having devoted most of his time to her for several days, delivering nine rabbits, he moved her to Guildford, to which he invited anyone who doubted the veracity of the reports he had been giving. St André, unfortunately for himself, accepted the invitation and made the trip to Guildford, taking with him Samuel Molyneux, secretary to the Prince of Wales, a scientist of great distinction, particularly important for his work in developing the reflecting telescope. Molyneux was not a medical man and made no pretence to knowledge of midwifery; St André, on the other hand, although he had taken no degree, had been apprenticed to a surgeon and had held the post of local surgeon to the Westminster Hospital Dispensary. It was the unoffending Molyneux, however, who bore the brunt of Pope's satire—perhaps because Pope knew more about telescopes (he had grown interested in the optical effects of the reflecting telescope) than about midwifery:[15]

> But hold! says Molly, first let's try
>   Now that her legs are ope,
> If ought within we may descry
>   By help of Telescope.
> The Instrument himself did make,
>   He rais'd and level'd right.
> But all about was so opake,
>   It could not aid his Sight . . .
>
> Why has the Proverb falsely said,
>   *Better two Heads than one;*
> Could *Molly* hide this *Rabbit's* Head,
>   He still might show his own.

Pope's satire on the "Rabbit Breeder" was one among many. He himself may or may not have contributed another "ballad" on the Tofts case to the *Flying Post*, published on 19 December 1726. In the *Flying Post* it was "Said to be Written by Mr. Pope to Dr. Arbuthnot"; the published title is simply "Mr. P—— to Dr. A——t." Here the satire is chiefly directed at Sir Richard Manningham, son of the Bishop of Chester and godson of Sir Hans Sloane, "society's most distinguished man-midwife," whose attention to Mary Tofts had been ordered by King George himself. Many others may be found in the Library of the Royal Society of Medicine in an apparently unique scrapbook, "A Collection of 10 Tracts" on "Mary Tofts, the celebrated pretended Breeder of Rabbits." Among these is a one-page set of verses, "The Rabbit-Man-Midwife," inscribed in an eighteenth-century pencilled hand, "by John Arbuthnot." Another is a tract of ten pages, *The Opinion of the Rev'd Mr. William Whiston concerning the Affair of Mary Tofts, ascribing it to the Completion of a Prophecy of Esdras*, written by William Whiston, formerly Lucasian Professor of Astronomy at Cambridge, Isaac Newton's successor. In the apocryphal book of Esdras, said Whiston, "Tis here foretold that there should be 'Signs in the Women' or more particularly that "Menstrous [sic] Women should bring forth Monsters."[16] Presumably writing years after the Mary Tofts affair, when the story had been "long laughed out of Countenance," Whiston insisted that he believed it to be true "as the fulfilling of this Ancient Prophecy before us." Still another satire in the Royal Society of Medicine scrapbook is a pamphlet of 1727, purportedly written by "Lemuel Gulliver, Surgeon and Anatomist to the Kings of Lilliput and Blefuscu, and Fellow of the Academy of Sciences in Balnibarbi": *The Anatomist Dissected: or the Man-Midwife finely brought to Bed*, London, 1727.[17] If one of the Scriblerians was responsible for this thirty-five-page pamphlet, it was Dr. Arbuthnot, who need not have concealed authorship since *The Anatomist Dissected* was far above the average tract on the rabbit-woman. It professes to be chiefly "An Examination of the Conduct of Mr. St André, Touching the late pretended Rabbit-bearer," based on St André's defence of himself, *A Short Narrative of an Extraordinary Delivery of Rabbits*. But scrutiny reveals that it is the work of a physician with extensive knowledge of anatomy and experience in childbirth. He points out inconsistencies in St André's account, pausing over matters of the temperature and pulse of woman in labour, and the influence of her demented imagination on the foetus.

I have strayed afield and treated the Tofts case at length because it stirred a controversy among physicians and other scientists that was to last in England more than forty years. Less than a month after the episode of the "rabbit breeder," James Augustus Blondel, a distinguished member of the College of Physicians of London, brought out a treatise denying the possibility of such an occurrence: this work was later advertised by Dr. Blondel as "My first Dissertation, *The Strength of Imagination in pregnant Women examin'd*, published upon the Occasion of the Cheat of *Godalming*, hastily, and without Name, as coming from one, who neither designed to be known nor to meddle any more in this Controversy." Trained in Leyden by Boerhaave, Blondel maintained that deformities in birth were caused by other factors—such as actual delivery—than the mother's imagination. He was challenged by Daniel Turner, another physician and Fellow of the Royal College of Surgeons, who dogmatically asserted the opposite.[18] The two physicians, both distinguished and both fellows of the same society, stirred considerable debate within the College of Physicians. Since Blondel felt he had been attacked personally by Turner, he responded with a one-hundred-and-fifty-page defence of himself: *The Power of the Mother's Imagination Over the Foetus Examin'd. In Answer to Dr. Daniel Turner's Book, Intitled a Defence of the XIIth Chapter of the First Part of a Treatise, De Morbis Cutaneis* (1729). In his preface Blondel stated his purpose: "My Design is to attack a vulgar Error, which has been prevailing for many Years, in Opposition to Experience, sound Reason, and Anatomy: I mean the common Opinion, that Marks and Deformities, which Children are born with, are the sad Effect of the Mother's irregular Fancy and Imagination." Without providing any historical survey of the controversy Blondel noted "that the Doctrine of Imagination, relating to the Foetus, had gone through several Revolutions," and continued to indict the "Imaginationists."[19]

> 'Tis silly and absurd; for what can be more ridiculous, than to make of Imagination a Knife, a Hammer, a Pastry-Cook, a Thief, a Painter, a Jack of all Trades, a Juggler, Doctor Faustus, the Devil, and all?
> 'Tis saucy and scandalous, in supposing that those, whom God Almighty has endowed, not only with so many charms, but also, with an extraordinary Love and Tenderness for their children, instead of answering the End they are made for, do breed Monsters by the Wantonness of their Imagination.
> 'Tis mischievous and cruel; it disturbs whole Families, distracts the Brains of credulous People, and puts them in continual Fears, and in Danger of their Lives: In short 'tis such a publick Nuisance, that 'tis the Interest of every Body to join together against such a Monster, and to root it entirely out of the World.

In less than six months the "Imaginationists" led by Turner retorted with a reassertion of the influence of the mother on her foetus. Parodying Blondel's title, Turner called his treatise *The Force of the Mother's Imagination upon her Foetus* (1730). This work was over two hundred pages and was a definitive defence of the majority view of the time. One of Turner's arguments was "the authority of Antiquity": he had culled hundreds of ancient and medieval medical writings and prepared a list of monstrous births in which the mother's demented imagination was the apparent cause. Most common among these, Turner affirmed, was her craving for exotic fruits—plums, cherries, grapes, prunes, and now pineapples. Unlike Blondel, Turner was not concerned with the physiological processes by which the foetus was actually "marked." He abstained from proving the truth of his argument by appealing to "sensation, the nerves, and the circulation of the foetus." Instead, he cited numerous ancient and modern authorities, known and obscure—Hesiod, Heliodorus, Jacobus Horstius, Ambroise Paré, Johann Schenkius, Thomas Bartholin, Charles Cyprianus, Robert Boyle, Sir Kenelm Digby—who had reported instances of deformed children; moreover, Mary Tofts herself, although "a cheat," had been frightened by rabbits while sowing in the fields, and in Turner's estimation there was a definite connection between the imagination and the foetus. Learned though his argument seemed, Turner was scurrilously satirized by his opponents in several pamphlets and poems, perhaps the most witty and scrofulous among them a burlesque set of verses written in Butlerian octosyllables entitled "The Porter Turn'd Physician," and published in 1731.

Although Blondel and Turner after 1730 did not publish works concerning the mother's imagination, the controversy over which they differed continued to be a topic of concern in medical and lay circles for at least three decades. Fellows of the Royal Society, many of whom were Smollett's personal friends, and other scientifically inclined gentlemen, hesitated to drop so controversial an issue. Doctors Hunter and Monro spent considerable time on the topic in their anatomical lectures, and we know that Smollett not only heard these but was in 1748–50 in medical dialogues with these men. As late as 1747, John Henry Mauclerc, an M.D. of no great distinction, published a lengthy treatise entitled *Dr. Blondel confuted: or, the Ladies Vindicated, with Regard to the Power of Imagination in Pregnant Women: Together with a Circular and General Address to the Ladies on this Occasion* (London).[20] Odd as it may appear, Mauclerc's book approved rather than confuted—his own term—Blondel's theory that imagination alone was unable to harm the foetus. "The Design of the Dissertation," he wrote in the preface of his book intended especially for women," is to prove that the Opinion, which has long prevail'd, that the Marks and Deformities,

Children bring into the World, are the sad Effect of the Mother's irregular Fancy and Imagination, is nothing else but a vulgar Error, contrary to sound Reason and Anatomy." Later in his preface Mauclerc writes as if the controversy were still inflaming the hearts of medical men, twenty years after the fact: "I don't despair of Success: Interest alone should prevail, upon the Party, which is chiefly concerned in this Controversy." Dr. Mauclerc disbelieving in old wives' tales and other odd superstitions, presents —to quote his own words—"a Sketch of the true Cause of Monsters—I hope, 'tis sufficient for the present, to give a general, and yet a clear Solution of those strange Phenomena [monsters]." If Blondel had his supporters, so did Turner, although both men had been dead for many years. In 1765, Isaac Bellet, a French physician residing in London, wrote *Letters on the Force of the Imagination in Pregnant Women*, in which he denied the possibility that pregnant women could mark their children, but was compelled to agree rather with Turner's explanations than Blondel's. The result was a second-rate medical work fraught with contradiction, but nevertheless one showing how very much alive the matter still was. Dr. Smollett, probably the author of the review in the *Critical Review*,[21] found the book very appealing: "We declare upon the whole," he wrote, "that he [Bellet] has fulfilled his scope, and executed his undertaking with great precision, and that he has clearly demonstrated the impossibility of a pregnant woman's marking her child with the figure of any object for which she has longed, or which may have made a deep impression upon the imagination." It is difficult, if at all possible, to state accurately what Smollett's views on the subject were almost twenty years earlier, when he was writing the early chapters of *Peregrine Pickle*, but there is every reason to believe that even the probability of a mother marking her child seemed remote to him. Hunter, Monro, and Smellie doubted the possibility, and medically speaking, they exerted much influence on his thought.

Throughout the 1740s cases of extraordinary childbirth of every sort continued to interest the English public, especially physicians and scientists. One could compile with ease a long list of works written in the decade about strange childbirths. Nor was the subject treated in books and tracts only. Popular periodicals that enjoyed large amateur audiences devoted much space in their issues to these freaks of nature. *The Gentleman's Magazine*, for example, contained no fewer than ninety-two articles (essays, reviews, and letters) on the question of extraordinary childbirth.[22] Curiosity was especially aroused by a woman who never became pregnant until she drank Bishop Berkeley's tar water in 1745. More specialized in its reading audience, the *Philosophical Transactions* of the Royal Society (to which Smollett never was elected but many of whose Fellows he knew) was flooded with communications about bizarre births attesting to the interests of its fellow members in the subject. Professor Knapp's biography makes it clear that Smollett was familiar with some of these publications. An idea of the range and diversity of such cases may be gained by listing a few of the titles of these articles:[23] "Account of a monstrous boy"; "Account of a monstrous child born of a woman under sentence of transportation"; "An Account of a monstrous foetus resembling an hooded monkey"; "Case of a child turned upside down"; "A remarkable conformation, or lusus naturae in a child"; "Part of a letter concerning a child of monstrous size"; "Account of a child's being taken out of the abdomen after having lain there upwards of 16 years"; "a letter concerning a child born with an extraordinary tumour near the anus, containing some rudiments of an embryo in it"; "An account of a praeternatural conjunction of two female children"; "Part of a letter concerning a child born with the jaundice upon it, received from its father's imagination, and of the mother taking the same distemper from her husband the next time of being with child"; "An account of a monstrous foetus without any mark of sex"; "An account of a double child born at Hebus, near Middletown in Lancashire." So interesting to laymen and amateur scientists were many of these cases that they were abstracted from the *Philosophical Transactions* and reported in abbreviated form as news items in *The Gentleman's Magazine*.

The controversy originally stirred by Blondel and Turner, and about which Smollett must have heard, also provoked considerable commentary in the 1740s in books (essays, novels, and poems). Fielding Ould, among the most famous male-midwives of his age and best known for *A Treatise of Midwifery* (1742)[24]—frequently called by historians of medicine the first important text on midwifery in English—considered the mother's imagination important in the health of the foetus, although he seems to have doubted the validity of Turner's views. Not infrequently the subject appeared in novels. Sir John Hill, an arch-enemy of Smollett in 1751, created a marvellous female character in *The Adventures of George Edwards, A Creole*,[25] who touched a robin-red-breast during pregnancy (her fancy having led her to this curious action!) and, thereafter, bore a child with a red breast—or red chest. In the same year that *Peregrine Pickle* was published, 1751, he also wrote a satire on the subject of curious births entitled *Lucina sine concubitu*. Here the reader finds the theories of preformation (according to which organisms are already fully formed in their seeds) and panspermism (minute organisms developed in fluids owing to the presence of germs) satirically treated, as well as those of the influence of the mother's imagination on her child. Although Hill was unable to attain membership in the Royal Society because of his disagreeable personality, his hoax *Lucina* was nevertheless widely read by such professional medical men as Dr. Smollett, who had good reason to take note of Hill in 1751.[26] The famous case,[27] two years earlier, of a woman "who carried with child 16 years," also helped to create the background for Smollett's witty treatment of the state of the mother's imagination.

Peregrine Pickle was published twelve years too early to bear any traces of awareness of George Alexander Stevens's *Dramatic History of Master Edward* (London, 1763). But this collection of extraordinary occurrences in 1730–1760—written, as the title page indicates, by the "Author of the celebrated Lecture upon Heads"—demonstrates how fully formed a type of writing (most accurately described as a *leit motif*) about abnormal births had emerged by the 1760s. In the opening pages (7–13), Stevens has Thomas recount to David a series of histories, all dealing with abnormalities during pregnancy and shortly after birth. The stories, culled from authors in different countries in Europe, are as bizarre and grotesque as scenes from gothic romances (then coming into vogue). Two histories in particular appeal to David, so much so that Stevens included illustrations of them in his revised edition of 1785. In the first, "*Aldrovandus* [a seventeenth-century naturalist] relates, that a woman in Sicily observing a lobster by a fisherman, and being moved by an ernest longing for it, brought forth a lobster, altogether like what she had seen and longed for." Stevens's "lobster woman" is not very different from Mary Tofts, the "rabbit woman." The second history richer in complexity and more touching relates, as Stevens writes, "something singular beyond all these:"

> . . . [it] is the tale of *Languis*, of a woman longing to bite the naked shoulder of a baker passing by her; which, rather than she should lose her longing, the good-natured husband hired the baker at a certain price. Accordingly, when the big-bellied woman had bit twice, the baker's wife broke away from the people who held her, would not suffer her to bite her husband again; for want of which, she bore one dead child, with two living ones.

Smollett himself had shown interest in cases of extraordinary childbirth five years before the composition of *Peregrine Pickle*. In *Advice: A Satire* (1746), the character Poet refers to the strange conception, or near-conception, of a hermaphrodite:[28]

> But one thing more—how loud must I repeat,
> To rouse th'engag'd attention of the great,
> Amus'd, perhaps, with C————'s prolific bum,
> Or rapt amidst the transports of a drum."

Here Smollett's own note reads: "This alludes to a phenomenon not more strange than true; the person here meant, having actually laid upwards of forty eggs, as several physicians and fellows of the Royal Society can attest, one of whom, we hear, has undertaken the incubation, and will, no doubt, favour the world with an account of his success. Some virtuosi affirm, that such productions must be the effect of a certain intercourse of organs not fit to be named." Smollett's source for "C——"[29] remains a mystery, although his satiric habit of mind was unlikely to fabricate a source. London newspapers in 1745–46 were filled with reports of such odd occurrences and the populace seemed to be diverted, if not instructed, by these accounts. In 1750, Smollett, while preparing for publication Dr. William Smellie's *Midwifery*, probably read about cases of unnatural birth in the hours he spent annotating. During that year he may have seen "Michael Anne Drouvert," the much talked about Parisian hermaphrodite who was displayed in London and written up as a case history in the *Philosophical Transactions;* may have read James Parsons's *Inquiry into the Nature of Hermaphrodites* (1741) or George Arnaud's new book entitled *Dissertation on Hermaphrodites* (1750); or may even have heard that John Hill's forthcoming book, *A History of Animals* (1750), contained a modern epitome of the subject. At any rate, Smollett's extensive reading in obstetrics in the library of Smellie, and earlier in Dr. James Douglas's library, would have revealed a wealth of real cases from which to create fictional characters and episodes relating to pregnancy. Smollett's own observations, printed in Smellie's *Treatise* (II, 4–5), "On the Separation of the Pubic Joint in Pregnancy," give ample testimony to and palpable evidence of his interest in cases of abnormal birth.

In fact, Smollett never lost interest in the subject and continued from 1750 to 1764 to edit and revise all Smellie's obstetrical works. Smollett's extensive medical reading coupled with his knowledge of the extraordinary case of Sarah Last,[30] who in 1748 underwent normal pregnancy without ever giving birth to her foetus, must have inspired him to draw a parallel case in Mrs. Trunnion in *Peregrine Pickle*. Readers will recall the bizarrely constructed chapters in which the pregnant lady is found to have been swelled with air! Smollett was reflecting contemporary fears about strange childbirth when he described the ultimate chagrin of the Trunnions:

At length she and her husband became the standing joke of the parish; and this infatuated couple could scarce be prevailed upon to part with their hopes, even when she appeared as lank as a greyhound, and they were furnished with other unquestionable proofs of their having been deceived. But they could not forever remain under the influence of this sweet delusion, which at last faded away, and was succeeded by a paroxism of shame and confusion, that kept the husband within doors for the space of a whole fortnight, and confined his lady to her bed for a series of weeks, during which she suffered all the anguish of the most intense mortification.[31]

II

The first pineapple grown in a hothouse in England may well have been planted during the Restoration. A well-known extant painting, bearing the inscription *Rose, The Royal Gardener, presenting to Charles II the first pine-apple grown in England*, is ascribed to the Dutch artist Danckerts and the gardener is John Rose.[32] Just how long before Monsieur Le Cour, a Frenchman residing in Leyden, Holland, "hit upon a proper Degree of Heat and Management so as to produce pine-apples equally as good as those which are produced in the West Indies."[33] is not known. Even in Leyden, where winters were less brutal than in England, Le Cour used stoves to grow the tropical fruit. Chambers's compendious *Cyclopaedia* (1728) reports that the gardens of England were supplied with pineapples by Le Cour himself, and John Evelyn wrote in his *Diary* on 9 August 1661: "I first saw the famous Queene-pine brought from Barbados presented to his *Majestie*, but the first that were ever seene here in England, were those sent to Cromwell, foure-yeares since" [1658].[34] Evelyn continued several days later with a description of the "rare fruite called the King-Pine," the first he had seen: he tasted it and found it not to his liking.

Whether or not those described by Evelyn were the first grown—it is at least plausible that an occasional fruit had been grown earlier—a more likely possibility is that pineapples were first artificially produced in quantity at any rate, in the hothouses of Sir Matthew Decker's famous garden in Richmond. He was a well-known London merchant (president of the East India Company) of Dutch origin who apparently enjoyed a "truly Dutch passion for gardening."[35] Richard Bradley, an authority on gardening in the early decades of the eighteenth century and Professor of Botany at the University of Cambridge, wrote that Sir Matthew's gardener, Henry Tellende, grew the first pineapples for his master "circa 1723."[36] Seven years before this, Lady Mary Wortley Montagu had eaten pineapples at the table of the Elector of Hanover. She wrote to Lady Mar about "2 ripe Ananas's, which to my taste are a fruit perfectly delicious," and continued to note surprise that pineapples had not yet been cultivated in her native land. "You know they are naturally the Growth of Brasil, and I could not imagine how they could come there but by

Enchantment. Upon Enquiry I learnt that they have brought their Stoves to such perfection, they lengthen the Summer as long as they please, gieing to every plant the degree of heat it would receive from the Sun in its native Soil. The Effect is very near the same. I am surpriz'd we do not practise in England so usefull an Invention."[37] From the lengthy discussion about pineapples that Horatio and Cleomenes have in Mandeville's *Fable of the Bees* (1714),[38] it may be assumed that Tellende and his lord, Decker, had raised the delicious and exotic fruit approximately in 1720–23. Mandeville's characters— not dissimilar to several enthusiasts in *Peregrine Pickle*—comment upon a new and "fine Invention" as well as on the intrinsic attributes of pineapples: Horatio says, "I was thinking of the Man, to whom we are in a great measure obliged for the Production and Culture of the *Exotick*, we were speaking of in this Kingdom; Sir Matthew Decker: the first *Ananas*, or Pineapple, that was brought to Perfection in *England*, grew in his Garden at Richmond." That garden was still viewed in the 1730s and Smollett, who had come to London in 1739, may have visited it.

As Richard Bradley had explained in his essay "A particular easy Method of managing Pine-Apples" (1726),[39] the difficulty of cultivation was due to poor hothouses and stoves. Pineapples required a full three years of growth, an exact temperature, ideal moisture conditions, and correctly constructed stoves. As soon as this was achieved, the fruit could be grown in domestic gardens, even if at great financial expenditure. Such was the case and it applied not only to pineapples but to other exotic fruits, limes, papayas, guavas, bananas, and even grapes. The cultivation of pineapples in the third and particularly the fourth decades of the eighteenth century became a hobby—not quite a popular sport—among expert gardeners and aristocrats. Prominent families who could afford the expense sent their head gardeners to Decker's hothouses to observe the new method and educate themselves. Among the first to display home-grown pineapples on their tables were the opulent Earls of Bathurst, Portland, and Gainsborough. The Duke of Chandos, long incorrectly identified as "Timon" in Pope's *Epistle to Burlington*, not only grew pineapples on his estate at Shaw Hall in Berkshire, but he also sold them "at a half a guinea a time,"[40] a price even Mrs. Grizzle would have been willing to pay for her sister-in-law!

Smollett may not have known first-hand the early history of pineapples in England, but he was old enough to be familiar with its more recent peregrinations. Few people were more excited about the new art of growing pineapples than Alexander Pope. Together with his gardener John Serle, whom the poet employed in 1724, Pope was growing "ananas" by 1734. He had, however, tasted the fruit long before this. On 8 October 1731, Pope wrote Martha Blount, "I'm going in haste to plant Jamaica Strawberries, which are to be almost as good as Pineapples."[41] In the spring of 1735, he wrote to William Fortescue that he was improving and expanding his garden, "making two new ovens and stoves, and a hot-house for anana's, of which I hope you will taste this year." Two or three pineapples grown in the Twickenham hothouse and sent to an intimate friend was perhaps the greatest honour Pope could confer. During this period he was continually experimenting for cheaper and better ways to raise the fruit. In August 1738, Pope and Serle "borrowed" Henry Scott, Lord Burlington's gardener who was an expert in growing pineapples, to consult with him "about a Stove I am building." It is possible that Pope was also reading modern handbooks on the subject. Whatever the case, by 1741 Pope thought he had discovered with the aid of Scott the long-sought method, and attempted to make it known to his friends. How well-circulated among the London *literati* Pope's "discovery" was, it is now impossible to tell; but by 1741, the magisterial poet was too conspicuous among men to veil any of his activities, even his pastimes and hobbies. Smollett, then young and still an *ingénu* among the "wits" in London, kept his ears and eyes open and possibly may have heard about the new pineapple method of Mr. Pope, his favourite author among all authors and a poet whose influence was to rub off considerably on his own writings. In any case, Pope soon wrote to Ralph Allen (to whom he occasionally sent a pineapple or two): "In a Week or two, Mr. Scot will make you a Visit, he is going to Set up for himself in the Art of Gardening, in which he has great Experience & particularly has a design which I think a very good one, to make Pineapples cheaper in a year or two."[42] Scott and Allen's gardener, Isaac Dodsley, were apparently successful in building the new type of hothouse with new stoves, for Pope wrote next year to Allen: "I would fain have it succeed, for two particular reasons; one because I saw it was Mrs. Allen's desire to have that fruit, & the other because it is the only piece of Service I have been able to do you, or to help you in."[43]

Poets and prose writers varied in their response to the fashionable king of fruits, some equating it with luxury and viewing it as a symbol of evil, others seeing in its beautiful colours and exotic shape an expression of the beauty of Nature and God. Pineapples were, as James Thomson wrote in "Summer" (a poem which Smollett singled out for praise in the preface of *Ferdinand Count Fathom*), the fruits of the Gods in the Primitive Ages of the world:[44]

> ". . . thou best Anana, thou the pride
> of vegetable life, beyond whate'er
> The poets imaged in the golden age:

Quick let me strip thee of thy tufty coat,
Spread thy ambrosial stores, and feast with Jove."

Still other authors wrote about the medical properties of pine-apples. In his didactic poem *The Art of Preserving Health* (1744), John Armstrong, with whom Smollett was on intimate terms throughout his life, chose the fruit as an example of a product raised that exhibited the differences and the extremes of cold and heat in diet:[45]

> . . . in horrid mail
> The crisp ananas wraps its poignant sweets.
> Earth's vaunted progeny: in ruder air
> Too coy to flourish, even too proud to live;
> Or hardly rais'd by artificial fire
> To vapid life. Here with a mother's smile
> Glad Amalthea pours her copious horn.

Smollett knew his friend's poem very well, had read it numerous times, and called it in *The Present State of All Nations* (London, 1768, II. 227), "an excellent didactic poem."

Long before the prose encyclopaedists (Ephraim Chambers, John Harris, Robert James) discussed the fruit, medical authors had commented upon it. From the time of Nicholas Culpepper's popular handbook, *A Directory for Midwives*, which Mrs. Grizzle had studied so assiduously, pineapples were strictly forbidden to ex-pectant mothers as one of the "Summer Fruits nought for her and all her Pulse." In *The English Physitian* (1674) Culpepper had devoted an entire section to the benefits and ill effects of the fruit: "It mar-velously helpeth all the Diseases of the Mother used inwardly, or applied outwardly, procuring Womens Courses, and expelling the dead Child and After-birth, yea, it is so powerful upon those Femi-nine parts that it is utterly forbidden for Women with Child, and that it will cause abortment or delivery before the time . . . Let Women forbear it if they be with Child, for it works violently upon the Feminine Part."[46] Seventeenth-century herbalists like Thomas Parkinson also warned their readers not to eat the artificial food. But it was not until pineapples were actually grown in English gardens that physicians and obstetricians became alarmed and abandoned superstition for medical science. Observation had revealed that pregnant women who ate this food miscarried again and again. Dr. Robert James, inventor of the famed "fever powders," writing in the London *Pharmacopaeia Universalis* (1742), commented: "This Fruit is esteemed cordial, and analeptic; and is said to raise and exhilarate the Spirits, to cure a Nausea, and provoke Urine. But 'tis subject to cause a Miscarriage, for which Reason Women with

Child should abstain from it."[47] One year later James (whose *Medicinal Dictionary* Smollett knew well) was even more precautionary, stating that pineapples definitely caused miscarriage. Similarly, dietitians and other authors on nutrition warned the pregnant women to refrain from the pineapple. M. L. Lemery, a prolific author on diet whose works were translated into English because of their popularity, wrote in *A Treatise of All Sorts of Foods*:[48] "Ananas is a delicious fruit, that grows in the West Indies, whose juice the *Indians* extract, and make excellent Wine of it, which will intoxicate. Women with Child dare not drink of it, because they say, it will make them miscarry." Francis Spilsbury, the author of *Free Thoughts on Quacks* (London, 1777), a treatise explaining the circumstances of Oliver Goldsmith's death, compared pineapples to gout (a strange comparison even for an eighteenth-century apothecary!) since he found a "universal comprehensiveness" in both. In his words, just as "the Ananas (vulgarly known under the name of *Pine-Apple*) is considered as containing the taste and flavour of many different fruits, so a great many disorders of the body are, under different appellations to be found in the Gout."[49]

Philosophers as well as medical thinkers pointed to the pineapple as a rare fruit with strange qualities and an exotic taste. Less concerned than physicians with the medicinal aspects of pineapples, they frequently referred to the fruit when discussing the sense of taste. As early as 1690, John Locke singled out pineapples as the best obtainable example of a food whose taste could not be comprehended without actually partaking of it. In a well-known passage in *An Essay Concerning Human Understanding* on "the Blind Man," to which Fielding referred several times in *Tom Jones*, Locke wrote of the impossibility of words replacing direct sensory experience:[50]

> He that thinks otherwise, let him try if any words can give him a taste of a pine apple, and make him have the true idea of the relish of that celebrated delicious fruit. So far as he is told it has a resemblance with any tastes whereof he has the ideas already in his memory, imprinted there by sensible objects, not strangers to his palate, so far may he approach that resemblance in his mind. But this is not giving us that idea by a definition, but exciting in us other simple ideas by their known names; which will be still very different from the true taste of that fruit itself.

Also speaking of the origin of ideas and the fact that they are grounded in sensory experience (i.e., direct sense experience), Smollett's countryman David Hume noted in the opening paragraph of his *Treatise of Human Nature* (1739) that "we cannot form to ourselves a just idea of the taste of a pineapple, without actually having tasted it."[51] That is, the rare and uncommon pineapple affords the student of philosophy a splendid opportunity to observe that "all our simple ideas in their first appearance are derived from simple impressions, which are correspondent to them, and which they exactly represent." And David Hartley, writing two years before the publication of *Peregrine Pickle*, may not have commented upon pineapples but he increased speculative interest in abnormal pregnancy by the inclusion in his *Observations on Man* of a chapter entitled, "To Examine How Far the Longings of Pregnant Women are agreeable to the Doctrines of Vibrations and Associations." Hartley, a physician by profession, underplayed the variety of longings found in pregnant women—an impressive range, as Smollett's female figures in the novels show—and demonstrated instead that abnormal cravings are caused in the first place by means of "nervous Communications between the Uterus and the Stomach." Both, Hartley maintained, are in "a State of great Sensibility and Irritability" during pregnancy, a view Smollett himself had taken in writing about the pubic joint. Smollett may not have read Locke, Hume, and Hartley—although that is highly unlikely—but he was certainly aware of popular references to pineapples and pregnancies in their works, ideas then so common that they probably required little documentation to a literate eighteenth-century man.

Thus, a decade before the publication of *Peregrine Pickle*, physicians, scientists, gardeners, philosophers, and literary men had all reacted in various ways to the new "King Fruit" which by 1751 had become much more popular than in John Evelyn's day; all had seen in the body of beliefs and superstitions embracing the fruit something different. If gardeners found it their delight and joy, philosophers were not far behind in using it as an emblem of singular sensory experience. If physicians, especially obstetricians, called it the bane of their pregnant women patients, other scientists (biologists, botanists, physiologists) were equally ominous in their belief that pineapples contained strange and unknown chemical properties.

It was therefore left to a literary man, who was a physician as well as a novelist, to see the comic possibilities in all these prevailing theories. It may also be that Smollett, himself editing the obstetric volumes of William Smellie at the time he was composing his novel, saw the fantastic (indeed absurd) theories of the mother's imagination together with the many muddles and mysteries that had grown up about pineapples could be wedded into one episode. The early chapters of *Peregrine Pickle* illustrate once again how adeptly Smollett used science, particularly medical learning, for the purposes of wit.[52] His satiric portraitures of characters such as Mrs. Pickle,

Mrs. Grizzle, and Mrs. Trunnion place great demands on the modern reader who wishes to comprehend the author's powerful wit. But his contemporary readers would have felt much more at home than we do in viewing his comic spectacle: they would have realized that he was using medical and scientific learning for pure levity and genial farce, and in this sense would have read his works as they were reading those of his great contemporary, Laurence Sterne.

We should not be surprised to observe a process of carry-over in Smollett's novels: from his medical writings to the novels and viceversa. Although he was never a successful physician, if daily practice is a yardstick of achievement, his entire life demonstrates a continuing interest in medical theory. It is, therefore, to be expected that Smollett's medical works—short essays, unsigned medical tracts written pseudonymously for financial purposes,[53] and virtually all the reviews of medical books in the *Critical Review* 1756–60 and possibly later—would have rubbed off on his fiction. Indeed, the sensibility pervading both worlds, medical and fictive, was one, and Smollett was at their centre. Such interaction serves to remind us, that the place occupied by medicine and by the social aspects of that science which daily seemed to take on ever greater consequence in the eighteenth century, is something of which we have yet to take account in our criticism and biography of Smollett.

NOTES

1. *Peregrine Pickle*, I. p. 32.
2. *Peregrine Pickle*, I. p. 31. Passages quoted in this paragraph are from *Peregrine Pickle*, I. pp. 32–36.
3. *Peregrine Pickle*, I. p. 32. Grown in elephantine stoves in specially-built hothouses, pineapples were considered an exotic and artificial fruit in the eighteenth century. I discuss the fruit more fully below.
4. *Peregrine Pickle*, I. p. 31: "She purchased Culpepper's midwifery, which, with that sagacious performance dignified with Aristotle's name, she studied with indefatigable care, and diligently perused the Compleat House-wife, together with Quincy's dispensatory, culling every jelly, marmalade and conserve which these authors recommend as either salutory or toothsome, for the benefit and comfort of her sister-in-law, during her gestation."
5. *Peregrine Pickle*, I. p. 31.
6. Some attention to embryological theory of the eighteenth century and *Tristram Shandy* is given in Louis A. Landa, "The Shandean Homunculus: The Background of Sterne's 'Little Gentleman,'" *Restoration and Eighteenth Century Literature*, ed. Carroll Camden (Chicago, 1963), pp. 49–68. I have discussed Smollett's novels and medicine in *Doctors and Medicine in the Novels of Tobias Smollett* (Princeton University dissertation, 1966).
7. *Letters from Edinburgh* (Edinburgh, 1776), "On . . . Gardening," p. 229.
8. *Aristotle's Compleat Master-Piece. Displaying the Secrets of Nature in the Generation of Man* (32nd ed.: London, 1782), pp. 33–4. See Fielding H. Garrison, *An Introduction to the History of Medicine* (4th ed. rev.: London, 1929), pp. 101 ff.
9. *An Essay for Abridging the Study of Physick* (London, 1735), p. 17.
10. *A Directory for Midwives* (London, 1684), p. 145.
11. The name given to the condition by Ancient Greek physicians, and also called "citta" or "malatia." See Hermann Heinrich Ploss, Max and Paul Bartel, "The

Longings of Pregnancy" in *Woman: An Historical and Anthropological Compendium* (London, 1935), II, pp. 455–60. A recent study of the medical aspects of *pica* is by M. Cooper, *Pica* (Springfield, Ill., 1957).

12. *The Female Physician*, p. 368. See also Part II, Chapter 7, which discusses numerous cases of foetuses that had been marked. Maubray was one of the first physicians in London to offer private instruction for midwives. See F. H. Garrison, *History of Medicine*, p. 399. A great believer in monsters, he earned notoriety in 1723 by assisting in the delivery of a Dutch woman, who produced a monstrous manikin called *de Suyger*, with "a hooked snout, fiery sparkling eyes, a long neck, and an acuminated, sharp tail." Maubray called it a moldywarp (mole) or sooterkin.

13. The most complete account is by S. A. Seligman, "Mary Tofts: the Rabbit Breeder," *Medical History*, V (1961), 349–60, which is based upon extant contemporary accounts. Another less extensive treatment is by K. Bryn Thomas, *James Douglas of the Pouch and his pupil William Hunter* (London, 1964), pp. 60–68.

14. *Correspondence of Alexander Pope*, ed. George Sherburn (Oxford, 1956), II, pp. 418–19.

15. I follow the text given by Norman Ault in *Minor Poems of Alexander Pope, The Twickenham Pope: Vol. VI* (London, 1964). pp. 259–64. St André was a Fellow of the Royal Society and contributed papers to the *Philosophical Transactions*. His appointment as Surgeon and Anatomist to the Court seems to have been made rather for his linguistic ability than his medical ability. Mary Tofts's confession put an end to his Court position, and he was never again to attain medical recognition.

16. According to the title page of the tract, these pages were copied from the second edition of Whiston's *Memoirs*, published in London in 1753. The interpretation of the Tofts case does not appear in the first edition of 1749, and, so far as I can determine, was not published separately. See K. Bryn Thomas, *James Douglas* (London, 1964), p. 65.

17. See Marjorie Nicolson and G. S. Rousseau, *This Long Disease, My Life: Alexander Pope and the Sciences* (Princeton, Princeton University Press, 1968), p. 114:

"Early in 1727 when the small talk of London seems to have been divided between Mary Tofts and Lemuel Gulliver—*Gulliver's Travels* had appeared the preceding autumn and provoked almost universal applause—it was inevitable that at least one pamphlet on the rabbit woman should be attributed to Jonathan Swift. Those who have done him that dubious honour have failed to notice that Swift had returned to Ireland a month before the Tofts affair, and while he probably heard of it in letters, he had no such background for parody as Scriblerians in London."

18. The chronology of works in the controversy was as follows: Turner, *De Morbis Cutaneis* (London, 1726; first published in 1714); Blondel, *The Strength of Imagination in Pregnant Women Examin'd* (London, 1727); Turner, *A Discourse concerning Gleets . . . to which is added A Defence of . . . the 12th Chapter of . . . De Morbis Cutaneis, in respect of the Spots and Marks impress'd upon the Skin of the Foetus* (London, 1729); Blondel, *The Power of the Mother's Imagination Over the Foetus Examin'd* (London, 1729); Turner, *The Force of the Mother's Imagination upon her Foetus in Utero . . . in the Way of A Reply to Dr. Blondel's Last Book* (London, 1730). Turner's first work, *De Morbis Cutaneis*, was written in part as a defence of Malebranche's theory that the mother marks her child. See *Father Malebranche's Treatise concerning the Search after Truth*, trans. T. Taylor (Oxford, 1694), "Book the Second Concerning the Imagination." As a conclusion to this book, Malebranche wrote: "When the Imagination of the Mother is disordered and some tempestuous passion changes the Disposition of her Brain . . . then . . . this Communication alters the natural Formation of the Infant's Body, and the Mother proves Abortive sometimes of her foetus" (p. 60). When the Tofts case revived the issue among medical men, Turner turned from Malebranche to a then real-life example. In this and other footnotes, I have dealt at length with these medical tracts because they were clearly read by the masses in their time and now are so little known.

19. *The Power of the Mother's Imagination*, p. xi. Blondel singled out from medical literature the six most common causes of spotted children: "1. A strong Longing for something particular, in which Desire the Mother is either gratified, or disappointed. 2. A sudden Surprise. 3. The Sight and Abhorrence of an ugly and frightful Object. 4. The Pleasure of Looking on, and Contemplating, even for a long Time, a Picture **or**

Whatever is delightful to the Fancy. 5. Fear, and Consternation, and great Apprehension of Dangers. 6. And lastly, an Excess of Anger, of Grief, or of Joy" (p. 2). Later (p. 4) Blondel notes that item (1) of the list above was the most common of the six, especially in the case of certain fruits, "the strong Desire of *Peaches*, or Cherries." Presumably he would have included in this list pineapples!

20. An earlier version of this work appeared in 1740 with the title page, *The Power of Imagination in Pregnant Women Discussed: with an Address to the Ladies in Reply to J. A. Blondel*. So far as I can learn Mauclerc published no other works.

21. *Critical Review*, XX (July 1765), 63–65. On pages 125–33, Bellet provides a fair estimate—in his opinion—and a history of the controversy from the time of Malebranche. There is reason to believe that Smollett and Bellet had met and that Smollett was impressed by his knowledge of medical history. I treat this in my forthcoming book, *Doctors and Medicine in the Novels of Smollett*.

22. A list of references is too long to be given here. The two cases that attracted the most attention were "A Foetus of Thirteen Years." *The Gentleman's Magazine*, XIX (1749), 415, and in the same publication, "Fatal Accident: Woman carry'd a child sixteen years," XIX (1749), 211.

23. Respectively *Philosophical Transactions*, XLI (1740), 137; XLI (1741), 341; XLI (1741), 764; XLI (1741), 776; XLII (1742), 152; XLII (1743), 627; XLIV (1747), 617; XLV (1748), 325; XLV (1748), XLVI (1749), 205; XLVII (1750), 360, Some of these cases were abridged and printed in popular monthlies such as *The Gentleman's Magazine* and *The Monthly Review*.

24. First published in Dublin and numerous times thereafter in London. For Ould's contributions to midwifery see John R. Brown, "A Chronology of Major Events in Obstetrics and Gynaecology," *The Journal of Obstetrics and Gynaecology*, LXXI (1964), 303; and Fielding H. Garrison, *An Introduction to the History of Medicine* (4th ed. rev.; London, 1929), pp. 338–40.

25. First published in 1751 and reprinted in *The Novelists' Magazine*, XXIII (1788). The complicated history of Smollett's interaction with John Hill is narrated in my forthcoming biography, *The Literary Quack: A Life of Sir John Hill of London*. One episode is discussed by William Scott, "Smollett, John Hill, and *Peregrine Pickle*," *Notes and Queries*, CC (1955), 389–92.

26. Two weeks before the publication of *Peregrine Pickle*, Dr. Hill anticipated Smollett's novel by bringing out *The History of a Woman of Quality: or the Adventures of Lady Frail*. While Smollett believed the presence in his novel of Lady Vane's "Memoirs" would enhance sales, Hill's earlier publication greatly diminished sales.

27. *The Gentleman's Magazine*, XIX (1749), 211.

28. *The Works of Tobias Smollett, M.D.*, ed. by James Browne (London, 1872) I, p. 294.

29. There is no mention of this case in the *Philosophical Transactions* or other scientific literature I have examined. Perhaps "C——" was the famous "Charing Cross hermaphrodite," about whom Dr. William Cheselden had written in the *Anatomy of the Humane Body* (London, 1713) and about whom Dr. James Douglas wrote many medical fragments in the 1720s. Smollett was too young to have seen that curious organism. By 1751 this hermaphrodite may have become too stale a subject for satire, although K. Bryn Thomas, *James Douglas and his pupil William Hunter* (London, 1964), p. 190, does not think so. I am inclined to believe it was a more recent occurrence, about which Smollett was informed, as the tone of his note indicates.

30. Among numerous accounts of her case the most interesting I have found is in the *The Gentleman's Magazine*, XXI (1751), 214–15: "About the beginning of August 1748, Sarah Last, a poor woman in Suffolk, had the usual Symptoms of pregnancy, which succeeded each other pretty regularly thro' the usual period, at times she was seiz'd with pains . . . the child did not advance in birth . . . after the pains were gone off, the woman grew better . . . her menses return'd at proper seasons as if she had been deliver'd of a child, and continued so to do for several months . . . the poor woman recover'd, and is now perfectly well." The editor commented that "the foregoing case is not singular; we see two of the same kind recorded in the Memoirs of the Royal Academy of Surgery at Paris for the last year . . . and [one] communicated to the French academy."

31. *Peregrine Pickle*, I. p. 72. Smollett's description of Mrs. Trunnion's expectant state tallies well with observations made in John Pechey's *Complete Midwife's Practice*

Enlarged (5th ed.; London, 1698), especially the section "Of False Conception" (pp. 57–62). According to a manuscript in the Hunterian Museum, Pechey was included among required authors to be read by students at the Glasgow Medical School, which Smollett attended 1736–39.

32. Without pretending to summarize the vast literature dealing with the date and author of this painting, I mention the following: George W. Johnson, *A History of English Gardening* (London, 1829), pp. 72–81; Alicia Amherst, *A History of Gardening in England* (London, 1910), p. 238 ff.; Miles Hadfield, *Gardening in Britain* (London, 1960), p. 126; J. L. Collins, *The Pineapple* (Honolulu, 1960), pp. 70–86; William Gardener, "Botany and the Americas," *History Today*, XVI (Dec. 1966), pp. 849–55, where the picture was most recently reprinted. In his *DNB* life of John Tradescant the younger, gardener to Charles I, G. S. Boulger writes: "There is a tradition that the younger Tradescant first planted the pineapple in England in the garden of Sir James Palmer at Dorney House, Windsor, where a large stone cut in the shape of a pineapple by way of commemoration early in the seventeenth century is still extant . . . The pineapple pits were therefore pre-Charles II. Surely then John Tradescant the younger grew pineapples here for Charles I. The fact that there is no painting of John the elder or John the younger presenting a home-grown pineapple to Charles I does not disprove the possibility. The Tradescants would have had ready access to pineapples thanks to Sir William Courteen who was one of their principal benefactors. Sir William took out the first settlers to Barbadoes in 1625. The West Indies were one of his regular trade routes." This theory is supported by M. Allan in *The Tradescants: Their Plants, Gardens and Museum 1570–1662* (London, 1964), pp. 143–45. Tradescant was known for his exotic fruits, as is seen in Tom Brown's *Amusements Serious and Comical*, particularly the section entitled "The Philosophical or Virtuosi Country."

33. Robert James, M.D., *A Medicinal Dictionary* (London, 1743–45), article entitled "Ananas."

34. *The Diary of John Evelyn*, ed. E. S. de Beer (Oxford, 1955), Vol. III, pp. 293, 513.

35. Hadfield, *Gardening in Britain*, p. 126.

36. *Dictionarium Botanicum* . . . (London, 1728), article entitled "Ananas," and "A Particular Easy Method of Managing Pine-Apples" in *New Improvements of Planting and Gardening* (London, 1726), p. 605. Bradley's assertion was challenged in 1780 by Horace Walpole, who wrote to the Reverend William Cole: "There is another assertion in Gough [*British Topography*, 1768], which I can authentically contradict. He says Sir Matthew Decker first introduced ananas. My curious picture of Rose, the royal gardener, presenting the first ananas to Charles II proves the culture here earlier by several years" (*Letters to the Reverend William Cole*, ed. W. S. Lewis [New Haven, Yale University Press, 1937] II, p. 239). Walpole had acquired the painting from William Pennicott in 1780. In his popular handbook, *The Gardener's Dictionary* (London, 1724), Philip Miller attributed the first pineapple to Tellende. See also E. S. Rohde, *The Story of the Garden* (London, 1932), p. 178.

37. *The Complete Letters of Lady Mary Wortley Montagu*, ed. by R. Halsband (Oxford, 1965–67), Vol. I, p. 290.

38. Edited by F. B. Kaye (Oxford, 1924), Vol. II, pp. 193–95.

39. Pages 605–6. Bradley, among other authors, notes that a forty-foot stove was necessary to ripen one hundred pineapples. An average pineapple took three years to ripen and *c.* 1726 its total cost from the time of purchasing seeds was £80.

40. Hadfield, *Gardening*, p. 166, and C. H. Collins Baker and M. I. Baker, *The Life of James Brydges First Duke of Chandos* (London, 1949), p. 103. See also George Sherburn, "'Timon's Villa' and Cannons," *Huntington Library Bulletin*, VIII (1935), p. 143.

41. *Correspondence of Alexander Pope*, Vol. III, pp. 233 and 453.

42. Ibid., Vol. IV, p. 360. See also Vol. IV, pp. 405, 420; and Benjamin Boyce, *The Benevolent Man: A Life of Ralph Allen* (Cambridge, Mass., Harvard University Press, 1967), p. 114. On March 25, 1736, Pope wrote to Swift about the new fruits in his garden: "I have good Melons and Pine-apples of my own growth. I am as much a better Gardiner, as I'm a worse Poet, than when you saw me: But gardening is near a-kin to Philosophy, for Tully says *Agricultura proxima sapientiae*" (*Correspondence*, IV, 6). Without documentation Hadfield, *History of Gardening*, p. 187, states that "a year later [1742] Allen was advised not to take Scott's advice." But Pope could not

have been the unmentioned person since he fully approved of Scott's method. For Pope's activities as a gardener and ideas about gardening during Smollett's mature years, see Edward Malins, *English Landscaping and Literature 1660–1840* (London, 1966), pp. 26–51.

43. *Correspondence*, IV, p. 429.

44. *The Poetical Works of James Thomson*, ed. by J. L. Robertson (Oxford, 1908), "Summer," lines 685–89.

45. *The Art of Preserving Health* (London, 1796), including a *Critical Essay* by Dr. John Aikin, lines 334–40. Aikin commented on foods like pineapples as an example of a "too luxurious diet" (p. 14). The medical aspects of pineapples were also discussed in scientific publications. For example, see William Bastard, "On the Cultivation of Pine-Apples," *Philosophical Transactions*, LXVII (1777), pp. 649–52, in which the author describes his hothouse in Devonshire and the effects of the fruit on the body. Armstrong, a Scotsman who practised medicine in London, probably did not taste pineapples in Scotland. Dr. John Hope, the Regius Professor of Botany at Edinburgh University and a popularizer of Linnaeus in Scotland, allegedly grew in 1762 the first pineapples in Scotland, although I can discover no certain means of verifying this allegation.

46. *The English Physitian* (London, 1684), pp. 189–90. Pineapples were not mentioned in the edition of 1651, presumably because they were then unknown in England. Smollett referred to Culpepper's medical handbooks in several novels, and Joseph Addison listed the *Directory for Midwives* among essential books in an eighteenth-century "Lady's Library." See *The Spectator*, ed. Donald Bond (Oxford, 1965), Vol. I, p. 155.

47. *Pharmacopaeia Universalis* (London, 1742), p. 118. John Quincy made the same point in his *Complete English Dispensatory* (rev. ed.; London, 1742), p. 194.

48. *A Treatise of All Sorts of Foods, Both Animal and Vegetable*, trans. by D. Hay, M.D. (London, 1745), p. 350 and pp. 75–76. The signatures of several distinguished physicians of the Royal College of Physicians appear on the frontispage as approving the medical aspects of the book: among them are Edward Brown, Walter Charleton, and John Woodward, whom the Scriblerians satirized. For other comments by dietitians about the medicinal aspect of pineapples, see A. Cocchi, *The Pythagorean Diet, of Vegetables Only, Conducive to the Preservation of Health* . . ., trans. from Italian (London, 1745), pp. 74–76; and Sir Jack Drummond and Anne Wilbraham, *The Englishman's Food* (London, 1939), pp. 228–29. Numerous comments about the danger of pineapples for pregnant women may also be found in Ephraim Chambers's *Cyclopaedia: Or, An Universal Dictionary of Arts and Sciences* (London, 1728), article entitled "Ananas," and in George Cheyne's *An Essay on Regimen* (2nd ed.; London, 1740), pp. 76–77. Chapter XIX of *Roderick Random*, in which the hero meets the French apothecary Lavement, makes it clear that Smollett was thoroughly familiar with the medical effects of different diets.

49. *Free Thoughts on Quacks* (London, 1749), pp. 164–65.

50. *An Essay Concerning Human Understanding*, ed. by Alexander Campbell Fraser (Oxford, 1894), Vol. II, pp. 37–38. Although Locke was an expert botanist and did a great deal of plant research in the Oxford Botanical Garden in 1650–60, there is no evidence that he himself ever grew pineapples. See Kenneth Dewhurst, *John Locke (1632–1704) Physician and Philosopher: A Medical Biography* (London: The Wellcome Historical Medical Library, 1963), pp. 8–9.

51. *A Treatise of Human Nature*, ed. L. A. Selby-Bigge (2nd ed. rev.; Oxford, 1928), p. 5.

52. I have borrowed this phrase from the excellent article of D. W. Jefferson, "*Tristram Shandy* and the Tradition of Learned Wit," *Essays in Criticism*, Vol. I (1951), pp. 225–48.

53. Some of these have recently been studied and attributed to Smollett by G. S. Rousseau, "Matt Bramble and the Sulphur Controversy in the XVIIIth Century: Medical Background of *Humphry Clinker*," *Journal of the History of Ideas*, XXVIII (1967), 577–90.

XIII
Smollett and Roger Dibon

In 1950, Francesco Cordasco published a short article, "An Unrecorded Medical Translation by Smollett" (*N. & Q.*, cxcv (1950), 516), in which he reported discovery in the Medical Library of Padua of a translation of Roger Dibon's (1687–1777) work entitled: *M. Dibon's Description of the Venereal Diseases, The Retention of the Urine & Diseases of the Uretra. With the Additions and Observations of T. Smollett*. Leyden: Samuel Dortas, 1751. Dibon was a notorious French quack doctor who specialized in the cure of venereal diseases. He strenuously defended his various nostrums and throughout his career was embroiled in petty and seemingly incessant squabbles with less controversial medical colleagues. Dibon had recourse to a ghost-writer to compose his first book called *Dissertation sur les Maladies Vénériennes* (Paris, 1724), which was followed by several others on the same subject, among them *Suite de la Description des Maladies Vénériennes: Ouvrage dans lequel on traite des Retentions d'Urine, et en Général des Maladies de l'Urethre* (Paris, n.d. [1748]).

Dibon's *Description of Venereal Diseases*, mentioned above, may be a translation of his *Suite . . . des Maladies Vénériennes*. But the rub is "may be". Despite diligent and extended searches in virtually all the major European and American libraries, we have been unable to trace this remarkably elusive translation. Even more curious is a recent letter we have received from the Curator of the Padua Medical Library stating that the book mentioned by Cordasco has not been found among the holdings of his library.

There can be no shadow of doubt that Dibon used a ghost-writer for his first book. It seems likely that in the case of Smollett's translation we are vainly trying to grapple with a genuine bibliographical ghost.

XIV
Smollett and a Victorian Editor

David Herbert (1830–99), classical tutor, journalist and aficionado of eighteenth-century literature and history, was born on 15 April 1830 in Glasgow, at the home of his parents on Castle Street.[1] He spent his early life in Glasgow where his father, James Herbert, worked in a shop.

Nothing whatsoever is known about his first twenty years; perhaps he completed his primary education in the Glasgow area, not wanting to travel, but this is conjecture rather than fact. In 1851 he matriculated in the Latin class at Glasgow University directed by William Ramsay (1806–65), the noted classical scholar who had been Professor of Humanity since 1831. Herbert graduated from Glasgow six years later with a Master's degree, probably in classics, but the available sources do not specify his subject.[2] It was during these years that he apparently met his future wife, Elizabeth McPhie (1826–1903), daughter of William and Margaret McPhie. Extant records show that he married Elizabeth on 4 June 1855; his bride had little distance to travel after her marriage since David and Elizabeth had been neighbours, David residing at 126 and Elizabeth at 130 South Thistle Street.[3]

The year following their marriage, Herbert, possibly owing to the influence of his wife, was among the first students to enrol in the theological course taught at the newly established Free Church College (now Trinity College), Glasgow, and he continued there until 1860. During this period his oldest daughter, Margaret, was born, but it has not been possible to establish more about her than the year of her birth, 1856.[4]

Upon completion of his course of studies at Free Church College, Herbert left Glasgow to assume the parish post of the Congregational ministry at Darwen, a small industrial town some ten miles southeast of Preston in Lancashire. His youngest daughter, Lucy, was born there during his first year in England (1860) and he continued in his post until about 1870, at which time he returned to Scotland and took up lodgings in Edinburgh at 1 Nelson Street.[5]

His return to Scotland marked the beginning of a fairly serious literary career and the year of his return, 1870, the appearance of his his first three works: *The Lost Father; or Cecilia's Triumph. A Story of our own day* (Edinburgh, 1870) and *The Young Mountaineer; or Frank Miller's lot in life. The Story of a Swiss Boy* (Edinburgh, 1870), both adaptations of novels by Louise d'Aulnay,[6] were published under the pseudonym Daryl Holme. The third work was composed in Edinburgh, published under Herbert's own name, and was entitled *The Works of Tobias Smollett. Carefully Selected and Edited from the best Authorities, with numerous original and Historical Notes and A Life of the Author* (Edinburgh: William P. Nimmo, 1870).[7]

Precisely when Herbert wrote the first two adaptations is not known; it is possible that he produced them during his spare time as a preacher in Lancashire and submitted them to the publisher by mail, or he may have brought them with him to Edinburgh in 1870. But no doubt exists about the time he prepared his edition of Smollett, for according to the Preface to this work, Herbert prepared his annotations in Edinburgh at "the Advocates, the Signet, the Philosophical Institution, and the University Libraries" (p. 6), and no reason is known to question his remark. The edition contained *The Adventures of Roderick Random, Peregrine Pickle, Humphry Clinker*, and Smollett's plays and poems. The wealth of original annotations, particularly in the two non-fictional sections of *Peregrine Pickle*—the memoirs of Lady Vane (Chapter LXXXI in Herbert's text, i.e., that of the second edition, 1758 [LXXXVIII in the first edition, 1751]), and the narrative of the life of James Annesley (Chapter XCVIII [CVI in the 1751 edition])—provides abundant evidence of Herbert's perseverance and skill in discovering original material. Only in the last ten years has his work in these areas been superseded by James L. Clifford's Oxford English Novels edition (London, 1964) and the volumes which will be devoted to *Peregrine Pickle* in the forthcoming Bicentennial Edition of the Works of Tobias Smollett.

By combining a close reading of the clues provided by the text with the commentaries on English and Continental life found in the letters of Horace Walpole, Lady Mary Wortley Montagu and their circle of friends—especially Sir Horace Mann, George Montagu, Lady Pomfret (Henrietta Louisa Fermor, Countess of Pomfret), and Lady Bute (Lady Mary's daughter, Mary Stuart Bute, Countess of Bute)— Herbert was able to restore for the curious reader what had been widely known to some of the *cognoscenti* of the mid-eighteenth century. A few examples will indicate his procedure. At one point in Lady Vane's memoirs the text reads: "He said, the Queen had told him that Lord ——— had renewed his addresses to me." Herbert has filled in the blank with "(Cholmondeley)" and has added the following note: "Perhaps [George, 3rd Earl of] Cholmondeley. The first and last letters of this name are given on the following page, and seem to refer to him. If Lord Vane were meant, his claims would scarcely be termed "addresses" ' (p. 359). On several occasions Herbert had to rely on his intuition and on such textual hints as "the first and last letters of this name."

In this case he presumably compiled a list of all possible peers whose names began with C and ended in y, and then, after studying the biographical materials for each, made the most logical choice. In this particular case, Herbert could choose from four "Lord C——y's" Robert MacCarty (1685–1769), styled Viscount Muskerry 1686–1734, titular Earl of Clancarty 1734–1769; William (c. 1688–1750), fifth Earl of Coventry; George MacKenzie (c. 1703–1766), third Earl of Cromarty (most commonly spelled Cromartie, however); and George (1703–1770), third Earl of Cholmondeley. None of the candidates has been associated with Lady Vane in extant sources, but of the four, the first two may be eliminated purely on the grounds that they were too old in 1735–6 for the twenty-year-old Lady Vane—all of her known lovers were born within the century. Moreover, all the candidates except Cholmondeley were married at this time, and Lady Vane is not known to have had any liaisons with married men. For these and a number of other reasons, Cholmondeley, a widower in his thirties, impressed Herbert as the most logical choice and continues to persuade Smollett's most recent editors of *Peregrine Pickle*, James L. Clifford and G. S. Rousseau.

On other occasions Herbert was able to make more definite identifications by this method. Confronted with the following claim in Lady Vane's memoirs: ". . . . he chanced to open a letter from Sir T—— A—— . . .", Herbert made the following deduction:

> The only individual with these initials, occupying a place in society such as would warrant a conjecture regarding his personality, was Sir Thomas Aston, fourth Baronet of Aston, Staffordshire. Sir Thomas Aston's lady died in May 1737, leaving no children, so that he had been a widower two or three years before the time of this adventure. He died in France, 17th Feb. 1744, having devised his estates to his eldest sister. Another of his sisters was Molly Aston, Dr Johnson's very intimate friend.[8]

Herbert's deduction is correct, and if Cunningham's edition of Walpole's *Letters* (upon which Herbert heavily relied) had contained all of Walpole's correspondence with Sir Horace Mann, he could have readily confirmed the identification.

In addition to these types of conjecture and his use of available eighteenth-century letters, Herbert also gleaned several identifications from the ephemeral literature surrounding the publication of *Peregrine Pickle*, such as the mysterious and anonymous *Letter to the Right Honourable the Lady V———ss V———, occasioned by the publication of her memoirs in the Adventures of Peregrine Pickle* (London, 1751), and, for the Annesley narrative, "The Memoirs of an Unfortunate young Nobleman", especially as it appeared in the *Gentleman's Magazine* for 1743. Occasionally Herbert was able to make identifications by means of assistance from helpful friends, such as James Maidment, Esq., an attorney whom he singles out in the preface and who was responsible for the identification of "Mr. C———" as John Christie of Baberton. Christie had attended Augustus, fourth Earl of Berkeley, on his travels to Europe during 1737–8 and it is a credit to Herbert, as well as Maidment, that Smollett's most recent editors have discovered nothing more about Mr. Christie.[9]

The Census schedule for 1871 lists Herbert's occupation as "journalist", and from manuscripts of four letters in the National Library of Scotland it is clear that Herbert attempted to make his living by producing short pieces of historical and literary interest for the Edinburgh magazines. One letter, dated 31 August 1870 (probably not too long after his return from Darwen, Lancashire), addressed to the editor of *Blackwood's*, reads:

> I have for some time thought that an interesting and timely article might be written for "Blackwood" on "Francis Rous". The Speaker of Barebone's Parliament, belonging as he did to a good old family and acting a great part in the setting up of Cromwell as the Lord Protector, might be made the centre of considerable interest. Rous's relation to the Scottish version of The Psalms should be made clear and the importance of the recent introduction of the "Hymnal" would be seen in relation to the history of that Version. I may say that I am familiar with ample sources of information on the subject, and would be glad to write such an article as I suggest, and submit it to your judgement, if I had the preliminary encouragement to write it, of knowing that the subject would not be unsuitable to your Magazine.[10]

Some indication of the difficulties of the aspiring journalist during this period are provided by two of the remaining three letters, dated 25 May 1876 and 23 July 1887 respectively, both of which offer this same article on Francis Rous to subsequent editors of *Blackwood's*.[11]

Possibly owing to the sales success of his edition of Smollett, Herbert was subsequently commissioned to provide editorial material for editions of the poetical works of Thomas Moore (Edinburgh,1872 [1871], the works of Henry Fielding (Edinburgh, 1872; reissued London & Edinburgh, 1877), and the works of Laurence Sterne

(Edinburgh, 1872). In 1875 Herbert edited *Great Historical Mutinies: the Story of the Mutiny of the Bounty, the Mutiny at Spithead, the Mutiny at the Nore* . . . as a volume in "Nimmo's National Library" (London & Edinburgh [printed], 1876 [for 1875]). Herbert also began to supplement his income by tutoring local undergraduates in ancient and modern languages. Still resident in Edinburgh, he may also have undertaken a good number of journalistic assignments along the lines of his article on Francis Rous. If so, he executed these anonymously for an extensive search has revealed no record of his authorship.

By 1881 Herbert had removed to a house at 136 Gilmore Place, in the residential area to the southwest of Princes Street. No. 136 Gilmore Place was then a tenement building of substantial and fashionable flats. The Census schedule for that year lists his occupation as 'private teacher of languages' and indicates that he and his wife had now taken in his niece Jessie McPhie, who was studying art at one of the local institutions.[12] Two years later appeared *Fish and Fisheries* (Edinburgh: Blackwood & Sons, 1883), edited by Herbert and containing a selection from the prize essays of the International Fisheries Exhibition which had taken place in Edinburgh during 1882.

No facts have come to light concerning Herbert's activities during 1883–91. Presumably he continued to tutor Edinburgh students and still contributed free-lance articles to the local magazines. The Census schedule for 1891 shows that he had moved to smaller dwellings at 25 Gilmore Place; his daughter Lucy, now thirty years old and unmarried, continued to live with him. At about this time he was introduced into the staff of W. & R. Chambers Ltd., an important publishing house based in Edinburgh. This was apparently on a free-lance basis, since the company's records do not confirm his full-time employment on their literary staff. It is known, however, from an album of contributors to the 1892 edition of *Chambers's Encyclopaedia* (which contains a photograph of Herbert from that period) that Herbert contributed the articles on "Smollett" and "Smuggling" to that edition, and he may also have contributed other articles anonymously.

Herbert died on 8 April 1899 at the home of his son-in-law, A. Peterkin Hope, at Sunwick, Hutton, Berwickshire, and was buried in the Hutton Churchyard on 12 April.[13] He was survived by his wife who died on 20 January 1903.

NOTES

1. For supplying us with biographical information we are indebted to Miss Patricia M. Baxendine of the Scots Ancestry Research Society, Thomas C. Collocott and

A. S. Chambers of Messrs W. & R. Chambers, and S. M. Simpson of the National Library of Scotland. Herbert's birth was registered at St John's Relief Church in Glasgow.

2. See *The Matriculation Albums of the University of Glasgow From 1728 to 1858*, transcribed and ed. W. Innes Addison (Glasgow, 1913), p. 495; *A Roll of Graduates of the University of Glasgow*, comp. W. Innes Addison (Glasgow, 1898), p. 263.

3. The full entry recording Herbert's marriage reads:

4th June 1855 at 45 Wallace Street, Tradeston, Glasgow. Marriage (after Banns) was solemnized between us according to the Rites and Ceremonies of the Established Church of Scotland. David Herbert, of 53 Burnside Street, Glasgow, usual residence, 126 Thistle Street (South), classical tutor, aged 25, born at Castle Street, Glasgow, on the 15th April 1830 and registered at St John's Relief Church. The son of James Herbert, shopman, and Mary McIntyre (deceased). AND Elizabeth McPhie, of 45 Wallace Street, usual residence 130 Thistle Street (South), aged 29, born and registered on the 26th March 1826 in West Parish, Greenock. The daughter of William McPhie, shopman, and Margaret Mitchell (deceased).

4. Her year of birth has been computed from information in various Census schedules; for instance, the Census schedule of 1871 lists her as "aged 15, born in Glasgow".

5. See the *Edinburgh Post Office Directory*, 1870–1871 edition, and Census schedule for 1871, both of which list this address.

6. Louise d'Aulnay, writing under the pseudonym Julie Gouraud, published more than twenty-five novels and novelettes during 1864–88, a large number of which were subsequently translated or adapted into English. Many of her works, simple romances dealing with family life and aimed primarily at younger reading audiences, appeared in the *Bibliothèque rose illustrée*, a series translated and reprinted in London (1874 ff.) as "The Rose Library". Her works include: *Mémoires d'un Caniche* (Paris, 1866), translated by S. Baker, as *Memoirs of a Poodle* (London, [1876]); *Cécile, ou la Petite Soeur* (Paris, 1867), from which Herbert produced *The Lost Father*; *L'Enfant du Guide* (Paris, 1868), from which Herbert produced *The Young Mountaineer*; *Les Quatre Pièces d'Or* (Paris, 1873), translated by M. M., as *The Four Pieces of Gold. A Story of Normandy* (London, 1875); and *Les Deux Enfants de Saint-Domingue* (Paris, 1874), translated as *The Two Children of St Domingo* (London, 1874).

7. The location of Herbert's own copy of his edition of Smollett is unknown and a limited search has failed to uncover it.

8. Herbert, *The Works of Tobias Smollett* (Edinburgh, 1870), p. 363.

9. Ibid. p. 361.

10. MS. 4262, f. 5.

11. MSS. 4346, f. 159; 4500, f. 244.

12. The entry in the Census schedule for 1881 reads:

Address: 136 Gilmore Place
David Herbert, head of house, aged 50, private teacher of languages, M.A., born in Glasgow
Elizabeth, his wife, aged 54, born in Glasgow
Lucy, his daughter, aged 21, born in England,
Jessie A. Macphie, his niece, aged 22, art student, born in Portnahaven, Isla and one servant.

13. The following obituary appeared on 11 April 1899 in the main Edinburgh newspaper of the period, *The Scotsman*:

HERBERT—At Sunwick Berwickshire (the house of his son-in-law A. Peterkin Hope) on the 8th April, David Herbert, 25 Gilmore Place, Edinburgh, in his 69th year of his age. Funeral tomorrow (Wednesday) at 1 o'clock from Sunwick to Hutton Churchyard 5 miles from Berwick-on-Tweed. Friends will please accept this (the only) intimation and invitation (no flowers, by request).

XV
Smollett and the Scholars

These books[1] deal with Smollett, the first peripherally, the others exclusively. Parker's study of rogue literature extends to 1753 (date of the publication of *The Adventures of Ferdinand Count Fathom*), on grounds that if *"Ferdinand Count Fathom* . . . is not one of Smollett's successful novels, it is the only one that is fully picaresque—the last European novel of any consequence that is directly within the tradition started by *Guzmán de Alfarache*." A footnote to this sentence urges the reader to compare this statement with a passage in the *Cambridge History of English Literature*, X (1952), p. 45: "The picaresque novel in general, which burst into activity soon after the publication of *Roderick Random*, was under heavy obligations to Smollett, and nowhere more so than in its first modern example, *Pickwick*." If Harold Childs, author of the *Cambridge History* comment, is misguided, Parker, a scholar of Hispanic Studies, is not much better informed. His reasons for labelling *Count Fathom* as Smollett's only fully picaresque novel and Smollett-at-large a picaresque novelist are never stated; they merely proceed from an *ipse dixit* argument. Worse yet, Parker does not like Smollett's novels, *Count Fathom* least of all, and esteems all English picaresque fiction of the eighteenth century as a bastardized version of the Spanish form that flourished in the sixteenth century. Two critical observations, supposedly analytical but really impressionistic *aperçus*, give Parker away. Both refer to *Ferdinand Count Fathom*: "His [Fathom's] conversion is just as unaccountable as his delinquency. Alemán, Quevedo, and Grimmelshausen could never have been guilty of such novelistic irresponsibility, for it was not in their age to permit it." "Unaccountable," "could never have been guilty of," "such novelistic irresponsibility," "it was not in their age"; all illustrate the quality of Parker's prose and understanding of picaresque fiction. My reasons for discrediting this account of Smollett's fiction, for dispraising Parker's effort, will become clear by turning to Spector's book.

The contrast is marked: Spector knows all Smollett's works, understands his literary and social environment, English and Scottish, and views Smollett's writings with gravity and insight. He demonstrated knowledge in depth a few years ago by publishing an extensive work, *English Literary Periodicals and the Climate of Opinion during the Seven Years War* (1966), and since that time has shown expertise in the English novelists of the mid-eighteenth century, especially Smollett. Naturally he had to follow the "Twayne formula" to survey all Smollett's writings; but even that has not warped the result, a sane and balanced view of his subject. Everything in *Tobias George Smollett* is as one would expect from a competent scholar and critic. Both the biographical and critical (interpretive) aspects of Spector's book reveal thorough familiarity with the best Smollett scholarship including the admirable biography by Lewis Knapp (1949) and secondary periodical literature of the last two decades. The author is doubtless correct in maintaining in his preface that "the time now seems most appropriate for the full-scale analysis of Smollett's literary achievement that I offer in this book," and he has executed his intention by examining Smollett's values and techniques in both well-known and barely known works. Precisely because everything on the factual side of Spector's book is in order, I have little to add to it; and nothing I write in subsequent paragraphs ought to detract from the general excellence of this volume—surely one of the best in the Twayne Series of English Authors. One might have wished for a more extensive treatment (one sentence only!) of Smollett's *History of England*, now rarely read, too often disparaged, and barely understood; but such minor qualms exist for every book.

Everything except one aspect—and the reader will now see why I delayed commentary about Parker's book—is sound. This aspect is (of course) the picaresque, and Spector himself is aware of the problem: "I have argued," he writes on the first page of his preface and his execution shows rock-like belief in his basic assumption, "contrary to most critical opinion, that Smollett maintained the picaresque form throughout his five novels, that *Humphry Clinker*, no less than *Roderick Random*, belongs to that genre." Thus Parker and Spector are immediately in disagreement; the former affirming that *Fathom* is Smollett's "*only* [underlining mine] fully picaresque novel —the last European novel of any consequence that is directly within the tradition started by *Guzmán de Alfarache*," and the latter contending that Smollett maintained "the picaresque form *throughout* his five novels." The problem is—as every scholar of the eighteenth-century novel knows—definitional. Some competent critics have shown that the picaresque can be meaningfully defined; others have successfully destroyed the possibility of meaningful definition by demonstrating that the picaresque is not a genre at all, and that its appearance, if it exists in eighteenth-century English fiction, is so disguised and has been so vastly transformed over two centuries, that it is in no sense properly "picaresque" and ought not to be called by that name.[2] The debate continues, and some of the most sensible men in our profession are prudent to avoid it altogether; we have all heard the arguments, or parts of it, at one time or another. Like recent symposia on the definition of such critical terms as "Augustan," "neoclassical," "humanism," and "rational," most discussions about *the picaresque* (and the article is deceptive because it implies there is a superlative picaresque to the exclusion of all others) conclude in one of three ways: (1) by insisting that *picaresque* can be a meaningful category, useful for critics of fiction, if it is sharply distinguished from quixotic fiction, romance, and certain kinds of rogue tales; (2) by admitting that by 1700 it was no longer (and probably never had been) a pure form and that, as a consequence, it can be of only limited use to critics who wish to discuss "blended forms" (e.g., the so-called "georgic" is another); (3) by realizing that the term is of no use whatsoever, and does not begin to describe meaningfully the main thrusts of even those works (e.g., *Moll Flanders, Jonathan Wild, Roderick Random*) most commonly labelled picaresque.

Parker clearly believes in the first; it is to Spector's discredit that he nowhere declares himself: *all* Smollett's novels are picaresque; *ipse dixit;* that is the beginning and end of it. Granting that Spector could not split hairs about the definition of picaresque in a Twayne Series volume, his interpretation nevertheless ought to have included at least some definition. Definition was all the more necessary in his case (as opposed to Parker's) because he realizes his argument is "contrary to most critical opinion"; and to this I would add, because he is maintaining that Smollett was consistently picaresque "throughout his five novels."

Given the three main patterns of discussion about picaresque and having noted that Parker and Spector are in total disagreement about Smollett, a subset of comments about Smollett and picaresque fiction needs clear statement, if for no other reason than the possibility that Spector's contention may gain footing among students of the eighteenth century. The first point to be made refers exclusively to Smollett's fiction. There are probably three major ways of writing a book about Smollett's five novels: to view his development and growth on internal grounds without reference to other novelists, especially Fielding and Richardson; to view his development year by year, decade by decade, keeping a close eye to other works produced in that year and adopting the idea of literary periodization as a valid critical assumption; finally, formal generic studies that isolate the form of Smollett's novels and tell us the key things we need to know in order to understand each and every detail. All three approaches are valid and all have been practised upon occasion, although it is a lamentable fact that no serious book entirely devoted to Smollett's fiction as yet exists. Regardless of the approach taken—whether of of the first, second, or third of those described above; or whether combining these approaches—I doubt that a serious student, aware of the perils and pitfalls of critical terminology, could conclude that Smollett "maintained the picaresque form throughout his five novels." If Jery Melford and Matt Bramble are classical and "analytical picaros" (p. 130), as Spector would have us believe, then almost all figures in English fiction of the eighteenth century may be thus described.[3] A critical study of Smollett's five novels—regardless of its choice or combination of the above approaches—has more chance of being accurate and winning adherents if it steers away from the picaresque altogether; for confrontation with it can only cause trouble for the author.

This leads to the second point—that of distinguishing between the advantages and disadvantages of the above approaches to the picaresque in the case of Smollett's fiction. Any such argument is bound to be complicated and lengthy, however simple its aims and conclusions, for in serious criticism the simplest points often necessitate the most intricate arguments and proof, and no review can offer the necessary space. Without giving reasons for my conclusions (and I am well aware of asking my reader's indulgence in taking these conclusions on faith although the intermediary arguments have in no way been substantiated), I would arrange priority backwards; that is, by preferring approach 3 to 2, 2 to 1, and 1 to all approaches that omit definition of the picaresque. Basically my choice is made on the grounds that Smollett's novels *defy* formal categorization. They not only cannot be accurately described by a single critical term (picaresque, satiric, comic, fable, apologue), but they radically depart, at least on formal grounds, from the novels of Fielding and Richardson —all of which are built into a formal structure best described as containing plot-realism-judgment. This formal structure does not apply to Smollett's novels, either to an individual novel or to the entire *oeuvre*, and it is curious that the difference has not as yet been clearly delineated by critics. While the novels of Fielding, Richardson, and Smollett, like all other novels of the mid-eighteenth century, are "moral," Smollett's novels are "Fieldingesque" only by dint of similarity in the moral imperfection of his (Smollett's) fictional figures and in the type of morality he wishes to draw. Smollett's heroes, unlike Richardson's exemplary heroines, wander in low life (Pickle, Fathom, Clinker) and demonstrate levels of human weakness and moral imperfection unknown in Richardson's figures. But here ends any similarity with Fielding or Richardson; for in all other aspects, especially in the formal mode and structural edifice of his novels, Smollett is different, nowhere in his five novels displaying a formal structure built upon the Fielding-Richardson formula of plot-realism-judgment.[4] If this difference is granted, and I think it must be, then one wonders how the generic-descriptive label *picaresque* can apply to novelists who are as formally different as Fielding and Smollett. Surely both novelists were well versed in genuine Spanish picaresque fiction (*Guzmán, Lazarillo*), and surely both had Cervantes' quixotic fiction (not picaresque fiction) firmly and everlastingly fixed in their minds; but that is a very different matter from postulating that *Tom Jones* and *Count Fathom* are picaresque novels, that Tom and Fathom are picaros, and that the structural features of a picaresque novel as opposed to a quixotic novel are here evident. Even if they were evident, though they are not (certainly not in Smollett's case), one would be forced back to the question, how many picaresque features are necessary for a novel containing elements of an older form to be called "a picaresque novel"? This is the same question as, how many neoclassical features are necessary for a poem to be labelled "a neoclassical poem," and several years' discussion, orally and in print, has made it painfully evident that the question is a bad one, cannot be meaningfully answered, leads nowhere except to confusion and chaos, and that similar questions ought to be thrown out of court, now and forever. The task of criticism, in Smollett's case at least, involves the description of a highly elusive and hybrid parodic form of the novel that both mocks and glances at any number of unique previous forms (e.g., Fielding, Butler, Restoration tragedy) but that also flirts in the most oblique manner imaginable with still other forms (satire, anti-satire, romance, melodrama, picaresque, and quixotic fiction) and artistic techniques (Hogarthian comic painting, delineation of grotesques, the configuration of imaginary worlds of mirth, stratagems, and games). It is a brave critic who champions just one of these—picaresque—as the key to unlock all Smollett's treasures. If Parker and Spector had distinguished between "genuine picaresque novels" (e.g., *Guzmán*) and "loose picaresque elements within a novel" (e.g., Fathom's wanderings amidst low life), they may not have disagreed so totally about *Count Fathom*. But even if they had been in agreement about *Fathom*, whether picaresque or not, their mode of critical exegesis helps us little in comprehending the formal mould of Smollett's narratives and the reasons for his artistic successes (*Humphry Clinker*) and failures (*Fathom*). Theirs is the kind of exegetical writing that pins labels to architectural structures by arguing *a priori* and without assembling the entire edifice, floor by floor, room by room, window by window. No one should be coerced into thinking that Smollett's five novels are genuine picaresques merely because Smollett knew Spanish and had translated *Don Quixote*, which is in no sense a picaresque fiction. Nor does a listing of picaresque elements in each of his novels enhance critical understanding of the unusual form of each novel: picaresque *elements* are incontestably present in novels from Defoe to Jane Austen, from Thackeray to Barth and Kerouac, and at this time of day Smollett's novels will not be illuminated by a witch hunt for more picaresque elements. To be sure, they exist in varying degrees in each of Smollett's novels; but that does not in itself make *Fathom* "a picaresque novel" to the exclusion of other types of a novel, any more than the presence of certain satiric elements in *Tristram Shandy* renders that *lusus naturae* "a neoclassical satire"—if by this phrase one means *Absalom and Achitophel* or *The Dunciad*.

Turning from critical interpretation to factual scholarship, Korte's checklist is handy and useful but ultimately disappointing, for it is but a paste-up of July *PQ* Smollett entries and this accounts for its slenderness. The year 1946 was chosen as a starting point "because this bibliography is intended to supplement Francesco Cordasco's *Smollett Criticism, 1925–1945: A Compilation* (1947)"; but Korte's assumption about Cordasco's exhaustiveness is questionable; besides, Cordasco's pamphlet is not easily available. If the University of Toronto Press had been willing, it would have been better to go back to 1925, possibly earlier. Another odd feature is Korte's listing of completed doctoral dissertations: what is the point of listing a dissertation if one omits its length? While length is no guarantee of excellence, it is nevertheless an important indication of breadth and scope. Can it be that the University of Toronto Press, which publishes so magnificently the Alexander Lectures (witness the opulent splendour and luxurious printing of its most recent volume, Maynard Mack's *The Garden and the City*, 1969), niggled at production costs for the Smollett volume? If so, then Korte should have taken his book elsewhere, for with certain additions the results would have been an indispensable tool for Smollett scholars.

Knapp's correspondence has been long awaited and now supplants Noyes's *Letters* (Harvard University Press, 1926). Thirty-two new letters are added to the seventy-five printed in Noyes, thereby extending to one hundred and seven the extant letters of Smollett. None of these thirty-two letters radically changes our biographical knowledge of the eminent novelist, but Smollett, unlike Pope or Swift, was not the kind of man who revealed himself intimately in letters. Professor Knapp, Smollett's most learned student in this century, has done an admirable job of editing and annotating, and his book must now become a companion volume to the exhaustive 1949 biography. On the advent of Smollett's 1971 bicentenary, let us hope that more of his letters are discovered, as well as other documents, and that Professor Knapp will periodically publish them in supplemental form.

NOTES

1. Alexander A. Parker, *Literature and the Delinquent: The Picaresque Novel in Spain and Europe 1599–1753*. Edinburgh: Edinburgh University Press, 1967. Robert Donald Spector, *Tobias George Smollett*. New York: Twayne Publishers, 1968. Donald M. Korte, *An Annotated Bibliography of Smollett Scholarship 1946–68*. Toronto: University of Toronto Press, 1969.

2. Literature on the picaresque is vast, but little of it is persuasive. The most extensive generic study I have seen is Joseph Virgil Recapito's doctoral dissertation, "Towards a Definition of the Picaresque" (University of California at Los Angeles, Department of Spanish and Comparative Literature, 1967, 2 vols., 792 pages). Other studies of varying quality include: H. W. Streeter, *The Eighteenth Century English Novel in French Translation* (1936); A. B. Shepperson, *The Novel in Motley* (1936); D. J. Dooley, "Some Uses and Mutations of the Picaresque," *Dalhousie Review*, 37 (1957), 363–377; Robert Alter, *The Rogue's Progress* (1964); Stuart Miller, *The Picaresque Novel* (1967). Eighteenth- and nineteenth-century secondary works afford little help and less critical insight: a list of such works would include Formey's *Elementary Principles of the Belles Lettres* (1766); Hugh Murray's *Morality of Fiction* (1805); and Henry Hallam's *Introduction to the Literature of Europe* (1837–39).

3. Immense critical chaos has been caused by confusing picaresque and quixotic elements in eighteenth-century novels. Confusion among critics extends back at least as early as the turn of the nineteenth century; a perfect example is Hugh Murray's *Morality of Fiction* (London, 1805), p. 125.

4. Before me is a list of all Smollett doctoral dissertations of the last twenty years, together with an abstract of the contents of each: it is a curious phenomenon that not one takes as its main thesis the discontinuities of form in Fielding and Smollett. If Smollett merely aped Fielding, and badly at that, then why bother with him at all? Rather than lump together his five very different novels and dub them "Fieldingesque," "picaresque," or "satiric," we would render future graduate students (as well as modern scholarship) a service by suggesting that they avoid these horrendous and obsolescent catch-alls and set out to discover the unique laws of each novel.

Index

Note: This index includes materials found in the text only; proper names in footnotes are not included. References to Smollett's minor works are listed under the title of the work, not under Smollett. There is a substantial entry under Tobias Smollett that includes subjects and topics as well as names.